SONG

of

BROOKLYN

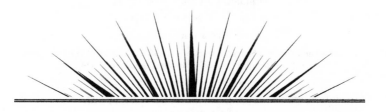

Song
of
BROOKLYN

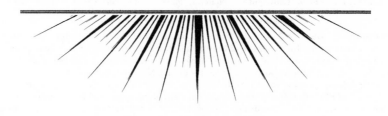

An Oral History
of America's
Favorite Borough

Marc Eliot

BROADWAY BOOKS
NEW YORK

BROADWAY

PUBLISHED BY BROADWAY BOOKS

Copyright © 2008 by Marc Eliot

All Rights Reserved

Published in the United States by Broadway Books, an imprint of The Doubleday Publishing Group, a division of Random House, Inc., New York.

www.broadwaybooks.com

BROADWAY BOOKS and its logo, a letter B bisected on the diagonal, are trademarks of Random House, Inc.

Acknowledgment is made to quote lyrics from:

"(I Used to Be A) Brooklyn Dodger" Words by Dan Beck, Music by Dion DiMucci, Mark Tiernan & Russell Steele Copyright © 1978 PKM Music, County Line Music & Megabucks Music Company c/o Publishers' Licensing Corporation, P.O. Box 5807, Englewood, NJ 07631. Used By Permission. All Rights Reserved. Recorded by Dion DiMucci for Lifesong Records on the album *Return of the Wanderer* (www.winthropmedia.com).
"Looking for an Echo" Copyright © 1996 Kenny Vance. Used by Permission of Kenny Vance.

Acknowledgment is made to quote excerpts from:

Best Seat in the House: A Basketball Memoir by Spike Lee with Ralph Wiley, copyright © 1997 by Spike Lee. Used by Permission of Crown Publishers, a division of Random House, Inc.
"Interview with Henry Miller," *The Paris Review,* issue #28, Summer/ Fall 1962. Used by Permission of the Miller Estate and *The Paris Review.*
Jackie Robinson Copyright © 1987 by Maury Allen. Used by Permission of Maury Allen.
Norman Mailer: His Life and Times, Updated Edition of the Authorized Biography by Peter Manso. Copyright ©1985, 2008 by Peter Manso. Excerpted with the permission of Washington Square Press/Pocket Books, a Division of Simon & Schuster, Inc.
Tales from the Dodger Dugout Copyright © 2001 by Carl Erskine. Used by Permission of Carl Erskine and CMG Worldwide, Inc.
Timebends: A Life Copyright © 1987 by Arthur Miller. Used by Permission of Grove/Atlantic, Inc.
Woody Allen Copyright © 1991 by Eric Lax. Used by Permission of Knopf Publishing.

Book design by Chris Welch

Library of Congress Cataloging-in-Publication Data

Eliot, Marc.
Song of Brooklyn : an oral history of America's favorite borough / by Marc Eliot.–1st ed.
p. cm.
Includes bibliographical references.
1. Brooklyn (New York, N.Y.)–Social life and customs–Anecdotes. 2. Brooklyn (New York, N.Y.)–Biography–Anecdotes. 3. Oral history–New York (State)–New York. 4. New York (N.Y.)–Social life and customs–Anecdotes. 5. New York (N.Y.)–Biography–Anecdotes. 6. Celebrities–New York (State)–New York–Biography–Anecdotes. I. Title.

F129.B7E45 2008
974.7'23–dc22
2007046871

ISBN 978-0-7679-2014-8

PRINTED IN THE UNITED STATES OF AMERICA

1 3 5 7 9 10 8 6 4 2

First Edition

FOR BABY COCOA BEAR

It'd take a guy a lifetime to know Brooklyn t'roo an' t'roo.
An' even den, yuh wouldn't know it all.

—Thomas Wolfe, "Only the Dead Know Brooklyn"

Stan: That's the first mistake we've made since
that guy sold us the Brooklyn Bridge.
Ollie: Buying that bridge was no mistake. That's going
to be worth a lot of money to us someday.

—Stan Laurel and Oliver Hardy in the comedy feature *Way Out West*

You see, the city is fundamentally a practical, utilitarian invention, and it always was. And then suddenly you see this steel poetry sticking there and it's a shock. It puts everything to shame and makes you wonder what else we could have done that was so marvelous and so unpresumptuous. . . . So it makes you feel that maybe you too could add something that would last and be beautiful.

—Arthur Miller in Ken Burns's documentary *Brooklyn Bridge*

The Brooklyn I was born in, near the end of the nineteenth century,
was still a city of churches, with their great bronze bells walloping to the
faithful from early dawn, and a city of waterfront dives where the old forest
of the spars of sailing ships was rapidly being replaced by funnels and
the Sands Street Navy Yard already had a reputation for girl chasers. . . .
[It was] a city of neat horse-plagued, tree-lined streets, connected by
a brand-new bridge to Manhattan.

—Mae West, *Goodness Had Nothing to Do with It*

✖

There was something about Brooklyn . . . that was magical . . .
the open fire hydrants, the spaldeens, the double-bill movie theaters,
the comic books in candy stores, the egg creams, the stickball games
with a broomstick handle.

—Jack Newfield, *Somebody's Gotta Tell It:
The Upbeat Memoir of a Working-Class Journalist*

✖

No one can hope to be elected in this state without being photographed
eating a hot dog at Nathan's Famous.

—Nelson Rockefeller, campaigning for the
governorship of New York

✖

Brooklyn was like a commonwealth, a colony of peoples,
yet at the same time it served as a gateway.

—Andrew Sarris

✖

I'm from Brooklyn. We talk plainly.

—Reverend Al Sharpton, reacting to comments by
Mexican president Vicente Fox

✖

One of the longest journeys in the world is the journey from Brooklyn to Manhattan—or at least from certain neighborhoods in Brooklyn to certain parts of Manhattan.

—NORMAN PODHORETZ, *MAKING IT*

✘

Can you tell me which is Brooklyn?

—PRISCILLA LANE AS PAT MARTIN IN ALFRED HITCHCOCK'S *SABOTEUR*

Contents

Dramatis Personae

Maury Allen: Brooklyn-born sportswriter for the *New York Post* and *Sports Illustrated* and author of several books about baseball, most focusing on the Yankees and the Brooklyn Dodgers. Grew up near Kings Highway. Attended James Madison High School.

Woody Allen: Legendary stand-up comic, writer, and filmmaker. Born and raised in Midwood, Brooklyn. Combines a Manhattan-style intellect with outer-borough humor.

Marty Asher: Editor-in-chief of Vintage Books and the author of the novels *Boomer* and *Shelter* and the nonfiction book *The 20-Minute Gardener.*

Maria Bartiromo: Business news anchor and reporter for CNBC television, the cable-based financial-news network. Popularly known as the "Money Honey." Also known as the "Econo-Babe."

Ralph Beatrice: Longtime resident of Brooklyn, owned a furniture gallery in SoHo, New York.

Mike Berger: Retired educator.

BRIAN BERGNER: Contemporary Brooklyn writer, co-editor with Marshall Berman of New York Calling.

MICHAEL BLOOMBERG: Mayor of the City of New York.

DEBBIE BOSWELL: Brooklyn-born writer, author of *Miriam's Journey*.

JIMMY BRESLIN: New York journalist.

MEL BROOKS: Comic legend, writer, performer, producer, director, librettist, Broadway musical composer. Early live-TV-sketch-writing pioneer and comedy album recording artist. Born in Williamsburg, Brooklyn.

AL BROWN: Brooklyn-born fireman stationed in Canarsie. A survivor of the 9/11 attack.

MAHOGANY L. BROWNE: Publisher of Penmanship Books.

AMANDA M. BURDEN: Chair of the New York City Planning Commission and director of the Department of City Planning.

BRIAN BURNS: Contemporary Brooklyn writer.

DIANA CARLIN: Organizer of the "No Condos in Coney" event.

JOHN "CHA CHA" CIARCIA: Brooklyn-born Coney Island restaurateur, actor, producer, boxing promoter, radio broadcaster. Cast member of *The Sopranos.* Unofficial mayor of Mulberry Street in New York's Little Italy.

HERB COHEN: Brooklyn-born author of the best-selling *You Can Negotiate Anything* and other books, international crisis management consultant, raconteur. Larry King's best friend.

CLARENCE COLLINS: Brooklyn-born founding member of Little Anthony and the Imperials.

CLEVELAND "CLEVE" DUNCAN: Brooklyn-born lead singer and founding member of the singing group the Penguins.

CARL ERSKINE: Legendary member of the 1955 World Championship Brooklyn Dodgers.

STEVE ETTLINGER: Popular science and popular reference writer. Lives in Brooklyn.

MICHAEL FRANK: Literary critic.

MICKEY FREEMAN: Actor, comedian; best known for his portrayal of Zimmerman in the 1950s TV sitcom *Sergeant Bilko* and his classic Catskill comic routines.

DARCY FREY: Author of *The Last Shot,* contributing editor at *Harper's* magazine and the *New York Times Magazine.*

BOB GANS: Brooklyn-born entrepreneur.

BRIAN GARI: Singer, songwriter, nightclub entertainer, and MC. Grandson of entertainer Eddie Cantor.

JOEY GAY: One of the present-day owners of the popular Sheepshead Bay comedy club Pips.

RUDY GIULIANI: Brooklyn-born Rudolph Giuliani is a lawyer, former district attorney, politician, and businessman. He was the mayor of New York City from 1994 to 2001.

HOWARD GOLDEN: Brooklyn borough president, 1977–2001.

DANIEL GOLDMAN: Spokesman for "Develop Don't Destroy Brooklyn," a coalition opposed to the Atlantic Yards development project.

TONY GOLIO: President of Tam Restaurants, the corporation that operates the legendary Lundy's in Sheepshead Bay.

"LITTLE ANTHONY" GOURDINE: Brooklyn-born lead singer, founding member of the pop and R&B singing group Little Anthony and the Imperials.

CARY GRANT: Actor.

DAVID HAGLUND: Managing editor of *PEN America: A Journal for Writers and Readers* and author of a blog, Essays and Criticism.

PETE HAMILL: Brooklyn-born journalist, newspaper columnist, memoirist, and best-selling novelist.

BILL HANDWERKER: Grandson of Nathan Handwerker, the original owner of Nathan's in Coney Island, credited with introducing the nickel hot dog to American cuisine.

GERALD HOWARD: Brooklyn-born book editor, literary critic.

CHARLES HYNES: Kings County district attorney, elected in 1990 and still serving in that post.

JEANELIA "J": Brooklyn-born writer, poet, rap artist.

SIMON JACOBSON: Rabbi, founder of the Meaningful Life Center, responsible for the publication of the talks of Rabbi Menachem M. Schneerson, the Lubavitcher Rebbe.

KENNEY JONES: Original member of the Small Faces, which later became the Faces. Joined the Who as the replacement for drummer Keith Moon.

JOHN KARLEN: Brooklyn-born TV and movie actor, best known for the role of Harvey in the long-running series *Cagney and Lacey*.

IVAN KRONENFELD: Principal in Koerner, Kronenfeld Partners, a consulting firm.

SPIKE LEE: Brooklyn-born filmmaker.

JONATHAN LETHEM: Brooklyn-raised novelist; author of *Motherless Brooklyn* and the bestseller *The Fortress of Solitude*.

MARK LOTTO: Journalist.

FRANK LOGRIPPO: Brooklyn-born aerospace engineer.

JOHNNY MAESTRO: Founding member of 1950s musical group the Crests and later of the Brooklyn Bridge.

FANNY SCHNEIDER MAILER: Mother of Norman Mailer.

NORMAN MAILER: Brooklyn-raised novelist, journalist, filmmaker, social critic, cultural figure, Pulitzer Prize winner.

STEPHON MARBURY: Brooklyn-born basketball player currently with the New York Knicks.

MARTY MARKOWITZ: Brooklyn borough president, 2002 to present.

ANDREW MILLER: A senior editor at Alfred A. Knopf.

ARTHUR MILLER: Brooklyn-raised playwright, whose greatest works include *Death of a Salesman* and *A View from the Bridge*.

HILLARY MILLS: Biographer of Norman Mailer.

BRUCE "COUSIN BRUCIE" MORROW: Legendary Brooklyn-born AM disc jockey and talk show host for WINS, WABC, and WNBC; now hosts a show on Sirius Satellite Radio.

ROSIE PEREZ: Brooklyn-born actress.

ANTHONY PETROCINO: Retired New York City fireman.

JOHNNY PODRES: Pitcher for the 1955 world champion Brooklyn Dodgers.

STEVE POWERS: Graffiti artist who helped restore much of the cartoonish look to the revitalized Coney Island.

SELWYN RAAB: New York–based journalist.

MILTON RADUTZKY: Brooklyn-born son of Nathan Radutzky, who founded the Joyva Corporation; currently the senior member of the family-owned and -operated business.

NATHAN RADUTZKY: Founder of the Joyva Corporation, headquartered in Brooklyn.

RICHARD RADUTZKY: Brooklyn-born grandson of Milton Radutzky. Original ambition was to be a comic actor; appeared on David Letterman's show once before being lured into the family business.

DON K. REED: Brooklyn-born New York disc jockey who hosted the Sunday-night *Doo Wop Shop* on WCBS-FM for twenty-seven years.

JOAN RIVERS: Brooklyn-born comic, actress, TV host, red-carpet icon.

MARV AND WALTER ROSEN: Sons of Harry Rosen, the founder of legendary Brooklyn delicatessen Junior's.

RON ROSENBAUM: New York–based journalist.

STEVEN H. RUDOLPH, M.D.: Director of the Stroke Center at Maimonides Medical Center in Brooklyn.

LOUIS SAVARESE: A retired sanitation worker for the City of New York.

J. K. SAVOY: Contemporary Brooklyn writer.

HARVEY SCHULTZ: Late city planner, former city commissioner, and real estate development executive; from 1977 to 1986 was executive assistant to Brooklyn borough president Howard Golden and was known as "the man behind the mayor."

NEIL SEDAKA: Brooklyn-born singer/songwriter.

MICHAEL SHAPIRO: Author of several books, including the definitive history of the Brooklyn Dodgers' last years, *The Last Good Season.*

AL SHARPTON: Alfred Charles "Al" Sharpton Jr., controversial Brooklyn-born, Harlem-based Baptist minister, civil rights and social justice activator.

JOSEPH J. SITT: Brooklyn-born founder of Thor Equities, currently redeveloping Coney Island.

BILLY DAWN SMITH: Brooklyn-born musician, club owner, songwriter; one of the legendary R&B singer-songwriters of the late 1940s and 1950s.

AMY SOHN: Contemporary Brooklyn novelist, magazine columnist.

DOUGLAS C. STEINER: Co-founder of Steiner Equities Group, owner-operator of Steiner Studios, which opened in 2004 at the old Brooklyn Navy Yard.

DAVID TAWIL: Brooklyn-born sports enthusiast, youth-camp athletic supervisor.

BOBBY THOMSON: Legendary New York Giant baseball player, who, in 1951, hit the home run that won the pennant for the Giants over the Dodgers—the "shot heard round the world."

ERICA TOWNSEND: Brooklyn-born contemporary writer.

KENNY VANCE: Co-founder of Jay and the Americans; founder and lead singer of Kenny Vance and the Planotones.

BEN VEREEN: Award-winning Broadway, television, and film actor, dancer, and singer.

LEONARD RANDOLPH "LENNY" WILKENS: Legendary Brooklyn-born pro basketball player and coach.

ERNEST WRIGHT: Brooklyn-born original member of Little Anthony and the Imperials.

BRUCE WULWICK: Brooklyn-born entrepreneur.

JULIUS ZOCAMPO: Longtime Brooklyn dockworker.

Song

of

BROOKLYN

INTRODUCTION

B ROOKLYN'S 70.61 SQUARE MILES are situated to the east
and south of its celebrated runway sister of a borough, Manhattan, the two separated by a river but connected by three
bridges, a tunnel, and the subway. To the north, Brooklyn remains
joined like a Siamese twin to homely Queens. To the south lies Staten
Island, remote both geographically and psychically from the rest of
New York City. Way to the northeast is the Bronx, a long drive or subway ride away. To the east there is nothing between Brooklyn and
Great Britain but Long Island.

The 1898 incorporation that united five individual, independent
territories—the Bronx, Brooklyn, Manhattan, Queens, and Staten
Island—into the single greatest city in the world was, according to the
late Harvey Schultz, who served as executive assistant to the Brooklyn borough president, "a day that New Yorkers still rue on both sides
of the river." The million-plus residents of Brooklyn were forced to
accept that their city had been reduced to a "borough." Ever since,

Brooklynites, Bronxites, Queenspeople, and Staten Islanders have been wallflowers hidden in the shadow of Manhattan, the glowing belle of the city ball. Indeed, to this day, when Manhattanites think of Queens (if they think of it at all), they regard it as little more than the location of the city's two major airports, a place of interesting ethnic restaurants, the first stage on the surface road to suburban Long Island or to their personal summertime shoreline playground in the Hamptons.

Staten Island offers a great view of lower Manhattan and the Statue of Liberty in upper New York Bay, but you need to take a ferry to get to Staten Island, and most Manhattanites wouldn't be caught dead on the ferry and couldn't care less about the statue, having last looked at it sometime in the second grade. No subway goes to Staten Island; the borough is linked to Brooklyn by the expensive, stand-offish Verrazano-Narrows Bridge. (The bridge is named after Giovanni da Verrazano, who in 1524 was the first European to sail up the Narrows into what is now New York Harbor. It is today perhaps best known as the bridge that Brooklynites Tony Manero and his friends dangled from in teenage existential angst in John Badham's 1977 movie *Saturday Night Fever.*) Overall, Manhattanites tend to think of Staten Island as little as possible.

As every first grader in the New York City public school system can tell you with great confidence and authority, the Bronx is the only borough with an article in its name, although few can tell you why. It was originally thousands of acres of quiet, remote farmland before being settled in the eighteenth century by Swedish-born Jonas Bronck and his wife and indentured servants. Other settlements soon followed. For most of the succeeding centuries, the Bronx was a place that defined upward mobility among the city's workers. It was often referred to as "the country" by working-class New Yorkers, and it was a place to move up to. The Bronx is famous for the New York Botanical Garden, the Bronx Zoo, the Bronx House of Detention for Men, the prestigious Bronx High School of Science, the Italian neighborhood highlighted by legendary Arthur Avenue, the Grand Concourse, and of course those damn Yankees and that storied stadium. No classic novels bear the Bronx's name; no songs exist dedicated to either its savagery or its sweetness. In the seventies the South Bronx became an international symbol of urban blight. Today, while poised on the brink of economic recovery, it nevertheless remains somewhat hidden from the outsider's view by a great, if invisible, wall.

But Brooklyn . . . ah, sweet Brooklyn. How she bursts with pride in her showy individualism, how she smiles out of the side of her mouth. And when she speaks, how she sings—with the broad, unmistakable accent that has come to stand for the urban dialect of the entire United States of America. "Whaddaya kiddin' me or sumthin'? Fuhgeddaboutit!"

If in the geography of American success Manhattan serves as the ultimate place to arrive, until recently Brooklyn has been the original place to leave. If Manhattan is where the city's greatest literature is published, Brooklyn is where much of it has been written. To put it another way, if Manhattan knows how to sell the city's culture, Brooklyn is where a lot of it comes from. In countless movies, television shows, plays, songs, and novels, Manhattan is the dream, Brooklyn is the reality. There lives the girl with the ruby red lips, a cigarette dangling from the side of her mouth, one hip to the side, her body perched atop black high heels, her hair piled on her head as high as the corned beef on a Junior's-on-rye. Or the guy with the big future who still lives at home, who can fix anything from a toaster to the space shuttle but can't figure out how to get himself over to Manhattan. He's Jewish or Italian or Irish or Italian-Irish or African American. Or Haitian. Or Russian, Norwegian, German, Lebanese. Or even Dutch. He sings doo-wop on the corner. He cries when he hears the name of his old high school. He loves women who treat him the way his mom does, and women who do things Mom would never do. He can be found in Walt Whitman's *Leaves of Grass*, in Betty Smith's *A Tree Grows in Brooklyn*, in Lawrence Ferlinghetti's *A Coney Island of the Mind*, in Hubert Selby Jr.'s *Last Exit to Brooklyn,* and in Arthur Miller's *Death of a Salesman.* He lives and breathes in the works of Hart Crane, Theodore Dreiser, Henry Miller, Thomas Wolfe, and Jonathan Lethem. He is in a hundred Hollywood movies, in the tuxedoed music of George Gershwin and washed-out jeans jingles of Woody Guthrie, in the street-corner harmonies of Kenny Vance and the Planotones, in the soaring voice of Neil Diamond, in the sultry sound of Barbra Streisand, in the street-tough singsong of Jay-Z.

Brooklyn is where the *madeleine* of choice is an egg cream, a charlotte russe, a bowl of matzo brei, a ball of mozzarella, a slice of Shabazz bean pie. It is the everlasting afterimage of the Brooklyn Dodgers—dem bums!—who once played in the glorious bandbox that was Ebbets Field, where the heights of success and the depths of failure were regularly foist (and second and toid) upon the ever-forgiving faithful.

It is in the smell of the docks of the waterfront and the storied Brooklyn Navy Yard, and in the Nathan's hot dogs and french fries of Coney Island. It is a ride on the Cyclone.

It is, ultimately, a time and place that holds the memories of the past and shapes the hopes of the future. It is at once the substance and the shadow of the American dream. It is in the lyric melody that Walt Whitman once called his Brooklyn and himself.

It is the harmony found in these voices that follow, Brooklynites famous and otherwise, who have come together here to celebrate, to mourn, to dream, and to reminisce. It is their song of Brooklyn.

As Henry Miller (raised in Williamsburg) once said, all you need to sing is something to say. This, then, is Brooklyn's song.

CHAPTER ONE

CONEY ISLAND

Not like Dante

Discovering a *commedia*

Upon the slopes of heaven

I would paint a different kind

of Paradiso

—LAWRENCE FERLINGHETTI,
"A CONEY ISLAND OF THE MIND"

N 1609, AFTER voyaging across the Atlantic under the sponsorship of the Dutch East India Company in search of a shortcut to China, English explorer Henry Hudson set foot on a clam-laden spit of wet land. Having anchored his ship, the *Half Moon*, just to the west of the main inlet, he and his men had just begun to explore the new territory when they encountered a band of native Canarsee tribespeople. Although initially friendly, the Canarsees boarded the ship at dawn the next morning and fiercely attacked the men they perceived as invaders. A sudden rain prevented Hudson's men from loading gunpowder into their pistols, and because of that many were killed, the first being petty officer John Coleman, victim of an arrow through his neck.

Hudson was mystified by the attack. He had come in peace and believed his party had been welcomed. What he didn't know was that the clam spit was considered by the natives to be sacred land, *konjin hok* (rabbit's breeding place), for the preponderance of the furry little things they believed were gifts from the gods to provide both food and fur.

The next morning the Canarsees returned to the ship and its still-reeling crew, but this time in peace, even bearing gifts for the explorers, as if the attack of the day before had never taken place. The day after that, Hudson took two natives as hostages to guarantee his continued safe passage up the river. That action marked the official beginning of what would eventually be the Dutch settlement in North America. Thirty-six years later, in 1645, having firmly established their presence in the New World, the Dutch (via the Dutch West India Company) granted a patent to Lady Deborah Moody, leader of a group of religious dissenters, to establish a settlement at an area called Gravesend. The next year, the director-general of New Netherland province, Willem Kieft, incorporated the municipality of Brueckelen, named after a town in the Netherlands. Although at war with the Canarsees, the Dutch believed the American "savages" would not kill settlers who were innocent women and children.

The Dutch were wrong.

The very day Lady Moody's group arrived at Konjin Hok, the natives furiously attacked. The forty English settlers put up a mighty battle and managed to fight off the surprised and impressed Canarsees, who, for the time being at least, let them occupy their holy turf. Over the next few years, despite periodic attacks, Moody's settlers developed the forty 16-acre parcels granted to them. By 1654 they had managed to establish excellent trading relations with the Canarsees, and on May 7 of that year, Chief Guttaquoh, who had grown wealthy from trading with the Dutch, peacefully ceded Konjin Hok to Lady Moody, who then anglicized the name into Conyne Island, or Coney Island."*

With the natives no longer restless, the English and the Dutch went

---

* Later on the Dutch would insist the name was a tribute to John Coleman, the first casualty aboard the *Half Moon*. Others believe the name is derived from one of the original thirty-nine landowner families, the Conyns.

to war with each other over the rights to the land on Coney Island. The first outbreak of violence was sparked in 1661, when the Dutch West India Company granted the father-and-son pair of Dirck and Abel de Wolff a monopoly to extract salt from the abundant deposits at Coney Island. The De Wolffs were quickly challenged by a band of armed British cattle farmers who regularly used Gravesend as pasture for their livestock. In response, the Dutch settlers demanded that Peter Stuyvesant, director-general of New Netherland, put an end to all illegal British cattle grazing on Coney Island. While Stuyvesant allowed the salt making (an important industry) to continue, three years later the British sent a fleet against the Dutch, and on September 8, 1664, Stuyvesant was forced to cede the entire island of Manhattan (New Amsterdam) to the British. A month and a half later, all of New Netherland was firmly in the hands of the British, who renamed it New York.

In 1683 the British divided the province of New York into counties, with Kings County (Brooklyn) being one of them. Each county was made up of several towns. To this day, the streets of Brooklyn do not form an orderly grid because each of the original municipalities created its own street plan.

In 1823 Gravesend town supervisor John Terhune formed the private Coney Island Road and Bridge Company and built Brooklyn's first beach resort, the Coney Island House, in anticipation of an influx of new vacationers from as far away as Manhattan. Terhune proved a commercial visionary. His bridge to the island helped turn Coney Island House into an extremely popular tourist destination, attracting not just the working class but the local literati as well as notables from the wider world. By the 1840s such figures as Washington Irving, Herman Melville, Swedish soprano Jenny Lind, and the wildly popular showman P. T. Barnum were regular visitors to the newest social getaway.

Society and literary figures and entertainers were not the only ones to frequent Coney's shores. Manhattan thugs and gamblers had begun to feel the legal heat generated by the great midcentury neighborhood cleanup and subsequent real estate boom led by John Jacob Astor and Cornelius Vanderbilt, and needed to find a new place to continue to operate their shady enterprises. They fled as far away from the streets of Manhattan as they could get, and wound up on the southernmost tip of the Brooklyn shore.

Waiting for them there was Manhattan's Tammany Hall crowd, an Irish working-class political organization whose leader was the notorious William M. "Boss" Tweed. Tweed's gang welcomed the thugs and gamblers with open arms and quickly incorporated them into his thriving tribute and protection scams, enlisting the new recruits to serve as his enforcers. With his blessing, they quickly and efficiently organized the illegal gambling and houses of prostitution that were to become Gravesend's primary attraction and best source of revenue for the next twenty years.

IN 1865 PETER TILYOU, a young and enthusiastic New York developer, moved his family to Coney Island in the hopes of developing a restaurant and resort business. Surf House, his first commercial establishment, was a combination hotel, restaurant, and cabana service, offering bathers a place to change out of their wet bathing suits after enjoying a day in the salty waters. Peter Tilyou's son, George C. Tilyou, had no trouble persuading the local politicos to rezone every available square footage of remaining unused and untaxed property to allow him to develop several more commercial amusement outlets. Not long after, the younger Tilyou presented the city with its first official amusement area. Steeplechase Park, named after the mechanized horse race ride that was its main attraction, also offered rides, games, and penny entertainments on a stretch of land between the Boardwalk and Surf Avenue, starting at West Sixteenth Street and ending at West Nineteenth Street.

GERALD HOWARD: I actually rode it several times as a boy. And my mother had a date or two with George C. Tilyou Jr. [one of the park owner's sons], although that did not get us a discount.

The success of Steeplechase sent other entrepreneurs scurrying to follow in his footsteps. In 1871, Charles Feltman staked his claim to fame on the hot dog, an anglicized version of the centuries-old German wiener. He set up a small stand on West Tenth Street and Surf Avenue, as near as he could to Steeplechase, to sell his ten-cent "miracles of flavor." So successful was Feltman's business that three years later he built the Ocean Pavilion Hotel. And three years after that he was able to add a hundred-foot-long pier that was the forerunner of Coney Island's wooden boardwalk.

The popularity of the Brooklyn shore began to attract serious investors. The Coney Island Jockey Club, the brainchild of a group of prominent New Yorkers that included Leonard Jerome (grandfather of Winston Churchill), New York City real estate baron William Kissam-Vanderbilt (son of William Henry Vanderbilt, grandson of Cornelius Vanderbilt), tobacco tycoon Pierre Lorillard (who'd claimed he invented the smoking jacket, which later became better known as the tuxedo), and legendary New Yorker August Belmont, the mastermind behind the nineteenth-century development of Times Square.

The Coney Island Jockey Club helped fill the nearby hotels and restaurants, but its embrace of horse racing at the nearby Sheepshead Bay Racetrack also signaled the return of some of the shadier characters to the area. By the late 1880s, rows of beer joints, rooms-by-the-hour hotels, and strip joints that offered topless (and, rumor had it, even bottomless) entertainment were once again flourishing in Coney Island. John McKane, another politician who, like Boss Tweed, did not mind looking the other way for the appropriate tribute, gave a leg up, as it were, to the brothels that catered to every perversion imaginable, and he also made it easy for illegal off-track gambling to operate.

By the turn of the twentieth century, the elite had ceded Coney Island to the city's undesirables and immigrant working class. With hundreds of arcades and attractions, it became known to some as the "Nickel Empire"—just about everything, from the rides to the hot dogs, cost the same. Others referred to it as the "Electric Eden," because of its nighttime glitter and gloss, its lit-up signs spreading across the area like giant street-theater poetry. It even attracted Sigmund Freud and Carl Jung as curious visitors.

In 1907 much of Steeplechase Park was destroyed in a fire, but soon George Tilyou came up with the brilliant idea of building a new enclosed amusement area, the Pavilion of Fun. One of the most popular new rides was the Human Roulette Wheel: riders mounted a giant disk, and when the ride started to rotate, riders would try to cling onto the ride against the mounting centrifugal force. The famous Steeplechase ride was also rebuilt, and at the end riders had to exit through the Blow-Hole Theater, where blowers lifted up women's long skirts, much to their horror and the corresponding delight of male onlookers.

Perhaps the best-known ride at Coney Island is the Cyclone, a wooden roller coaster that opened in 1927. Its 2,640 feet of ups and downs produce a stomach-churning sensation not unlike that of being trapped in a horizontal runaway elevator, complete with twelve terrifying drops and six hairpin turns. The Cyclone had been the dream of Jack and Irving Rosenthal; it was designed by Vernon Keenan and built at a cost of $175,000, an astounding amount of money back then, by Harry C. Baker to produce nearly two minutes of soaring, gasping thrills.

Indeed, completing a ride on the great wooden monster without falling to the ground was considered a sign of divine deliverance, which needed to be celebrated with nothing less than a Coney Island hot dog, slathered with mustard, its bun soaked from the juice of a mound of fresh steaming sauerkraut. This was always accompanied by slices of golden fried potatoes and yellow corn drowning in melted butter, all of it topped off with an ice-cold bottle of soda or cup of foamy beer that magically reversed the Cyclone's temporary ascent into the heavens by effectively bringing heaven straight down to earth.

The key to the eventual dominance of Nathan's Famous hot dogs over Feltman's had as much to do with marketing as with the taste of the competing dogs. For decades, Feltman had been the unchallenged food king of the boardwalk, known especially for its incredible clams and lobsters, all washed down by ice-cold beer. By 1915, the year Coney Island reached the peak of its popularity, Feltman's was serving upward of seven thousand meals a day, with the specialty of the house the ten-cent frankfurter. The atmosphere was festive, with live entertainment provided by young and enthusiastic singing waiters.

BRIAN GARI: My grandfather, Eddie Cantor, worked with Jimmy Durante, who was his piano player, at a restaurant with singing waiters. They would be asked to do certain songs. They never turned any song down; their job was to please the audience. If my grandfather didn't know a song, he would simply sing the title to your face, do a little dance, and sing the title again. That was the trick. That's how they made their living.

Nathan Handwerker, a young Jewish immigrant who had arrived in Coney Island looking for work, soon landed a job at Feltman's.

BILL HANDWERKER: The story goes that Durante and Cantor took Nathan aside and said, "You know, Feltman is charging ten cents for a hot dog. Why don't you open up a place and sell it for a nickel?"

So in 1916 my grandparents took their life savings, three hundred dollars, put it into a little stand, and called it Nathan's because they couldn't fit Handwerker on the sign.

Nathan Handwerker began selling his "red hots" at the stand he set up on Surf Avenue, using every attention-grabbing sales technique he could think of, including a public hot-dog-eating contest to see who could down the most dogs in the least amount of time.* After a scandal broke out about what actually was in the nickel Nathan's "hot dog," Handwerker forbid the use of that term by any of his employees. Thus was born the all-American "frankfurter," named after the city of Frank-

---

* The current record for this contest is held by Joey "Jaws" Chestnut, of San Diego, who in 2007 ate sixty-three Nathan's hot dogs and buns in twelve minutes.

furt, Germany, which sold a similar type of sausage that itself was named the wienerwurst, after the city of Vienna.

BILL HANDWERKER: My grandfather's lesson to me, very early on, was never to use the word "hot dog" . . . so no one would think the ingredients were dog food because the price was half of what Feltman's was charging.

Nathan went to extraordinary lengths to make sure that everyone knew his food was first-rate.

BILL HANDWERKER: My grandfather went to Coney Island Hospital and borrowed doctors' coats and stethoscopes and dressed guys up as if they were doctors, and had them eat hot dogs in front of the stand. People then figured if it was good enough for doctors, it was good enough for them! The rest is history.

Handwerker's nickel treats became Coney Island's biggest sensation. It was not uncommon for customers to stand fifteen deep to wait for service from one of the fifty men behind his new corner counter. On weekends auto traffic often had to be rerouted off Surf Avenue because of the crowds. By 1920, a new subway stop at the corner of Surf Avenue and Stillwell Avenue, across the intersection from the stand, made Handwerker look like a real-estate genius, since for everyone who came to Coney Island, the first stop always had to be Nathan's.

During this time, numerous future celebrities paid their professional dues working at Coney Island's many sideshows.

MICKEY FREEMAN: In 1934 or so, I had a peanut stand at Coney Island when I was a kid, right below the Thunderbolt ride. I sold Indian nuts, pistachio nuts, and peanuts. There was a big "5 Cents a Pound" sign, with a very small "half" squeezed in. I knew it was there, but I had to look for it whenever I wanted to check to make sure. People would come up to me and say, "Let me have five cents' worth of peanuts," I'd give them the bag, and they'd almost never question that it was half a pound.

I had a very good first season, so the next year I opened in Luna Park. One day a guy came by and asked for a nickel's worth of peanuts. I gave it to him, and he complained, saying I was cheating him. He actually starting beating me, so I yelled, "Hey, Rube," the code word for trouble at all sideshows. Guys came running from everywhere and quickly broke it up. I came home and told my mother and she said I couldn't work there anymore, it wasn't for me, I had to get a legitimate job. I protested, insisting this was a legitimate job, but she said no, so I had to do something else. So I became a barker.

I worked all along the boardwalk. The thing was, Ravenhall Baths was on one side and Washington Baths was on the other. They all had pools. I was in the middle, working for Majestic Baths. My job was to convince people to come to ours. "Come in, thirty-five cents, we got all the water you want. . . ." One day a guy walks by while I'm barking and he says, "Aren't you Mickey Freeman?" I said yes. "Well, I'm Dave Fishkin. I was the social director at the Waldheim [a Catskills resort located in White Lake, New York], where my family used to take a bungalow and see you. I used to go to that hotel and sing a few tunes, do Eddie Cantor impersonations." We talked for a few minutes and then he said, "I'm an agent now for the Catskills. Come to my office in the Strand Theatre and we'll talk."

I went up there with my sister and he got me a summer job in Sharon Springs, where the sulfur baths are. That's how I began my career as an upstate tummler. It was a good job, but it smelled bad because of all the sulfur. The rest of my career didn't stink.

Of all those who worked the Coney Island beat during their salad days, none would become more famous than a certain young out-of-work music hall performer from England by the name of Archie Leach, whose acrobatic proclivities led him in his late teens to a summer job as a Steeplechase stilt walker, years before Hollywood rechristened him Cary Grant.

CARY GRANT: After a few jobless weeks [in New York City the summer of 1922] my savings were spent, and I began nibbling into the emergency money put aside for return passage to England. Eating, for such a ravenous appetite, was a bit of a problem; but fortunately, being a tall dark-blue-suited young bachelor who wouldn't arrive wearing brown shoes, fall off the chair, or drink from a finger bowl, I was often invited at the last minute to round out the guests at dinner tables on which were some fine spreads. . . .

At the dinner I met a man named George Tilyew [*sic;* George Tilyou Jr.]. We exchanged the "and-what-line-of-business-are-you-in?" genialities, and he told me he had offices at Coney Island in Steeplechase Park, which I gathered his family owned, operated, leased, or managed; I wasn't fully listening at that point because my mind, always alert to the possibility of a job, was wondering how best to benefit from the introduction. Steeplechase? Hmmmm! An amusement park, wasn't it?

I remembered seeing a man walking on stilts along Broadway advertising something or other, and heard myself suggesting to Mr. Tilyew that perhaps I could do the same for him. He agreed that perhaps I could. I said, yes, well, perhaps I could advertise Steeplechase Park by walking up and down in front of the place. I didn't care to invade that other fellow's stilt-walking territory and risk getting my comeuppance or, rather, comedownance. Mr. Tilyew said yes, perhaps I could, it might be a fine idea, and would I see him at his office whenever convenient? *Would* I?

This wasn't the only gimmick the attractions at Coney Island came up with to lure customers. The city had, for many years, a Miss Subways contest (later spoofed as "Miss Turnstiles" in *On the Town*, the 1944 Comden/Green/Bernstein Broadway musical love letter to New York City). The contest allowed many young female subway riders to dream that someday their photo would be up there, and young single male riders to imagine that the girl of their dreams might very well be riding alongside them on the D train.

Coney Island's version of this hearty hucksterism was the Queen of Coney Island contest, which at one time was held in such well-established beachside restaurants as Childs on the Boardwalk, with its friezes of sailing ships and great King Neptune. During the contest's heyday, such burlesque luminaries as Milton Berle were enlisted to help crown the next lucky lady.

In the years immediately following the end of World War II, interest in the contest and all of Coney Island itself peaked—July 3, 1947, is generally agreed to have been the single busiest day in the history of the beach, with estimates running as high as seven million visitors.

But it was all downhill after that.

After a few years the postwar air of celebration began to give way to a sense of malaise, most evident in 1948, when more judges than contestants showed up for the Miss Coney Island pageant and the prize dipped to $2,000 (from a high of $20,000). When a scantily clad bathing beauty couldn't attract patrons to the beach, times were surely bad.

In 1954, Feltman's, which had been so popular in the early decades of the twentieth century and which had managed to withstand the Nathan's onslaught for nearly forty years, closed its legendary doors for good. The beloved 262-foot-tall Parachute Jump, originally built as a promotion by the Lifesavers Company for the 1939 New York World's Fair, then bought by Edward Tilyou (George's eldest son) and moved to Coney Island, stopped operating in 1968.

DON K. REED: You know what killed me about that? When they tore down the Steeplechase, I think it was 1964, the square block it had been on stayed empty *for more than thirty-five years,* until the city built Keyspan Park for the Cyclones, a minor-league ball team owned by the Mets, which didn't open until 2001.

Even the immortal Cyclone was threatened with demolition. It was closed in 1969 and slated to be torn down, but in 1971 it got a last-minute reprieve from the city, which bought it for a million dollars from its then owner, Silvio Pinto. However, when it was unable to find anyone willing to run it, the city reluctantly leased it back at a steep loss to Pinto, who in turn leased it to the father-and-son team of Dewey and Jerome Albert for $57,000 a year. The Alberts, who owned and operated Astroland, on Surf Avenue, one of the four once-great Coney Island boardwalk amusement parks, restored the Cyclone, and they continue to run it to this day.* Beginning in the last third of the twentieth century, as the economic wheel turned once more, a slowly accelerating revival occurred along the sparsely populated beaches of Coney Island. A notable turning point came in 2004, when graffiti artist Steve Powers was hired to restore some of the old signs and, hopefully along with them some of the old glory, to the barely surviving shops along Surf Avenue. The first one he did was for the Eldorado Bumper Car concession.

STEVE POWERS: Coney Island is the most beautiful place in the New York City and we are dedicated to keeping it that way. . . . Once I did it, everyone else wanted a sign too. It went from 0 to 60 . . . celebrating that grimy, hustling, bustling commercial end.

Word of the popularity of the signage revival reached Creative Time, a nonprofit public art agency whose president and artistic director, Anne Pasternak, decided to get behind the movement. With twenty or so up-and-coming artists and $80,000 in seed money, the group set about restoring and updating the art that had defined Coney Island at the dawn of the twentieth century.

Along with corporate interests came the reappearance of some of Coney Island's most colorful characters, with their own ideas about revival.

---

* The other three parks were Dreamland, destroyed by fire in 1911; the New York Aquarium, still in operation; and Luna Park, designed to resemble old Baghdad, which was torn down; today its site is a housing development.

JOHN "CHA CHA" CIARCIA: I used to go to Coney Island every day when I was a kid living on the Lower East Side, with my aunts on the beach. We used to get on the subway, the Sea Beach or the West End, whichever came first. I preferred the West End because at a certain point it would come out of the ground and be outdoors, elevated. I used to stand in the first car, put the window down, and spit out of it, and then get out of the way and see how far the spit would fly back into the car.

I remember going down to the St. George Hotel, in downtown Brooklyn [Brooklyn Heights], because it had a big public pool. A quick ride on the Foster Avenue bus. Coney Island? Went there all the time. It was the thing to do. The Steeplechase? Great. There were the big three–the Cyclone, the Thunderbolt, and the Tornado. The Bobsled was another big ride. And having a hot dog at Nathan's on a hot summer night, that was the best. Walk around, guys selling things, games, throw a dart, blow up a balloon, perfect place to take a girl.

Everything in those days was all woody and great. All the old places that are long gone–Ravenhall, Washington Baths, Steeplechase Park, the steam rooms. When I sit in my restaurant near the boardwalk today and look out on what I call the Brooklyn Riviera, I think to myself, I remember sitting on the boardwalk or lying on a blanket on the beach, eating a tuna fish and egg sandwich with sand in it, this was better than being in Portofino. The only difference is that when I was a kid, Coney Island was a European culture, Irish, Jews, Italians, Norwegians. Now it's an international, worldwide culture. There's Asians, Russians, blacks, Puerto Ricans. When people say Coney Island is not what it used to be, it's because they don't understand the whole world is changing culturally, not just Coney Island. For a while it went all the way down, controlled by the pimps selling prostitutes and drugs, but now it's on a big comeback. With the price of gas and all the problems with the airlines, people want to stay closer to home. Where better than Coney Island? Instead of having to go to the far corners to see the world, the far corners have come to the beach.

I opened up a hot dog stand in Coney Island.

Joe Sitt, "Joey Coney Island" to his friends, named his real estate and development company Thor Equities after his favorite comic book hero. Thor was the "protector of the Planet Earth's buildings from the evil goblins from outer space seeking to destroy them." A few years ago Sitt began buying up the rights to a ten-acre parcel that included Coney Island's Boardwalk. Sitt's vision of a reimagined and rebuilt Coney Island came with an initial budget of $1 billion and a backup portfolio of more than $2.4 billion.

At first glance Sitt may have seemed to be merely the latest in a long line of visionaries whose signature projects dragged along the pejorative description of "folly," but today it looks as though he knew exactly what he was doing. Despite the generally dilapidated state of Coney Island, more than 10 million people visited the beach in 2005—five times as many as had been there only seven years earlier. Bodies, Sitt knew, meant traffic; traffic meant money; and money meant profit.

And profit meant votes. That was the clear message to New York City's first mayor elected in the twenty-first-century, Michael Bloomberg, a billionaire at home in the world of real estate development and profit. No sooner had Thor Equities begun making revisionist plans for Brooklyn's past than Bloomberg gave the go-ahead for a new Stillwell Avenue terminal featuring solar panels to be built for the D, F, B, and Q trains.

JOE SITT: I was born in Gravesend to Middle Eastern Jewish parents . . . right next to Coney Island. I went to a private parochial school near Flatbush, even though I was Jewish. My parents thought I'd get a better quality of education there. Still, like all kids from Brooklyn, I grew up tough, maybe in my instance a little too tough, and my parents sent me there to "straighten me out." I then went to NYU [New York University], where I discovered my entrepreneurial skills. Even as a kid I had always been ambitious, doing anything to make a buck. When I was fourteen years of age I would go door-to-door in Gravesend offering to clean people's fish tanks for a couple of bucks. I was a Brooklyn disc jockey for a while, and did a lot of work in local flea markets, at Aqueduct and Roosevelt Raceways, getting there on weekends at four in the morning to make sure I got the best spot to sell my stuff.

It was during my time at NYU that I formed Thor Equities. One day I came across an article that some tax-seized properties were being sold at One Police Plaza, and became interested in real estate. During my undergraduate years I did a lot of traveling, particularly in the Far East, which I became quite interested in. After I graduated, I moved back, because my heart was always in Brooklyn. I knew early on that I was in a special place, like no other, really, in the world.

Twenty years ago, when I returned, it was at its low point. People were actually embarrassed to say they lived in or were from Brooklyn. Now, it's once again become a cool place to live in, that people are proud of. And with good reason. All of Brooklyn, but I think especially Coney Island and its environs, has a special history.

As a kid growing up, I had so much fun at Coney Island, all the rides, the walks along the boardwalk. People tend to remember things like the Steeplechase that were a part of the fabric of their childhoods. Or their first Nathan's hot dog. People everywhere know Coney Island, even if they've never been there or never even seen a photo of it. A Nathan's hot dog is the most famous symbol of America in the world.

Many years ago there were raging fires throughout Coney Island, and most of what was older and less secure simply burned down and disappeared. A hundred and seventy-eight residential buildings were destroyed in the blazing infernos of 1932. Those buildings were never rebuilt. There was over a million dollars' worth of damage, and thousands were rendered homeless. Then there was the great fire that leveled the original Steeplechase Park and Dreamland Park in 1944, and that put an end to Luna Park.

The Coney Island that once was had been irrevocably lost, gone forever. And something else was destroyed as well, something far more subtle. Many of the families that had first moved to Coney Island owned a small piece of land that the first generation had operated a small food stand or a ride on. The businesses may have fallen away, but the families held on to the land mostly for nostalgia, and that was what, to a large degree, was responsible for the stagnation and neglect that became so much of Coney Island.

When I first thought about revitalizing Coney Island, I was struck by how pitiful this was, all those small parcels of mostly useless land going to waste. The other thing I noticed was that the newer immigrant communities, the Russians and the Chinese, were creating a huge demand for housing. So was the Orthodox Jewish community from Ocean Parkway, the African Americans, the Hispanics–they were all growing and eventually expanding to wherever housing was cheap, even if dilapidated, and that was Coney Island. Beginning in the '80s, although largely unnoticed, there was a lot of movement toward the beach, which started to draw large crowds again. People wanted to swim and sit in the sun, and did so even amidst the burned-out rubble that surrounded Coney Island.

I first got the idea to redevelop the entire area one morning in 2003 while jogging on an early Sunday morning with my wife along the water, which happens to be magnificent. Not far from my home, in Gravesend, the view into the ocean is simply breathtaking. I don't think the Hamptons or the Jersey Shore are nearly as beautiful. Then we hit the empty lots. I saw a broken-down boardwalk, but in my mind I saw a revitalized community, with volleyball courts, restaurants, and a café life that could spur Coney Island back to the greatness it once had. Every once in a while I'd have a shot of vodka with some friends at one of the new Russian bars and then go back to jogging. That may have helped my vision.

I remember thinking how Brighton Beach and Manhattan Beach had both survived long enough to witness the early stages of a comeback boom, while Coney Island was still this long strip of run-down, neglected land. I just said to myself, I'd love to own this and bring it back to its glory days.

I did some research and found that the city had indeed taken notice of the fact that Brooklyn was still very economically viable. After 9/11 they spent $47 million to redo the Aquarium, and close to a hundred million dollars to build a minor league baseball field; $87 million was invested in a brand-new boardwalk, $280 million for a new solar-powered train station. If the legacy of the Giuliani administration is the restoration of Forty-second Street in Manhattan, the legacy of Bloomberg will undoubtedly be Brooklyn.

When, in 2003, as I saw all this infrastructure happening, I thought the time was right to get involved. I began to accumulate property, with the goal of owning as much of Coney Island as I could, so I could redevelop and restore it. The key to it is the brand Coney Island and the larger one it belongs to: Brooklyn, the mythic, legendary borough, and its historic playground on the southern tip. I now own at least 80 percent of the non-government-owned and/or landmarked amusement areas in and around Coney Island.

What was Coney Island always known for? Excitement and fun on the retail level, hotels, and to some degree summer homes, which is why, referring to the latter, we're working on a time-share program of trendy condominiums, to take advantage of the summers. In the grand plan, I see Coney Island as a year-round opportunity, and with the right kind of development it can be, as opposed to a summer resort and amusement park facility.

I'm sure old George C. Tilyou's smiling face should somehow hover over the entire redevelopment.

A lot of people thought I was out of my mind when I started to talk about Coney Island as a place of the future. My dream is to see Coney Island restored to greatness as the most incredible urban entertainment venue anywhere in the world, with hotels, rides, restaurants, all of it—just the way it once was.

Nostalgia, though, can only take you so far. Nothing but time will tell if Joey Coney Island's dream is the real thing.

As for Astroland, as the summer of 2007 commenced, it was announced that this was to be the final year of existence for the stretch of amusements between the landmarked (and therefore protected) Cyclone and Nathan's. All the rides, carny attractions, and boardwalk businesses in between were set for demolition, to make way for high-rise condos and hotels. Among those slated to go were the fondly remembered batting cages that stood in the shadows of the new, upscale Brooklyn Cyclones minor league ballpark. It was in those cages that every kid with a nickel could pretend he was Duke Snider for a day.

Then, in the winter of 2007, an ad hoc committee that called itself No Condos in Coney began holding rallies to defend what it considered hallowed land.

DIANA CARLIN: This is going to be a celebration of the true spirit of Coney Island, which I believe [developer Thor Equities] can't comprehend.

JOE SITT: Thor Equities shares the view that Coney Island needs to be saved . . . which is why Thor's plan calls for the largest investment ever made in new amusements.

Even as some shed tears for the end of an era, others were lining up to be the first to buy one of the new condos, before so much as a single brick had been put in place.

And then in October 2007, just as the hammer of Thor was about to come down, Brooklyn councilman Domenic Recchia Jr. helped broker a one-year lease extension for most of Astroland's commercial renters, including Carol and Jerome Albert, the children of the family that has run Astroland for generations. The deal gave new life to Ruby's Bar and Grill, the red and blue rocketship ride, Dante's Inferno, the pirate ship ride, the annual Mermaid Parade, the Lola Staar Souvenir Boutique on the Boardwalk, Shoot the Freak, and of course Cha Cha's place. However, beyond the end of the 2008 season, no one knows what will happen.

Through it all, the cyclonic roller-coaster ride that is Coney Island's future continues to soar and dip, thrilling some and scaring the life out of others.

✖ ✖ ✖

KEY DATES IN BROOKLYN'S HISTORY

- 1683—Kings County and "six towns" created: Brooklyn, Bushwick, Flatbush, Flatlands, Gravesend, and New Utrecht.
- 1816—Village of Brooklyn incorporated with Town of Brooklyn.
- 1827—Village of Williamsburgh incorporated within Town of Bushwick.
- 1834—Town of Brooklyn (including Village of Brooklyn) becomes City of Brooklyn. Kings County now includes one city (Brooklyn) and five towns (Bushwick, Flatbush, Flatlands, Gravesend, and New Utrecht).
- 1851—Village of Williamsburgh secedes from Town of Bushwick and becomes City of Williamsburgh. Kings County now includes two cities (Brooklyn and Williamsburgh) and five towns (Bushwick, Flatbush, Flatlands, Gravesend, and New Utrecht).
- 1852—Town of New Lots secedes from Town of Flatbush. Kings County consists of two cities (Brooklyn and Williamsburgh) and six towns (Bushwick, Flatbush, Flatlands, Gravesend, New Lots, and New Utrecht).
- 1854—City of Williamsburgh and Town of Bushwick consolidated into City of Brooklyn. Kings County now one city (Brooklyn) and five towns (Flatbush, Flatlands, Gravesend, New Lots, and New Utrecht).
- 1886—Town of New Lots annexed to City of Brooklyn. Kings County now one city (Brooklyn) and four towns (Flatbush, Flatlands, Gravesend, and New Utrecht).
- 1894—Towns of Flatbush, Gravesend, and New Utrecht annexed to City of Brooklyn. Kings County now one city (Brooklyn) and one town (Flatlands).
- 1898—The city's great unification becomes official with incorporation; Brooklyn joins with the Bronx, Queens, Manhattan, and Staten Island to form New York City.
- 1903—Williamsburg Bridge opens.
- 1907—Brooklyn and Manhattan are connected by the IRT, New York's first subway system, through the Joralemon Street tunnel.
- 1907—The Vitagraph company begins film production in Midwood. The site will later house studios owned by Warner Bros. and NBC-TV.

- 1909—Manhattan Bridge opens.
- 1911—Brooklyn Botanical Garden opens.
- 1913—Ebbets Field opens.
- 1916—"Nathan's" opens on Coney Island.
- 1926—The main entrance to Prospect Park is renamed "Grand Army Plaza."
- 1928—Brooklyn Paramount Theatre opens.
- 1928—"The Cyclone" debuts on Coney Island.
- 1934—Lundy Brothers Restaurant opens in Sheepshead Bay.
- 1938—Ebbets Field is the site of New York City's first-ever night baseball game, in which Johnny Vander Meer pitches the second of his record two consecutive no-hitters.
- 1947—Jackie Robinson of the Brooklyn Dodgers becomes Major League Baseball's first African American player.
- 1950—Brooklyn Battery Tunnel opens.
- 1950—Junior's Restaurant opens.
- 1951—Dodgers lose playoff for National League pennant on Bobby Thomson's "shot heard 'round the world."
- 1951—Jackie Gleason's *Honeymooners* characters from Bensonhurst first appear on TV.
- 1955—The Dodgers defeat the New York Yankees in seven games for Brooklyn's only World Series victory.
- 1957—Dodgers play their last game in Brooklyn.
- 1964—Verrazano Narrows Bridge, the word's largest suspension bridge, opens.
- 1966—Brooklyn Navy Yard closes.
- 1972—A botched bank robbery in Gravesend will become the story of the movie *Dog Day Afternoon*.
- 1977—Fulton Mall opens in downtown Brooklyn.
- 1977—*Saturday Night Fever* movie about Brooklyn disco scene opens.
- 1977—Parking ticket issued to David Berkowitz at the scene of the final "Son of Sam" murder leads to his arrest.
- 1978—Brooklyn political boss Meade Esposito, having "delivered" the mayoral election, starts a corruption time bomb ticking on Ed Koch's administration.

- 1986—Gambino crime family mobster Frank Decicco is killed by a car bomb explosion in Bensonhurst. The intended target is John Gotti, who is not there.
- 1989—Formation of Brooklyn Philharmonic.
- 1989—The murder of a black teenager named Yusef Hawkins by a mob of white teenagers in Bensonhurst sparks an explosion of protesting and riots.
- 1990—Boycott of Korean grocery "Red Apple" highlights racial tensions in Flatbush.
- 1991—Crown Heights rioting begins as racial tension explodes over car accident.
- 1995—Brooklyn Brewery opens.
- 1999—Mayor Giuliani vs. Brooklyn Museum over "Sensation" exhibit.
- 2001—44 years after the departure of the Dodgers, professional baseball returns to Brooklyn as the Cyclones, a Mets minor league affiliate, begin play on Coney Island.
- 2005—The NBA's New Jersey Nets, under new principal owner Bruce Ratner, announce plans to move to Brooklyn.

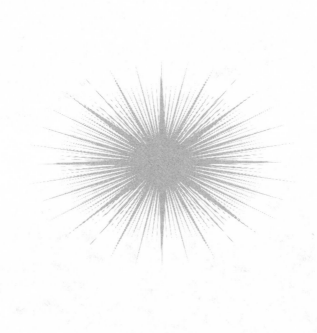

CHAPTER TWO

SHEEPSHEAD BAY

So I get into a cab and the driver asks me if I want to be fixed up with a real hot babe who puts out . . . I say sure and he shows me a picture of my wife.

—RODNEY DANGERFIELD, FROM A ROUTINE
HE OFTEN PERFORMED DURING HIS EARLY DAYS
AT PIPS NIGHTCLUB IN SHEEPSHEAD BAY

N AMED AFTER A LOCAL FISH, Sheepshead Bay was one of the last areas of south Brooklyn to be developed. In 1880 the shore's bulging population had become wealthy enough to justify the founding of the Sheepshead Bay Racetrack. While the elite enjoyed the sport of kings, working-class ethnics, mostly Jews and Italians, benefited from the area's development, as inexpensive housing sprang up along the shore to accommodate those who worked at the track and its various offshoots and, after betting at the track was banned in 1910, in the party-boat fishing industry that developed there.

Hungry after a day out fishing, people could find a good meal at Dubrow's, a classic help-yourself-style cafeteria. Brennan and Carr has been serving its famous thin-sliced roast beef sandwiches since 1938. And Randazzo's Clam Bar still offers an extravaganza of fresh seafood. But probably the most famous eatery of all was Lundy's, which started as a clam bar built on pilings over the water in 1907 and twenty-eight years later moved to the site on Emmons Avenue it occupied for the next seven decades.* Lundy's was able to seat as many as 2,800 diners at a time in its Spanish-mission-style stucco structure, as hundreds more eager bodies crowded into the front bar area, drinking, socializing, schmoozing, all the while downing luscious fresh raw ocean clams. Evenings, Lundy's became the gathering spot of choice for the borough's remaining gamblers, local whales who bet on anything—when no sport was available, they'd play the numbers game, with the winning number often based on specific digits in payoff amounts at the racetrack.

Two years after the death in 1977 of Irving Lundy, the last of the establishment's original founder-operators, economic hard times, endless labor disputes, and a dwindling of foot traffic finally forced the original incarnation of Lundy's to close its doors. It reopened in 1995, as the economic rebound of the 1990s reached all the way from Wall Street to the shores of the bay. Although the new Lundy's was smaller, it still featured the legendary old Lundy's 1,200-gallon lobster tank filled with crustaceans the size of raccoons. Besides size, the biggest difference was that there was no longer a Lundy at the front door. What had once been a family operation was now wholly owned and operated by a corporation, Tam Restaurants.

Until it finally closed again in 2007, Lundy's had many Russian customers. So many Russians had immigrated to Sheepshead Bay and adjacent Brighton Beach in the early 1990s that it became known among its residents (both Russian and non-Russian) as "Little Odessa." This kicked off a boom in high-rise luxury development within skipping-stone distance of the beach.

At some of the Sheepshead Bay restaurants a visitor might have seen Mafia chieftain Carlo Gambino or another mob figure indulging

---

* Lundy's seafood took on an even more legendary reputation after the publication of Philip Roth's *Portnoy's Complaint,* in which the eponymous Portnoy does something quite loathsome in the bus back to New Jersey that he blames on having eaten the "forbidden" seafood at Lundy's after a Dodgers game.

in a little scungilli, a cold beer, followed by a satisfying, definitive belch. The Gambinos were more or less the ringleaders of ringleaders, with the late Carlo Gambino the acknowledged *capo di tutti capi*, boss of bosses, who, from his modest Brooklyn home, ruled Brooklyn, the rest of the city, and other mobbed-up capitals across the country.

PIPS, IN SHEEPSHEAD BAY, is the oldest continuously operating comedy club in the country. It is situated on the relatively remote Emmons Avenue, beyond the encompassing limits of the Belt Parkway (the main roadway that loops the entire borough and links it by car to Manhattan, Queens, and Long Island), within walking distance from the last stop on the Q line. For Manhattanites, a trip to Pips for a night out is the rough equivalent of taking a drive to Arizona for the weekend.

The club first opened its doors in 1962, the dream child of Brooklyn-born-and-raised stand-up comic George Schultz, then one of the group of comics who used the lunch counter at Hanson's drugstore in midtown Manhattan as their unofficial clubhouse. The inner circle included the notorious and still young Lenny Bruce, the wildly off-color Borscht Belt comedian Buddy Hackett, the aluminum-siding salesman Jacob "Jack" Cohen (who first started performing under the stage name Jack Roy and later changed his name to Rodney Dangerfield), and the comics who would form the nucleus of TV comedy entertainment for generations to come. Performers who appeared at Pips included such future Broadway, movie, and nightclub comedy stars as Billy Crystal, David Brenner, Jerry Seinfeld, Robert Klein, Joan Rivers, George Carlin, Andy Kaufman, Jackie Mason, and Woody Allen.

The story is told that after one particularly bleak Thanksgiving day on the road, Schultz, alone, lonely, and pining for his wife and family, had an epiphany and decided then and there to move back to the borough of his childhood and open a club. His vision was inspired: rather than having to pack bags and hit the road every time he wanted to collect a paycheck, he would put out his shingle and make the road come to him.

Schultz built his comedy roster on the talents of his old Hanson's cronies. Woody Allen was so excited about the idea of the new club that he tried out to be house MC, a position for which Schultz offered a then-whopping $200 a week, but didn't make the final cut. (Allen used the club as the backdrop for his 2003 film *Anything Else*.)

Besides the original Hanson gang, regulars who appeared at Pips included Andrew Silverstein (later known as Andrew "Dice" Clay), Steve Landesberg, Richard Lewis, Adam Sandler, Robert Guillaume, Ray Romano, Paul Reiser, Elayne Boosler, and Jackie "the Jokeman" Martling (occasionally barred from performing because he drank too much).

BRIAN GARI: My friend Alan Colmes, the television commentator who was at the time trying to be a stand-up, auditioned with me for a spot at Manhattan's Comic Strip, which had just opened. I tried out as a singer/songwriter, Alan as a comic, and we both made it. In those days it was rare to have singers at these clubs, but I sort of fit in with the general feel. Of course, the other reason they hired us was they had nobody else willing to work for nothing.

We both started playing the club regularly. One of the other comics there, a fellow by the name of Ellis Levinson, liked my music, and told me he worked at this club in Brooklyn, a place called Pips, where he knew the owner, George Schultz, and would recommend me to him.

At the time I had never heard of Pips. The next day while I was sitting in my kitchen the phone rang and it was George Schultz. He introduced himself and said he wanted to give me a shot. He wanted me to play all the familiar pop songs, but I told him I'd only do original stuff. He said okay, and that he'd give me fifty dollars for four shows that weekend, and I felt like I had just scored a fortune. All I had to do was show up.

I didn't realize how far away from Manhattan the club was. I was living on the Upper West Side at the time, and it took nearly two hours by subway to get to it.

One of the great things about Pips was that you not only got your fifty bucks, you also got to eat there, which meant free cheeseburgers and hot fudge sundaes, a big deal to struggling entertainers. I remember Andy Kaufman, in particular, used to go nuts over those sundaes. He used to drink the hot fudge directly, without even pouring it on the ice cream.

The club itself was a raunchy-looking place. The owner, George, lived with his sons, Seth and Marty, in the same building above the nightclub. Anyway, I went over so well, George asked me to come by the following week, and that was it, I was a regular at Pips, from 1976 till the early eighties. I quickly learned that the Pips audiences were the toughest in the country and that if you could go over with them, you could actually make it in show business. A gig at Pips was more often than not the deciding factor in whether or not a comic or a singer continued pursuing a career. By the end of my run, I was doing twenty-five-minute sets, making about a hundred and fifty bucks a pop.

What can I say about the audiences? It was what we called "outer borough," real Guido time, with the gold chains on the men's necks, the women with the frozen hair, and they were college-age! They could relate to the scene and didn't suffer fools. They wanted bottom-of-the-line, easy-to-understand comedy, which was perfect for the entertainers trying to learn the rhythms of telling a joke and getting a laugh. The audiences didn't like to think or make connections; they were not an intellectual crowd. These were people who worked all week, got dressed up on weekends, wanted to go out, laugh, have a few drinks, smoke like chimneys, have a bite to eat, and be entertained. If you could win over this tough Brooklyn neighborhood crowd in that smoky, dingy room, it meant you could conquer any audience.

MICKEY FREEMAN: All the New York City and Catskills comedy acts, including me, wanted to work at Pips, primarily because it was a great place to break in new material. Rodney Dangerfield, all of those guys started in Pips. It was like a breaking-in-material club that happened to get a lot of attention and had a lot of influence and therefore got you noticed.

JOAN RIVERS: I went into comedy long after I had decided to pursue a career as an actress. Comedy became a means of supporting myself. My father was very funny, so was my sister, so comedy ran through the family. I could always make people laugh. One day someone approached me and said, "This is only temporary, but I know where you can make six dollars a night in comedy clubs." I thought, wow, what a great way to make a living, certainly better than sitting in an office all day as a typing temp.

I played Pips maybe twice. Once Rodney Dangerfield took me out there—and, by the way, drove like Looney Tunes. And I went once with David Brenner. It was like a sixties coffee shop, only it served drinks. Young comics would come on and perform, and everyone pretty much knew everyone else on the circuit. We'd get paid a little bit of money, and after the show we'd all go over to Lundy's to get some real dinner and drinks and talk through the night.

BRIAN GARI: So many people who came through Pips got their big career boost there. Jerry Seinfeld, Larry Miller, Robert Klein, Jose Feliciano, Stiller and Meara, Gilbert Gottfried, Rodney Dangerfield.

Unfortunately, during the years I was there, a lot of cocaine began showing up, and that helped to bring down the whole New York and Brooklyn club scene, mainly because it became increasingly hard to deal with some of the talent, while others began to taste real success and lost interest in the club. George was old, tired, divorced, and eventually got fed up with some of the younger kids who wanted in but who, to him, just didn't have it. As time went on, talent got less and less, and that made it more difficult to make the club work. An enormous dark side developed that clung to Pips like a suckerfish, when a couple of the regular comics, Adam Keefe and Bernie Travis, whose careers weren't going anywhere, committed suicide. They were two promising but troubled comedians whose untimely deaths cast a deep shadow over the club.

In the 1980s, Pips fell into a sort of emotional and economic despair that roughly coincided with the arrival of the Russians, whose sense of humor was, to say the least, not in sync with the zingy one-liners that had been for so many years the calling card for Pips' comics. By the summer of 1994, things had gotten so bad George was about to sell the place to a guy looking to turn it into a Greek restaurant. Then a couple of boys from the old neighborhood, Louis Torelli, Joey Gay, and Gene Burshtein, decided to try to save Pips.

JOEY GAY: I felt like I was the only Yankee fan and they were tearing down the stadium. The blue bloods of American comedy started here. That meant something to me.

Gay looked around for partners and found Louis Torelli, a restaurateur he'd gone to Catholic school with who was thinking of opening a fast-food franchise somewhere in Sheepshead Bay. With a third partner, Gene Burshtein, they bought Pips instead and have kept the doors open to this day.

"*Did you hear the one about the cab driver . . .*"

✶ ✶ ✶

FAMOUS BROOKLYNITES

AALIYAH: Real name **AALIYAH DANA HAUGHTON**. Notable for several hit records, including five number-one R&B hits, one number-one pop hit, and seven top-ten singles, Aaliyah sold more than twenty-four million records worldwide during her career and starred in two motion pictures before her death in a plane crash in 2001 at the age of twenty-two.

ZAID ABDUL-AZIZ: Born Donald A. Smith in Brooklyn, 1946. Professional basketball player. Played for the Milwaukee Bucks, Seattle Supersonics, Houston Rockets, Buffalo Braves, Boston Celtics.

WARREN ADLER: Novelist. Several of his books were made into movies, including *The War of the Roses* and *Random Hearts*. Attended Brooklyn Tech.

DANNY AIELLO: Movie, TV, and stage actor and nightclub singer. Nominated for an Oscar for Best Supporting Actor in Spike Lee's *Do the Right Thing* (1989).

FRANKLYN AJAYE: African American stand-up comedian, film, and TV star

(*Convoy, Car Wash, Deadwood*). Born in Brooklyn, raised in Los Angeles, currently lives in Australia.

MARV ALBERT: Sportscaster. Was the voice of the New York Knicks for thirty years. Member of the Basketball Hall of Fame. Born Marvin Philip Aufrichtig in Brooklyn in 1941. Two brothers, Al and Steve Albert, are also professional sportscasters.

STEW ALBERT: Co-founder of the Yippies (Youth International Party), 1960s anti–Vietnam War activist. Named as an unindicted co-conspirator during the trial of the Chicago Seven, following the riots that took place during the 1968 Democratic Convention. Born in Sheepshead Bay, 1939.

WOODY ALLEN: Comedian, film director, screenwriter, essayist, actor. Allen Stewart Konigsberg was born and raised in Flatbush. Allen attended New York University but dropped out because of a poor academic record. By the age of nineteen he was writing material for the *Ed Sullivan Show* and the *Tonight Show*. Emmy winner, 1957. Won three Academy Awards: Best Director and Best Original Screenplay for *Annie Hall* (1977); Academy Award, Best Original Screenplay, *Hannah and Her Sisters* (1986). Allen holds the record for most Best Screenplay Oscar nominations with fourteen.

LYLE ALZADO: Born in Brooklyn to an Italian-Spanish father and a Jewish mother. Played professional football for the Denver Broncos, Cleveland Browns, Los Angeles Raiders. Alzado was also an actor and an amateur boxer. He died of brain cancer at the age of forty-three.

DARREN ARONOFSKY: Film director. Born in Brooklyn, attended Harvard. In 2001 made a notable film of Brooklyn-born Hubert Selby Jr.'s *Requiem for a Dream*.

ISAAC ASIMOV: Born in Russia, raised in Brooklyn. Attended Boys' High School, earned a Ph.D. from the City University of New York. Worked as a civilian at the Brooklyn Navy Yard during World War II. Best known for his intellectual, philosophical, visionary science-fiction novels, including *I, Robot*, written in 1950.

RED AUERBACH: Arnold Jacob "Red" Auerbach was born in 1917 in Brooklyn, the child of Russian immigrants. He attended Eastern District High School and made the All-Scholastic second team. After being discharged from the military, in 1946 he started his professional career with the Washington Capitols and joined the last-place Celtics four years later and turned them into the perennial leaders of the NBA. He is tied with Phil Jackson for the most NBA championships with nine. In 1980, he was named the best NBA coach in basketball history by the Professional Basketball Writers Association of America.

KEN AULETTA: Brooklyn-born Ken Auletta grew up in Coney Island and attended Abraham Lincoln High School. A respected journalist, he is the author of eight books, including the best-selling *The Streets Were Paved with Gold* (1979) about the fiscal crisis of New York City. Since 1992 he has written the "Annals of Communication" column for *The New Yorker*.

LAUREN BACALL: Born Betty Joan Perske in Brooklyn to Jewish immigrant parents. Starred on Broadway in the 1940s. Became a Hollywood leading lady with her role in Howard Hawks's 1944 *To Have and Have Not*, after being spotted by Hawks's wife, Slim, on the cover of *Harper's Bazaar*. Married Humphrey Bogart, with whom she co-starred in that movie.

BRIAN BACKER: American film actor, born in Brooklyn, best known for his role in *Fast Times at Ridgemont High*. After that he appeared in several popular movies and on TV.

RALPH BAKSHI: Noted animated feature film maker. Born in Krymchak, Haifa, part of the British Mandate of Palestine (Israel). He was raised in Brownsville, Brooklyn, and attended Jefferson High School. His most famous animated films are *Fritz the Cat* (1972), *Heavy Traffic* (1973), and *Coonskin* (1975).

INA BALIN: Actress. Born Ina Rosenberg in 1937 in Brooklyn. She appeared on television, in movies, and on Broadway.

JEFF BARRY: Pop music songwriter, record producer, singer. Born Joel Adelberg in Brooklyn, he lived there until the age of seven, when his divorced mother moved to New Jersey, where he lived for several years before returning to Brooklyn. Attended Erasmus High School. After military service, he changed his name to Jeff Barry (after his screen idol, Brooklyn-born Erasmus alumni Jeff Chandler), turned to songwriting, and wrote a series of Brill Building hit songs, including such rock-and-roll and pop classics as "Da Doo Ron Ron" and "Then He Kissed Me" for the Crystals, "Be My Baby" and "Baby,

I Love You," for the Ronettes, and "Christmas (Baby Please Come Home)" for Darlene Love, all of which were produced by Phil Spector. Wrote and/or produced "Chapel of Love" and "Iko Iko" for the Dixie Cups, and "Remember (Walking in the Sand)" and "Leader of the Pack" for the Shangri-Las. In 1991, Jeff Barry and his former wife, Ellie Greenwich, were inducted into the Songwriters Hall of Fame.

PAUL BARTEL: Actor, director, screenwriter. Born in Brooklyn in 1938. Best known for his 1982 film *Eating Raoul*.

MARIA BARTIROMO: Famed "Money Honey" financial reporter, hosts the *Closing Bell* program on CNBC. Born in Bay Ridge, as a teenager she worked at her parents' Italian restaurant while attending Fontbonne Hall Academy and NYU. Punk icon Joey Ramone wrote a song about her in tribute.

JEAN-MICHEL BASQUIAT: Born in Brooklyn in 1960. Gained early fame as a graffiti artist and became a proponent of the burgeoning East Village art movement of the late 1970s, gaining widespread recognition in the 1980s. Died of a drug overdose in 1988.

PAT BENATAR: Rock musician. Patricia Mae Andrzejewski was born in Brooklyn, but while still a child moved with her family to Long Island and then Virginia. She was discovered at an amateur night show in New York City's Catch a Rising Star in 1977. Her creative pairing with guitarist Neil Giraldo (whom she married in 1982) produced many hit records.

WILLIAM BENNETT: Born in Brooklyn in 1943, William John Bennett served as U.S. secretary of education from 1985 to 1988. Was the director of national drug policy under President George H. W. Bush. Bennett has been a long-time Republican conservative activist.

DAVID BERKOWITZ: David Falco Berkowitz was born in Brooklyn in 1953. Better known by his murderous pseudonym, "Son of Sam." Currently serving a life sentence for murdering six people in New York City's outer boroughs during the 1970s.

OTIS BLACKWELL: American singer, songwriter, musician. Born in Brooklyn in 1931. Wrote classic rock-and-roll hits for Elvis Presley ("All Shook Up," "Don't Be Cruel," "Return to Sender"), Jerry Lee Lewis ("Great Balls of Fire," "Breathless"), Dee Clark ("Hey Little Girl"), and many others. He also wrote, under the pen name of John Davenport, the Peggy Lee standard "Fever." He was inducted into the Nashville Songwriters Hall of Fame in 1986 and the National Academy of Popular Music's Songwriters Hall of Fame in 1991. He died in 2002 of a heart attack.

MR. BLACKWELL: Richard Blackwell, born Richard Selzer (sometimes spelled Seltzer) in 1922 in Brooklyn. As the peripatetic Mr. Blackwell gained fame as a fashion critic, producing the highly entertaining "Worst Dressed" lists.

JOSEPH BOLOGNA: Noted American actor. Born in 1934, in Brooklyn. Married to actress Renee Taylor. Starred in numerous plays, movies, and TV shows, including *Lovers and Other Strangers* (1970), *My Favorite Year* (1982), *Blame It on Rio* (1984), and *The Woman in Red* (1984). He was a frequent guest on the *Tonight Show* starring Johnny Carson.

JULIE BOVASSO: American actress and writer. Born in Brooklyn, best remembered as John Travolta's mother in John Badham's *Saturday Night Fever* (1977) and as Rita Cappomoggi in Norman Jewison's *Moonstruck* (1987).

CLARA BOW: Born in a Brooklyn tenement in 1905. Began working in New York–based silent movies in 1922. She was discovered by Paramount Pictures' Budd Schulberg. The studio publicity department declared her the "It Girl," and she became an international film star.

BARBARA BOXER: Born in Brooklyn. Attended Brooklyn College and graduated in 1962 with a degree in economics. Relocated to California and was elected a congresswoman in 1982 and a senator in 1992. Her daughter married Hillary Rodham Clinton's brother.

CARL BRAUN: Brooklyn-born basketball player. Played for the Knicks for twelve of his thirteen years in the NBA (he played his last season with the Boston Celtics).

JAMES L. BROOKS: Film and TV actor, producer, and director. Born in Brooklyn in 1940. Produced classic TV sitcoms, including *The Mary Tyler Moore Show, The Simpsons, Rhoda, Taxi,* and *The Tracey Ullman Show.* He won the Best Director Academy Award for 1993's *Terms of Endearment* (which also won two other Academy Awards) and a total of nineteen Emmy awards.

MEL BROOKS: Actor, director, writer, producer, comedian. Born Melvin Kaminsky in Brooklyn, 1926. Served in the army during World War II as an engineer in North Africa. Began his show business career as a stand-up comic, which led to a writing stint on Sid Caesar's classic TV comedy variety series *Your Show of Shows*. Created legendary comic routine "The 2000 Year Old Man" with Carl Reiner. In 1965 created the successful TV series *Get Smart*. In 1968 wrote and directed *The Producers*, for which he won an Academy Award for Best Screenplay. In 1974 he directed and wrote *Young Frankenstein* and *Blazing Saddles* (co-written with Richard Pryor). In 2001 turned *The Producers* into an award-winning Broadway musical. A film of that version was released in 2005. Among the select few who has won at least one Oscar, Emmy, Tony, and Grammy award.

FOXY BROWN: Born Inga Marchand in Brooklyn, of Trinidadian and Asian descent. Grammy-nominated hip-hop singer, rapper, model for Christian Dior and Calvin Klein.

LARRY BROWN: Born Lawrence Harvey Brown in Brooklyn in 1940. Played high school basketball for Long Beach and college ball at University of North Carolina under Dean Smith. As a coach, was the first man to win collegiate national and NBA championships. Most recently, he has been the coach of the New York Knicks.

STEVE BUSCEMI: Steven Vincent Buscemi was born in Brooklyn to an Irish American mother and Italian father. A popular character actor and director who has appeared in numerous films, including Quentin Tarantino's *Reservoir Dogs* (1992) and *Pulp Fiction* (1994), and in a memorable recurring role on *The Sopranos*.

CHAPTER THREE

MUSIC

At Erasmus Hall High School we used to harmonize
Me and Benny and Ira and two Italian guys
We were singing oldies but they were newies then
And today when I play my old 45s I remember when . . .
    —"LOOKING FOR AN ECHO"

BROOKLYN'S POSTWAR R&B and jazz movement was the razor's edge of the coming 1950s teen scene. The singers, songwriters, and instrumentalists blacktopped and slicked back young Brooklynites' fantasies and wore them like a generational badge, a crucial barrier between kids, who were hip, and parents the kids thought couldn't possibly be. What emerged from it in the fifties was rock and roll, the great cultural divide, the ultimate chronicle of teenage loneliness and longing, its catchy lyrics and minor-key melodies making life and the greasy-kid-stuff angst that came with it all more heartbreakingly beautiful. But tight group harmonies had ruled the street corners of Brooklyn for nearly a decade before Memphis' own Elvis first appearance on the *Ed Sullivan Show* in 1956 brought R&B to the attention of the rest of America.

BILLY DAWN SMITH: I been in music all my life, really. I began singing when I was six years old in the Church of God and Christ up on Bergen Street. I graduated from Thomas Jefferson High School in 1950 and immediately began singing on the streets. I remember sitting on the benches in the project and watching all the girls follow Sonny Till and the Orioles around, who had big local hit records at time, "It's Too Soon to Know," "Forgive and Forget," "Crying in the Chapel." That was it for me. Sonny was a Brooklyn kid. His success with girls and records inspired me to want to be a part of what was happening.

I recorded my first record in 1953, "This Is the Real Thing Now," backed with "Cryin' for My Baby," with the Billy Dawn Quartet, on the Decatur label. We played Bay Ridge in a place called the Steeple, a catering hall that happened to be owned by a friend of mine. Then we began singing in all the black clubs in Brooklyn, including the two biggest at the time, Club Ebony and Purple Street.

Soon enough we started getting some airplay on WWRL, which was *the* black station in New York City at the time, and that really made us popular. Dr. Jive got on us. When Jocko, who came out of Philadelphia radio as the "Ace from Outer Space," arrived a little later, he played us as well. Jocko came to New York around the same time as the legendary DJ Alan Freed, and they changed everything.

All of a sudden a lot of other groups started singing just like us. There would be dances at the school gym Friday nights, and guys would get in a corner, rehearse, then come up onstage and sing. When they finished another group would get up. Even though we were professional, we used to get together with a lot of those street-corner groups and head uptown to Harlem or the Audubon Ballroom, where we'd do R&B shows long into the night.

SPIKE LEE: Once you got into high school, the stakes changed. Girls came into the equation, and girls liked guys who could sing and guys who could play sports—particularly basketball. It became a manhood thing, who had "game."

KENNY VANCE: If you weren't in a gang or didn't play basketball, you were in a group, and soon enough there were battles between the groups, musical rumbles so to speak, battles of the bands. Groups had different turfs. Every Friday night we'd get dressed up in some kind of suits, most of the time gray sharkskin, no lapels, white shirt, blue thin tie, and go down to the boardwalk on Brighton Beach to try to sing whatever we'd heard on the radio that we liked. I remember a group that called themselves the Concords on one side and a group called the Accents on the other, and a group called the Quotations would be down the way a bit. We'd challenge each other to see who had the best sound. That's all we would do on a Friday night.

There was an underground of music and hipness we knew about that simply didn't exist in the mainstream, the mainstream being everything that was going on in Manhattan. Flatbush Avenue, Garfield's, Dubrow's, these were the places we'd hang out. For five cents you could sit with a cup of coffee all night at Dubrow's and sooner or later everybody would come in through the front door. The guys I hung out with as a kid were older than me, real fake tough guys. They wore sport coats with open collars and ties that weren't really tied, their uniform signs of rebellion. They were mostly bookmakers and numbers runners, while we were trying to be beatniks. They thought being tough was as good an identity as any, especially when they came to getting real jobs. Most everyone else in that generation, street-corner guys from the late forties and early fifties, before rock and roll, was looking for an angle.

Meanwhile, we were looking for an echo. Once I discovered music, I never thought about anything else. I went to school, the Brooklyn Academy on Lafayette Place, Erasmus summer school, and Far Rockaway High School, but I never saw those as institutions of learning. I went there strictly to have fun.

During this period of my life, before rock and roll proved to the major labels there was money to be made with it, there were hundreds of small record labels, like Bellnote, and the guys who owned them all considered themselves big shots in show business. Every furrier with an extra hundred bucks might finance a record that could conceivably, if it somehow broke through, make him a million dollars. To the rest of the musical world, especially in Manhattan, before Alan Freed legitimized it, outer-borough street-corner rock and roll was seen by the big labels, guys like Mitch Miller, the head of Columbia, as nothing more than musical porno.

After knocking around for a few years, I found myself on one of those indie labels as a member of Jay and the Americans. Jay Black, the leader of the group, was also born and grew up in Brooklyn. Because of the way he looked, with his greased-back hair and his neo-operatic voice, everyone thought he was Italian, which was a good thing since most of the bands were either black or Italian, but he was actually Orthodox Jewish from Borough Park. He'd replaced the original Jay—John Traynor, who was either Italian or Irish.

Anyway, Jay used to come home from yeshiva with a yarmulke on, and because it was a mixed neighborhood sometimes he got a smack in the head by Italian tough kids, until one day he decided the only solution was for him to become Italian. When John decided to pursue a solo career, we replaced him with this very clean-cut kid, the new Jay, who we were sure would have no problems.

Some guy in my neighborhood knew Jerry and Mike and brought us over to audition for them. They liked us, we made a record of one of their songs, and it became a hit. In those days, if you were young and you scored a hit, you were in show business, it was as simple as that. We were lucky, we had a couple—"She Cried," "Only in America," "Come a Little Bit Closer," "Cara Mia," "Walkin' in the Rain." What was important to me was that even though songwriters Jerry Leiber and Mike Stoller were Brill Building veterans, we managed to keep the kind of Brooklyn sound that had already been co-opted by Tin Pan Alley as sellable pop, softened, whitened, and commercialized into three-minute ditties.

The truth was, although we didn't know it at the time, real, uncut Brooklyn rock and roll had already come and gone. It had been strictly local and either black—typified by the Strangers ("My Friends"), the Jive 5 ("My True Story"), Bed-Stuy's the Velours ("Can I Come Over Tonight"), songs that, with a great and unique Brooklyn sentiment, epitomized the adolescent mating rituals the way we knew them to be in our borough— or white, the Italians, like Cirino and the Bowties ("Rosemarie"), from Red Hook. Cirino was a guy who learned how to play guitar in a local barber shop. In those days, every Italian barber who cut hair in Brooklyn also knew how to play a diminished seventh chord on the guitar. There was "Blanche" by the Three Friends, "Runaround" by the Three Chuckles, "Just to Be with You" by The Passions, Nicky Marco and the Venetians, Anastasia, Johnny Restivo, they were all out of Bay Ridge, all Italian, all with fierce local followings and all managed by the same guy. Neil Diamond, Neil Sedaka, the Tokens, Carole King, Jeff Barry, Barry Manilow, they came after Elvis, and all of them more or less copied his sweet, pure sound and broadened the appeal of Brooklyn rock to universal pop, heavily commercialized, cleaned up. I don't know how but it was sold to the world as authentic Brooklyn rock and roll.

NEIL SEDAKA: Maybe it was because of the egg creams or the lime rickeys we drank at the corner candy store. It was made with cherry syrup, lemon and lime syrup, crushed limes and ice.

I was born and raised in Brighton Beach and lived there for the first thirty-five years of my life, throughout all the success and fame that I've had. If it were up to me I'd still have a place there, but my wife hates it! The reason why I stayed in Brooklyn for so long is because I'm a mama's boy and always have been. My mother said she would cut me off if I moved away from her. I lived across the street, a place called Sea Coast Towers. She was in charge of my money. So I stayed there, my children were born there, I loved it and still do. I love the fact that the Russians have moved into Brighton Beach and have kept the neighborhood at such a great level. There's a street named after me today on the corner of Coney Island Avenue and the Boardwalk, "Neil Sedaka Way," and I still go back once a year to reminisce, to go on the Cyclone, to visit Lincoln High School, where I went, to Nathan's for a hot dog and French fries and to Junior's.

When I was a kid I started a group in Brighton called the Linctones, because we all went to Lincoln High School. Then we changed our name to the Tokens. I left the group to become a solo and they went on to have several hits, of course, including "The Lion Sleeps Tonight."

We would rehearse on the beach, on "Bay 3." We sang a cappella, sometimes our friends would join us, like Carole King, who lived nearby and also went to Lincoln High. I always felt very safe in Brooklyn. It was very *haimish*; you never had to lock your door. You could walk into your neighbor's house at any time and feel welcome. We watched fireworks every Tuesday night from the boardwalk, pizza was a brand-new thing so going for a slice was a kind of event, we played games like stickball, kick the can, Chinese handball against the wall. The big deal was to take the train and go from Brighton Beach into Manhattan on the weekend. My father was a taxi driver, so once every couple of weeks he would take us into Manhattan, to a place called the Brass Rail, a famous restaurant which I thought at the time must be the center of the universe.

I used to go to the Brighton Beach Baths and learned how to play tennis. And I'd hear the local bands play at the Brighton Beach band shell by the baths. Rock and roll was just beginning, and I heard it for the first time on the juke box at Andrea's pizza parlor on Brighton Beach Avenue. The first song I ever heard there was "Earth Angel," by the Penguins. I was with Carole Klein, who later on changed her name to Carole King.

That's when I started making my own music. Howie Greenfield lived in my building, 3260 Coney Island Avenue. At the time I was studying to be a concert pianist. One day, it was October 11, 1952, I was thirteen, his mother, who had heard me play, asked him to knock on my door. He was sixteen. We got along and he asked me if I'd be interested in writing pop songs with him.

I used to go to the Forty Thieves, a small candy store on Brighton Beach Avenue and Coney Island Avenue. It was called the Forty Thieves, by the way, because the guys who owned it were real *goniffs*, or thieves. I used to pass the Pink Elephant, it was a bar and I was too young to go in, but I could hear the music coming out the door and I was fascinated by it. Same thing with the pool halls.

The first song Howie and I did together was something called "Mr. Moon." I sang it at Lincoln High School at a "ballyhoo" night in the auditorium. The principal, Abraham Lass, came to me after the first of what were two scheduled performances and told me he didn't want me singing that song again in the second show. This was the beginning of rock and roll and the song had nearly caused a riot, with the kids bumping and grinding to it all throughout my singing. The song made me a big *macher* at Lincoln High. Before that I had been a total nerd. That all changed with "Mr. Moon."

I met Mort Shuman, who with Doc Pomus wrote a lot of the pop songs that became hits for Elvis, the Drifters, Dion. I met Mort while I was peddling songs as a teenager at Atlantic Records, which was owned at the time by Ahmet Ertegun and Jerry Wexler. I managed to get a few of my songs recorded by their artists. Mort told me about this new publishing company, Aldon Music, up at 1650 Broadway, which was turning into the new Brill Building. The old Brill Building, at 1619, had been the home of Tin Pan Alley, where a lot of "The American Songbook" had been written. Rock and roll was becoming so big it had moved to a separate locale to hold all the new publishers. I walked in, met Al Nevins and Don Kirshner, who were just starting their new venture, Aldon Music, and we, Howie and I, were the first writers they signed. By now I was eighteen. Donnie knew Connie Francis, who was the top female recording artist of that year, 1958. We went to her home in New Jersey, played her "Stupid Cupid," she recorded it and it became an international hit. I played a lot of ballads for her, because I figured that's what she'd want, something to follow up her smash recording of "Who's Sorry Now?" But it was the novelty record, "Stupid Cupid," that she loved.

My recording career followed and I became one of the rock and roll icons from Brooklyn, New York, part of the "Brooklyn sound." It was Carole King, Barry Mann, Barbra Streisand, Neil Diamond, Barry Manilow, and me. The Cookies were my first backup group, who later became the

Raelettes, Ray Charles's back-up singers. There was a certain ring, a sound, a harmony, a lingo. Everyone from Streisand to me had it. Maybe there was something in the egg cream.

I love where I came from. Brooklyn was the best.

DON K. REED: I was born in St. John's Hospital, on Atlantic Avenue, downtown. I grew up in Flatbush, on Bedford Avenue between Newkirk and Foster, down the block from Brooklyn College. As a kid I explored a lot on my own–Prospect Park, the museum on Eastern Parkway, the big library by Grand Army Plaza. But the thing I loved to do most was go to the movies. In those days it was part of the Brooklyn ritual, and the theaters were magical places. I could walk down Flatbush Avenue towards Church and hit the Rialto first, then the Loew's Kings, which was a nifty four-thousand-seat theater. I remember when I first saw *A Summer Place* because I couldn't get the theme song by Percy Faith out of my head.

A little further there was the Albemarle, then a little art theater, right next to Erasmus, called the Astor. Then, past Church, on the left, there was a Dutch Reformed Church, and the Kenmore theater. Theaters were all over the place and they held cruise-ship-size audiences. My friends and I would go every Saturday morning to see a film, sit on the side into the afternoon when, after three o'clock we'd be chased by the matron, as they warned us with those ten-pound laser-beam steel flashlights they wielded to keep our feet off the seats.

Up on the screen, meanwhile, there was always some guy like William Bendix, whose character was from Brooklyn. That was all we needed to know–he was a good guy, honest, tough, brave, even if he wasn't particularly handsome in the traditional matinee-idol fashion. A lot of us strongly identified with him, like he was some perfect giant-size version of our older brothers or father.

But the film that stands out from all the others, the one that changed everything in my life, was *Blackboard Jungle*. I can remember sitting in the Loew's Kings and hearing the first notes of "Rock Around the Clock" leap off the screen. It was thunderous–the drumbeat, the tension, the excitement. Here was a movie about so-called juvenile delinquents, set on the city's streets, with el trains and school yards and racially mixed and extremely tense student bodies. I knew that world and thought the film was speaking directly to me; its riveting and unforgettable title song by Bill Haley and the Comets rang out like a clarion call.

That film helped turn rock and roll from something of a novelty into a defining cultural force that changed the world, and that's no exaggeration. After that, to the guys who sung on the corners, the kids who bunched together in cliques, the kids who hung at the candy store, rock and roll meant everything. I know because I was one of them.

While I was still in grammar school one of my friends came up to me and asked if I'd heard this new guy by the name of Alan Freed on the radio, on WINS, playing rock and roll. I hadn't. Up until then I didn't listen to the radio all that much. My dad had a '48 Ford and would play the radio on the long and boring drives we went on, but only the pop stuff like Patti Page and "(How Much Is) That Doggie in the Window?" I even liked some of it, but it wasn't rock and roll.

Alan Freed gave us that. I found out later that he had been imported from Cleveland after scoring huge numbers there playing what was then called "race music," really R&B, a lot of Chuck Berry, all the black harmony groups. WINS brought him to New York City for what was then the astonishing sum of $75,000 a year to play those records. After hearing him on the radio I became obsessed, not only with the music, but the medium that was bringing it to me.

KENNY VANCE: Alan Freed starting playing rock and roll in the early fifties in New York. Every kid in Brooklyn listened to his show religiously. It was the single most important part of the day.

BEN VEREEN: I remember Brooklyn in the late fifties and early sixties. There was a rhythm in the air, early Motown, Chuck Berry, Ray Charles, Sarah Vaughan, the Soulsters, the Blind Boys of Mississippi, Little Anthony and the Imperials. All these cats put that rhythm there.

DON K. REED: In 1956 I got a Webcor tape recorder that was so big if I took out the guts it could have doubled as a suitcase. My grandma passed away and left me a couple of bucks so I went out and bought myself one. I wanted it because I was by now addicted to Alan Freed and wanted to play disc jockey like every other kid in Brooklyn. Kids listened to him outside in the summertime on little transistor radios, in the car with the top down, everywhere. And then we expanded and listened to all the new rock-and-roll stations that suddenly sprang up all over the city—WMCA, WABC, WINS of course, and even down at the end of the dial, what we called the black stations at the time.

I remember the names of the men I listened to as a kid on the radio. The morning man on WABC was Herb Oscar Anderson, someone an entire fraction of New York kids woke up to. Each station had its own, distinctive roster that every kid knew—on MCA it was Joe O'Brien, Harry Harrison, Jack Spector, Dandy Dan Daniel, B. Mitchel Reed, and Dean Anthony. On ABC it was Brooklyn-born Cousin Brucie, "the Cuz" (who started out at WINS), Dan Ingram a little bit later, and Scott Muni, every one a legend in New York radio. The countdown survey was as important to us as the front page of the *New York Times,* telling us the pick hit of the week, the number one song, all of it.

I went to Erasmus High School. It was huge, more like a college campus than a public high school, with a grassy square on the inside of the walls, and eight thousand neighborhood kids in attendance. Erasmus was a rite of passage for so many of us who grew up in Brooklyn. Many famous and legendary names went to Erasmus, including Jimmy Durante, Barbra Streisand, Susan Hayward, Jeff Barry, Jeff Chandler, Bobby Fischer the chess champion. Gilbert Price, the Broadway star, sat in front of me in history.

I began high school in 1956 and was there until 1960. I used to hang around with four other guys I knew as far back as first grade. My four buddies were Catholic, I'm not, but I joined their local church to be able to go to the dances, the only place to meet girls because we were too young to go to bars, and the teen club scene had not yet materialized.

Nobody went to church for the religion, everyone was there for the dancing. We were after close dancing–grinding, we sometimes called it–provided by doo-wop groups like the Five Satins ("In the Still of the Night") or the Students ("I'm So Young") or the Schoolboys ("Please Say You Want Me").

A few blocks from Erasmus there was a community center. I used to play Nok Hockey, a very New York City game played on a miniature wooden hockey field, with pucks and sticks that looked like drumsticks, or listened with some of the other guys to 45s on a small stackable record player. After the night center would close, we'd go to the nearest street corner, where guys would be standing facing each other singing a cappella, or doo-wop style, which meant singing without instruments, trying to sound like the record we had just been listening to.

BRUCE "COUSIN BRUCIE" MORROW: By the time I went to Madison High School, in the late fifties, I had begun to find myself. I had been very shy in public school and to get rid of that I joined "the sing." Every high school in the city had one–an inter-class competition between the freshmen and the sophomores and the juniors and the seniors, a half-hour, forty-minute show where we'd make fun of each other, using popular songs with our own lyrics. I was given a solo in mine, as Guba the Cave Man. I was dressed in a leopard-skin suit and all the Cave Girls were at my feet. I sang a song to the tune of "Kisses Sweeter Than Wine." We won the sing, and that opened my eyes to wanting to be on the stage, to be some type of performer.

There was a high school teacher, Mrs. Siegel, who also thought I had some kind of a talent and referred me to what was then called the All-City Radio Workshop. The workshop was a product of the New York City Board of Education, housed at Brooklyn Technical High School, or Brooklyn Tech as it is universally known. It had its own actual radio station, WNYE-FM. I auditioned to be on it, passed, and stayed with them for three years. At that time I was known by my real name, Bruce Meyerowitz. The Cousin Brucie thing came years later.

BILLY DAWN SMITH: I started running with Sam Cooke and Luther Dixon, and singing at Towne Hill. All the big black acts played there and because of it they packed the people in. They'd always have a black comedian opening for the groups, like, say, a Flip Wilson or a Godfrey Cambridge. Things sometimes got pretty raunchy, but that was cool because Towne Hill was meant for an adult crowd. The Gallo brothers, one of the mob families that came from Brooklyn, hung out there all the time. Especially Crazy Joey Gallo. It was his favorite homey place. Management loved it, because if there was ever any problem it was taken care of in a second. *Any* problem.

KENNY VANCE: Towne Hill was on the corner of Bedford and Eastern Parkway. It was a black nightclub. As an underage white kid in the late fifties, I used to go to see Sam Cooke there. The format of the shows was always the same. They'd have a comedian, Flip Wilson, Irwin C. Watson, maybe Nipsey Russell, followed by a jazz or fast-blues trio, and then an exotic dancer who in those days looked like she might have been someone's older aunt from the neighborhood up there on the stage actually taking her clothes off. The comedian would then come on again to introduce the main act—the Coasters, or the Drifters, James Brown, Jackie Wilson, the Olympics, names of that caliber. The whole thing would cost me five dollars.

BILLY DAWN SMITH: I began to write hit tunes for white rock groups like the Crests, whose lead singer, Johnny Maestro, eventually became the lead singer for the Brooklyn Bridge. My piano player in the Billy Dawn Quartet was Larry Brown, and he played on many of the early Johnny Maestro and the Crests' records, like "My Juanita" and "Sweetest One."

JOHNNY MAESTRO: Brooklyn had a sound all its own, and it was that sound that made up the core of the musical neighborhood. You didn't have to live in Brooklyn to recognize what that sound was. I was born and raised on the Lower East Side of Manhattan, on the Manhattan side of the

Brooklyn Bridge. As a kid, I always listened to the radio, hearing songs by people like Frankie Laine and Johnnie Ray, and I used to mimic them. Then one day a different kind of music started coming over the airwaves, played by this new fellow, Alan Freed, with his Moondog show on WINS. He played a lot of harmony groups, like the Flamingoes, the Harptones, the Moonglows, and that sound fascinated me, so much that I wanted to re-create it. I looked for guys who could sing and when I found them I put my first group together, the Crests.

BILLY DAWN SMITH: In 1957, I bought the Colonial Inn with Otis Blackwell and Bert Keyes, down by Ebbets Field, on Washington Avenue and Park Place. We knew the Dodgers were leaving, but we bought the place anyway. There already was a Dodger Café, on Flatbush, and that was doing great business. When they said they were going to actually tear down the field and put up public housing in its place we just figured, great, that would bring us a lot more customers. Sure enough, we were packed every night and became the most important R&B club in Brooklyn. The whole music business used to come in to see our shows. I mean, we had the biggest stars of the day, and although we were in a predominantly black neighborhood it didn't matter. White guys, black guys, Spanish guys, everybody came and everyone was welcome. You could get drunk in my place and you could live fifteen, twenty blocks away, and you could stagger home on your hands and knees to your house, and if somebody came along they'd pick you up and take you home. You could have a thousand dollars in your pocket, nobody would ever touch a nickel of it. *Never.* Of course today they'd cut your head off.

Things eventually changed. One day in the early sixties a porter at the club came to me and said, "We gonna have to get outta here 'cause nobody in this neighborhood speaks English anymore." I knew what he meant and he was right. Things were changing. So I moved the club over to Flatbush.

JOHNNY MAESTRO: We were like a lot of other doo-wop groups in those days, we'd stand on the corner and sing. We really began to find our future on the Brooklyn Bridge IRT subway station, one evening in 1957. A woman on the station heard us, came up, and offered a business card. She was the wife of bandleader Al Brown, who was connected with many labels, one of them being Joyce Records. "You should call this person, he may be able to help you out. You have a nice sound," she said.

The next day we went to see him, sang, and he too liked what he heard. He brought us to Joyce Records for a formal audition, and they signed us up immediately. The Crests' first record was "My Juanita," backed with another hit, although not as big, the more regional "Sweetest One." Both were very street-oriented, New York–sounding songs, written by this cat Billy Dawn Smith. We recorded them in Brooklyn, in a small studio on Avenue U. The total budget for the entire session was something like $15. My first royalty check from them was $17.50, and I was ecstatic! After that we started touring, doing record hops, then we switched to Co-ed Records and recorded "Sixteen Candles," which made us national.

JOHN KARLEN: Summer nights in Brooklyn, it's ninety degrees, you're sweating your skin off sitting on the stoop, and suddenly you hear Roy Orbison singing "Only the Lonely" floating in the airwaves, because everybody had a transistor radio and was tuned to the same station, WABC. That kind of echoing electric sound always gave me the chills. It was like Brooklyn was right in tune with the whole world. Or the other way around. That it *was* the whole world.

DON K. REED: I used to go down and see every one of Alan Freed's shows at the Brooklyn Paramount, and they mesmerized me. To see the Moonglows or the Flamingoes live, in green or orange suits doing those steps, or the Cadillacs, that was pure heaven. And when Alan Freed would come out, everybody in the audience went crazy! There he was, that spectacular voice on the radio, in person! It was a near-religious experience.

MARTY ASHER: I lived in Canarsie, where the Impalas came from. They had one hit record, "Sorry (I Ran All the Way Home)." They were like God to me. They used to drive around the neighborhood in a big white Cadillac.

KENNY VANCE: As a kid I used to take the train down Flatbush Avenue and get out at Nevins Street to see Alan Freed's rock and roll shows at the Brooklyn Paramount. I remember seeing the crowd, the police on horseback, and feeling the excitement. The thought of seeing the people I was hearing on the radio was almost unbearably exciting. Alan Freed put on what were, conceivably, the first East Coast, urban, fully integrated rock-and-roll shows, in gigantic movie theaters, meant for white *and* black *and* Puerto Rican kids. Groups like Eddie Cooley and the Dimples, Cirino and the Bowties, Screamin' Jay Hawkins, Chuck Berry, Buddy Holly, Lee Andrews and the Hearts, the Heartbeats. My mind was blown a thousand miles away. Rock and roll was born in Brooklyn, birthed by Alan Freed at the Paramount Theater.

DON K. REED: I could go out of my house, take the Flatbush Avenue bus all the way to DeKalb Avenue, almost to the bridge, get out, and there I was, at the Brooklyn Paramount, where I'd have the privilege of standing in line for two hours–all day and all night there was always a humongous line–and for two bucks I could get in and see everybody. And I mean *everybody.* Bill Haley and the Comets, Jerry Lee Lewis, the Everly Brothers, Paul Anka, Frankie Lymon and the Teenagers, Larry Williams, the Moonglows, Jackie Wilson, Buddy Holly and the Crickets, Eddie Cochran, and on and on. They did six shows a day, with a film that *also* starred Alan Freed and a couple of the bands he controlled.

It was possible to discern the music by borough, the sounds were that distinctive. The Mello-Kings and the Earls, for example, were unmistakably from the Bronx. They had a toughness and a style that clearly identified them, while groups like Johnny Maestro and the Crests were soaked in a Brooklyn sweetness. There was a certain difference in bravado.

I always thought how lucky I was to be born in Brooklyn and able to get to see all this. A lot of kids from the Bronx never got to because their parents wouldn't let them go. They lived too far away, all the way up there in some exotic land above Manhattan. I don't think I was ever there more than once or twice all the years that I was growing up. But for me, and for all the kids of Brooklyn, Mecca was just a long walk or a short bus ride away.

JOHNNY MAESTRO: Our first big show was with Alan Freed, at the Brooklyn Paramount, on the same bill with Richie Valens, Dion, the Big Bopper, Buddy Holly, the Everly Brothers, Bobby Darin, and my idol, Johnnie Ray. It was a dream for me, to work with all these great singers and groups I'd grown up admiring. We'd each do five, sometimes six shows a day. It was fun. I really enjoyed those days so much.

"LITTLE ANTHONY" GOURDINE: We always used the big town clock on the Williamsburg bank as a way to guide us, a kind of urban North Star. They tried to tear it down but weren't able to succeed and it's still there to this day. That thing saved our lives. We used to use it to find our way home, or to show us the way to get to Junior's, which is still there–it never changes–where we'd love to go and stuff ourselves after singing all night on a street corner or in a church. Or if we'd snuck into the old Albee Theater or the Brooklyn Paramount. We never paid. They were so *easy*, far easier than even the Peerless or the Loew's. Unlike the Apollo, uptown, which was impossible to get into. I used to sneak into the Alan Freed shows at the Paramount and say to myself, "One day I'm going to be up there."

The Imperials were formed mostly at Boys High. We all hung out at the Fort Greene projects. Everybody was singing. I was the first to break into the business, in '56, with a group called the Duponts. The Imperials were originally the Chesters until Alan Freed started calling me "Little Anthony" because he thought I was so small. Or small-sounding, actually.

When I started singing, we'd do schools, parties, wherever we could. We had all kinds of places to learn how to do it in front of other people before we ever had a hit record. A lot of that was Brooklyn–the sense of neighborhood and friends and family gave us the chance to learn how to be who we were. When we got good enough we were signed by End Records, had our first hit, "Tears on My Pillow." The other side was also a hit, "Two People in the World." We joined the chitlin' circuit–the Apollo, the Howard Theater in D.C., and all over the South. But we always came home to Brooklyn, because we had homes here, and by that I mean more than just four walls. It was a place where life blossomed for us. And still does.

ERNEST WRIGHT: I grew up in the Fort Greene projects in downtown Brooklyn, near the Navy Yard. As far back as I can remember we used to sing. [Little] Anthony's mother was a gospel singer at church. I met the other guys when I was in public school. We started singing on street corners. The A train subway stations (for the echo) down at the Jay Street and Borough Hall stops, in the Church of the Open Doors near the Farragut projects, right off Flatbush Avenue, two streets over from the bridge.

We'd heard about a guy named Richard Barrett, a record producer who'd made a lot of hit records with city kids. We went looking for him at 1650 Broadway, a famous music-publishing building in Manhattan. It was 1957 and he was riding high with the Chantels, Jo Ann Campbell, the Valentines, that kind of sound.

Growing up in Brooklyn made all the difference for us. It had a sense of neighborhood that no place else in New York City or maybe even the country had. We had the biggest local following in the world, because Brooklyn is in a very real sense the world. It's everywhere. People from Brooklyn have spread out, like colonists, but they always retain something of Brooklyn wherever they go.

CLARENCE COLLINS: I was born at Brooklyn Jewish Hospital on Bergen Street and raised in the Fort Greene projects. It was rough but fun. We played stickball, ringolevio, kick the can, all those kid games. And we sang, all the time. We loved the feel of being in a neighborhood with our friends. Compared to the Bronx, say, which was like a war zone to us, the streets of Brooklyn back then were one big playground. By the time

I was fourteen, "Tears on my Pillow" was a hit and everything changed. No more playing. It was all work, make a dollar, but it was great work. In those days, that's about all it was. End Records was run by George Goldner, who came into the streets of Brooklyn and plucked groups out he thought could make money for him. That's the way the business worked back then. All the things we did were great, being rock-and-roll stars and all that, but he made all the bread. We did tours for Irving Feld, for Dick Clark, we did shows for Alan Freed, but all of the money went to everyone but the artists.

But hey, my father bought his house in '63 on Carlton Avenue, a three-story brownstone. He paid $16,000 for it. When he passed away, I settled his estate and the house brought in nearly $4 million. Some things in Brooklyn did change!

CLEVELAND "CLEVE" DUNCAN: I was the lead singer of the Penguins. We played the Brooklyn Paramount back in 1955 with Alan Freed. We came east every year to play the big rock-and-roll shows. We had to stay at a place in Harlem, which I found a bit jarring, because this was New York City, not the South. We had to travel to Brooklyn every day to do the shows, five a day. We stayed not too far from where Frankie Lymon lived. I can remember seeing him playing stickball in the streets before he headed downtown to do the shows. He must have been about fifteen years old.

I remember coming out of the Brooklyn Paramount stage door and being confronted by a local white gang who didn't want to let us out because we were black. They didn't like the fact that white girls were hollerin' and screamin' over us. They cornered us and we fought it out. Right then and there.

BRUCE "COUSIN BRUCIE" MORROW: My love for radio just grew and grew. WNYE-FM was not a music station, it was an educational outlet, and we did a lot of plays, primarily aimed at classrooms, where big radios were set up and all the students listened. I played Paul Bunyan for a whole series, things like that. There was always a moral message, God help us!

When I graduated from high school, I went to Brooklyn College for six months. I felt completely lost there. I was never able to find where the French class was. I guess I just wasn't ready and very politely they asked me to leave. It was a hard lesson for me to learn but a good one, that my parents were no longer there to protect me and now I had to make it on my own.

I then entered New York University, NYU, where my life really began in radio. I eventually received my degree in communications and education. I also founded the radio station there, WNYU, which I'm still affiliated with. The university gave me the freedom to literally build, from the ground up, a real radio station. I didn't attend that many classes, but I really learned my trade. Tell a Brooklyn kid he can do something and it's get-out-of-his-way time.

DON K. REED: My first and only non-radio job was working for the Bank of America, which is where I met my wife. People kept on telling me my voice wasn't that bad, and I thought I sounded pretty decent, so I went to all the New York radio stations and knocked on their doors, looking for a job as a DJ. On my own I went to WMGM, a rock-and-roll radio station at the time, or at least one that played a rock-and-roll show just before Peter Tripp. It was called *Music with a Beat.* The host was Bill Reddick, and when I went down to the station, he actually came out and talked to me. Then I went to WABC, and I met the guard out front, who let me go up to where the studio was. I remember looking through the glass and seeing Scott Muni. I was blown away.

BRUCE "COUSIN BRUCIE" MORROW: We took a closet for our station at NYU. We had no budget–I think the dean gave me $28 to build the radio station, just to get rid of me. I bought cable, speakers, we had some microphones, and a little Dynavox phonograph to spin records on. It was magical to me, like the equivalent of an HDTV set to me at the time. I dropped the wire four stories down to the lounge and hooked it up to an old hanging speaker from our microphones–our "broadcasting system"–and that's how I started. I kept on getting a little more money and I'd add another lounge until the entire downtown college was wired to hear our broadcasts. I went to London Records and begged for some albums and they gave them to me. Once one label did, then they all did it because they wanted a piece of this new phenomenon, college radio.

I put all kinds of shows on and that's where I learned the business of radio. Otherwise I'm sure I would have been a gynecologist.

DON K. REED: I started making my own tapes, trying to imitate what I heard on the radio. WLIR was my first job, in Long Island. I got paid $1.10 an hour, and it was for one hour a day, and I thought I was the richest and the luckiest guy in the world. My next gig was one to five in the morning. It was a tough schedule but I jumped at it, part-time at first, and then I worked my way into the regular rotation, first one day a week, and then on a regular basis. That led to twenty-seven years hosting *The Sunday Night Doo-Wop Shop* on WCBS-FM, a celebration of New York City rock and roll with a lot of local Brooklyn groups. I got the show because the station manager knew I was a Brooklyn guy and knew the type of music to play, and he was right. The show, with its slight echo meant to sound like a high school hallway, became a city institution floating through the streets of Brooklyn, from the bridge to Coney Island.

BRUCE "COUSIN BRUCIE" MORROW: When I graduated from NYU, in 1956 I think, I sent out eight minutes of demo tapes of me on the radio. Six came back telling me to find another career. I did get a call from Panama City, Florida. I'd sent it there because I'd wanted to live in a warm climate. The station manager called me and offered me a job. I had my father, who was a savvy garment center worker, negotiate the deal for me for $82.50. Nice money for a young kid. But what killed the deal was when the manager said I would work half the time at the radio station and half the time at his other business. My father insisted on knowing what that business was. "A car wash," the manager said. That ended that deal.

About a week later, a station in Paradise, Bermuda, called. There was no car wash involved, so I took the job. I stayed there for a year, where I learned my skills. I got my first nickname there, "the Hammer."

I grew up listening to Alan Freed, the father of rock-and-roll radio. He was the first person who sounded like the music. He used to pound on a Brooklyn telephone book to keep the beat on the air. I tried to model myself after him. My banging was what got me the handle of "the Hammer." It was the first time I ever faced racism, anti-Semitism, anti-Catholicism, everything. I used to go home at night with a lead pipe in my hand, an old trick I'd learned in Brooklyn.

Eventually, I landed in New York City, at WINS, Alan Freed's former station. I knew enough now that everyone in this business needs some kind of shtick, otherwise you tend to fall in with the chorus. I never wanted to be a chorus member, I always wanted to be the lead. That was something that came along with the Brooklyn water and air. It does that to you. It makes you want to get up and capture the hill—"Get out of my way, I'm from Brooklyn."

Anyway, I was on ten to midnight as Bruce Morrow, and one day a guard asked me if he could bring a lady into the studio to see me. I said, "Sure, but she has to know that I'm playing records at the time." This little old black lady with white hair and twinkling eyes sat down next to me. I knew that she wasn't a regular listener to rock and roll, but she was up there for a handout. "Mr. Morrow," she said, "do you believe we're all related?" Oh boy, I said to myself. "Yes, ma'am," and then I put a record on. "Well, cousin, lend me fifty cents. I'm broke and can't get home." "Okay, cousin," I said, "I'll be happy to do that for you." She left immediately, and that night, going home to Brooklyn, in the middle of the Brooklyn Battery Tunnel, a light went on in my head. *Cousin, lend me fifty cents . . . cousin . . . Cousin Brucie . . .* And that's how and when Cousin Brucie was born.

The next day I went to the station manager and said that from now on I wanted to be known as Cousin Brucie. "Kid," he said to me, "that is the stupidest, corniest thing I've ever heard in my life." "You're right," I said, "it might be corny, but there's no one cornier than a New Yorker. We are all cornballs." I finally convinced him to let me try it and that was it. Goodbye Bruce Morrow, hello Cousin Brucie!

My next stop was WABC-AM, and that's when the legend of AM rock radio was solidified in New York City. We were very much like a family. You became a nation during those years and Brooklyn was my personal capital. I never strayed too far from that image I had of myself as a Brooklyn boy, and through all the shows, the ones at the Palisades Amusement Park, the ones I hosted in New York City, everywhere I went, I was everyone's Cousin Brucie from the nation of Brooklyn, which represented, really, everyone's hometown neighborhood. You know, one of the guys.

JOHNNY MAESTRO: Sometime in 1961 I left the Crests and started performing with a different band, until a couple of years later Beatlemania happened and we had to learn different kinds of songs to stay relevant. The harmonies were still there, but now real instruments came to the forefront. The whole reason we had sung a cappella was because none of us could afford to buy, let alone learn to play, instruments. That's how four- and five-part street harmonies had come to be in the first place.

In 1967 I formed a new group. We were eleven people, and our management group said it was going to be very difficult to sell such a large number to promoters. "It would be easier to sell the Brooklyn Bridge!" he said. So that's what we decided to call ourselves.

DON K. REED: The Brooklyn Bridge became the house band at the Cheetah Club, in midtown Manhattan off Eighth Avenue. Clubs were springing up everywhere. There was the Peppermint Lounge in midtown, whose house band was Joey Dee and the Starliters, who had the hit single "Peppermint Twist." All these clubs were driven by outer-borough talent. During the disco era, of course, Brooklyn had the 2001 Odyssey

club, which became immortalized in the movie *Saturday Night Fever.**
I remember as a kid going to the 802, the Odyssey's original name, and
also to the Elegante on Ocean Parkway and the Town and Country on
Flatbush Avenue and Avenue U. The Town and Country was the biggest
nightclub in New York City at the time, and it was always filled with
Brooklynites. Very few people from any of the other boroughs came to
the Town and Country, despite the fact that some of the biggest stars in
the country played there.

GERALD HOWARD: There was something odd about living in Bay Ridge
when *Saturday Night Fever* burst upon the world in the early seventies.
I had graduated from Cornell in 1972 and come back to live in Bay Ridge
with my parents until I got my own apartment, over a store, still in Bay
Ridge. One day *New York* magazine published a cover story by Nik Cohn,
"Tribal Rites of the New Saturday Night."

It was interesting to see how all the Italian kids duded themselves
up every Saturday night to go to the club to dance. This was their relief
from the boredom of living in Bay Ridge, which was something I could
appreciate. The thing I knew about this club, that called itself 2001
Odyssey, was that it was just down the street from the Crazy Country
Club, whose memorable motto was "Warm beer, lousy food." When I
found out that there was this sort of discotheque in the neighborhood—
such clubs were previously found only in Manhattan—I knew some corner had been turned.

I never actually went into the club—I was, emphatically, not that kind
of person—but I had gone to grammar school with the Tony Maneros of
the world. I have to say, they're a lot cuter in the movies than they are
sitting behind you in Sister Mary Othilia's class giving you noogies on
the back of your head during catechism.

---

* The 2001 Odyssey (later called Spectrum) closed and was demolished in 2005. A dispute
over the Odyssey's storied floor, featured in the film and danced on by an iconic John Travolta,
is currently the object of a lawsuit over ownership—just the floor, not the walls or the ceiling.

Essentially, Nik Cohn got it right, even if the actual Tony Manero never existed. He was made up, a sort of composite. The article got picked up for development and eventually was made into the film *Saturday Night Fever*, which turned outer-borough torpor and yearning into Hollywood mythology. It was so strange to me because the street where Tony Manero grows up in the film was precisely the block I grew up on–Seventy-ninth Street. And so I had this sensation of witnessing the place of my childhood turned into media fodder, not just for all of America but for the entire planet. Because of it, hundreds of millions of people to this day think of Bay Ridge as a guy walking along Eighty-sixth Street under the "El" with a bunch of paint cans in his hand eating two slices of pizza one on top of the other, happy as a lark.

DON K. REED: The clubs disappeared in Manhattan first, but eventually they all went away, even the ones in Brooklyn, eaten up by the same hunger and greed for real estate profits that worked itself through the entire city.

KENNY VANCE: I recently went down to where the Brooklyn Paramount was. It's completely transformed. It's now a part of Long Island University. But it still retains some of the character it had when it was a beautiful, ornate, rock-and-roll temple. The floor is still there, the seats are all there, the gargoyles and all the silver and gold painting, the banisters, all of it still exists as part of the gymnasium, meant to help us remember rock and roll for the royalty it was.

BRIAN BERGNER: To me Brooklyn hip-hop from 1988 to the present is at least of equal cultural importance, if not more so, than anyone besides [author] Jonathan Lethem in terms of understanding what working-class life and the creative struggle in contemporary Brooklyn is all about, from an African American and a West Indian perspective, language, geography, that is often completely missing from the mainstream media, or for that matter, in contemporary literature either. One of the most unique things about it is that it's fairly divisive and at the same time it's very popular; it's a form of popular culture that people can identify with about their inability to relate.

The first major Brooklyn rapper was Big Daddy Kane. He was the father of Brooklyn hip-hop, he advanced it in a lyrical way. He crystallized it and took it to another level. But the nature of hip-hop is disposability as a corporate meaning, I suppose, for mortality, a very big issue in hip-hop. *Real* street music. With very few exceptions there are no long career arcs, as there are in rock, for example. The Notorious B.I.G., Biggie Smalls, was from Bed-Stuy. He's a Brooklyn icon and another dead guy, a beloved figure who really stands at the top of the heap. There's no getting away from the reality and the romance of early death, especially when it reflects a kind of norm rather than the unusual. Another guy is Ol' Dirty Bastard, who was a member of Wu-Tang Clan, mostly from Staten Island, but if you talk to people around the world about Brooklyn, two of the best people they liked were Notorious B.I.G. and Ol' Dirty Bastard, and they're both dead.

JEANELIA: I'm twenty-three and live in East Flatbush, Brooklyn, New York, where I was born and raised. My mother works in a hospital, has since I was born, to make sure my brother and I never have to want for anything. I don't have too much contact with my father, but I did have father figures in my life that helped me out, taught me lessons to stay the right way and prevent me from being caught up. I went to elementary and middle school in Brooklyn, and college near Boston, Newbury College in the Brookline area. That was cool. Boston is very similar to New York, the people are just as rude and aggressive, so I felt like I wasn't too far from home.

My goal is to be successful, to make a difference, preferably in my writing work. I do music; I also write for newspapers. I like to spread the word either through my music or on the page. I used to write poems and short stories before I got into doing investigative journalism. I enjoy the whole research and reporting process.

I also really got interested in writing about music when I did my internship, and that became my real love, writing about the entertainment industry. Music has always been around me. My family is into music; my cousins, my brother, they used to do hip-hop music. My poetry, I used to turn it into rhymes and he'd say, "Lexie, you got a talent!" I was eighteen when I went to college and I met up with another female who does rap music. That was the first time I took it seriously. Other people were looking at me and saying, "Hey, you're good."

We began as journalism majors, which allowed us access to the radio station 24/7. So we'd write something and go do a session on the air. People outside the college heard about it and we were able to open up, and that led to other artists coming up to us and producers and saying they wanted to do tracks with us. What we considered fun suddenly became something serious, and then it became harder.

Truthfully, I would like to get an independent distribution deal and allow them to be like parents, pushing, but I'll be independent. I don't want to sit on some major label's shelf. I would have my own label and they would give me the money so I could distribute my music on my own, private label. Eventually it would be in stores, bootlegged, the Internet, wherever music is that's where mine would be.

I write about my own struggles, growing up, the type of family I grew up in, the neighborhood, the environment, the high school I came through. I was raised in a single-mother home, family problems, money issues. There have been times when I wanted to give up and then I realize I have the strength to keep going. Man issues, going through relationships, this is what I went through when I was growing up, or what I seen my friends do as they were growing up. And people getting lost to the streets.

I believe no matter where you are, everyone's a person and everyone's going to go through the same things, of course, depending upon your neighborhood it's gonna be different. Every place is a ghetto, every place has poverty and rich folks. Everybody is going through the same thing in different areas in just a different way. Just how you might see the white boy's cell phone playing a DMX song and you wonder, "How can he relate?" Maybe some part of it makes sense because he sees the troubles in his own neighborhood. Different in some ways, the same in others.

Brooklyn gives you this certain type of pride, and in my music you can hear the pride. Everything I talk about has Brooklyn in it or represents Brooklyn. There is a definite Brooklyn sound. Kinda gritty. Like when you know somebody from Brooklyn and they got that real street, rough, rugged edge, that's the Brooklyn sound—like Biggie, like Jay-Z, the way they swagger, their confidence, only Brooklyn hip-hop and rap has that.

Brooklyn makes me cautious and careful and street-smart. I'm never afraid to walk the streets of Brooklyn because this is home. I'm not afraid of the people that I live with. It just makes you cautious to know that something can happen to you in the neighborhood. But I don't walk around scared.

Brooklyn is in me, so I don't have to stay in Brooklyn to identify with the sound. I was born and raised here, so it's not going to leave me, you know what I'm saying? I've been in different countries and different states, I don't mind leaving, but Brooklyn is someplace that I'll always come back to 'cause it's home.

My favorite artists are Tupac, Biggie, myself. I listen to the oldies, I would put them on once in a while, and I guess they did affect me as far as my sound, the way they performed. Some artists make me feel a certain way about my written words, some people make me feel a certain way about my performance. James Brown is a great performer, so I look and see how he got the crowd going, and I like that; next time I do something, I'm going to try to do that too.

The Four Tops, groups my parents listened to, that's what gives you soul, all those soulful songs. I might use a sample of it to give my music a soulful sound at some point, so it provides the feeling for your music. If I want a nice mellow song, I might go back to a jazz beat.

Everything I write about is something I feel, something I been through, so it's like you looking into my diary, or you reading into me. I'm important to myself, so my music is very important to me. If I feel good, I listen to feel-good music. If I want to feel depressed, I put on some depressed music. If I'm angry and I don't know how to express myself, a 'Pac CD. "Fuck this and this is how I feel . . ." I couldn't express my anger as well as he did his. The anger in his voice and in his songs might make me feel good because somebody identified with what I'm going through. It might not be the same thing but he's feeling an emotional feeling and I feel good by listening to him.

Brooklyn teaches you how to live. How to survive. Brooklyn does what it does. It has its good points and it has its bad points. History repeats itself and never changes. It may be a little easier, but racial issues are still around. I mean, just last week there was a story about some neighborhood thug, a white guy who beat up a black guy in Bensonhurst. Come on! I guess on some level I'm kind of numb to it. I know it's out there, I know it's gonna happen; you just gotta stay away from the ignorance. You sooner or later get numb to the pain and just live your life. In Brooklyn that's how it is; you really don't worry about too many other people except you and yours.

In Brooklyn you have the Crown Heights section, which is predominantly a Jewish community; you have East Flatbush, which is predominantly West Indian culture; then you have Park Slope, predominantly Hispanic, and others. As far as that goes, you drive in the wrong neighborhood, it's like, "What are you doing here?" Maybe not to white people, but certainly to black people. That's maybe why there's still a lot of gang stuff in Brooklyn. But no mistake, they not there to protect you or anyone. They there to protect themselves and to make money, by whatever they do. That's what the gang says they about. Make money. In reality, you just learn to live with your surroundings. It's really about taking care of myself.

Brooklyn, I live it, it's always been there for me, given me a lot of love, and I'll always be there for Brooklyn. There's no other place like it.

Time is money and I got neither to waste exposin' the waste will
  quickly make them open the safe
Slip up evidence will make them reopen the case

Would have been good, cast a mask over your face, avoid the mistakes
Show young G's to manage bit business
My apprentice sixteen fillin' OG britches
Start with consignment
Put myself in alignment
Major moves makin' money is all about the timin'
For the line that's major movement, your money, it's all about
The timin',
Then many places but Brooklyn's zone,
Where we wear our squad on shirts
And recognizes by the stroll

For real!

BILLY DAWN SMITH: I'm not a rap fan. I don't get it.

PETE HAMILL: If hip-hop is poetry, what the hell do we call William Butler Yeats? God?

BILLY DAWN SMITH: It's young people's music, I believe.

✳ ✳ ✳

MORE FAMOUS BROOKLYNITES

HUGH CAREY: Hugh Leo Carey, born in Brooklyn in 1919, was the governor of the state of New York from 1975 to 1982. Served as an enlisted man during World War II, entered the U.S. House of Representatives in 1960. He was the first congressman from Brooklyn to oppose the Vietnam War. Was instrumental in the start of the long-range redevelopment plans for the outer boroughs.

JEFF CHANDLER: Popular movie star. Born Ira Grossel in Brooklyn and attended Erasmus Hall High School. Studied acting and did some professional work before serving in World War II. Upon his discharge appeared on several nationally broadcast radio shows before breaking into the movies in

1947's *Johnny O'Clock*, directed by Robert Rossen. Other movies include George Sherman's *Sword in the Desert* (1949), Joseph Pevney's *Away All Boats* (1956), and Samuel Fuller's *Merrill's Marauders* (1962). Nominated for an Academy Award for his portrayal of Cochise in Delmer Daves's *Broken Arrow* (1950).

SAUL CHAPLIN: Hollywood composer Chaplin (Saul Kaplan), born in Brooklyn. Known for his many outstanding scores, also produced several Hollywood movies. He worked on several memorable musicals, including Alfred Green's *The Jolson Story* (1946), for which he did the score and wrote "The Anniversary Waltz." Orchestrated Stanley Donen and Gene Kelly's *On the Town* (1949), George Sidney's *Kiss Me Kate* (1953), Charles Walters's *High Society* (1956), and was one of the composers of the hit song "Bei Mir Bist Du Schoen." Inducted into the Songwriters Hall of Fame in 1985.

LARRY CHARLES: Wrote several episodes of *Seinfeld*. Charles and Larry David, one of the show's creators, both grew up in Brooklyn, which Charles often credits for the two of them speaking the same "native tongue."

ANDREW "DICE" CLAY: Controversial stand-up comic and actor. Born Andrew Clay Silverstein in Brooklyn. Gained notoriety in the late eighties for his use of profanity. Unable to adjust his act for mainstream TV, faded into relative obscurity in the nineties. Appears frequently live in Las Vegas.

BETTY COMDEN: Born in New York City, attended Erasmus Hall High School and New York University, where she first met Adolph Green, who was to become her performing and writing partner for numerous Broadway revues and shows, including, with Leonard Bernstein, 1949's *On the Town*.

CHUCK CONNORS: Born Kevin Joseph Connors in Brooklyn to Irish immigrant parents, attended a private high school, briefly played basketball for the Boston Celtics and baseball for the Brooklyn Dodgers and the Chicago Cubs. Became good friends with Carl "Oisk" Erskine. While playing minor league ball in Los Angeles for Chicago's farm team, he was spotted by a Hollywood director. Best remembered for his role in the TV series *The Rifleman* (1958–1963).

JIMMY CONWAY, aka **JIMMY BURKE:** Born in Brooklyn, sent to an orphanage by his Irish American parents at the age of two, grew up to be the gangster known as "Jimmy the Gent." Best remembered for masterminding the $6 million Lufthansa airport heist in 1978. A character based on Conway was played by Robert De Niro in Martin Scorsese's *Goodfellas* (1990). Died of lung cancer in prison in 1996, at the age of sixty-four.

PAT COOPER: Born Pasquale Caputo in Brooklyn, of Italian parents. Stand-up comic with heavy ethnic brand of humor.

AARON COPLAND: Brooklyn-born composer, son of Lithuanian Jews; his father's surname was originally Kaplan before anglicizing it in England prior to immigrating to the United States. Best known for his compositions *Appalachian Spring* and the score for the ballet *Billy the Kid.*

JEFF COREY: Brooklyn-born actor whose film and stage performing career was cut short by accusations of communist sympathies that led to his being included in the notorious blacklist of the fifties. Founded the Actors Lab and became one of the most important and influential acting teachers in Hollywood. Corey returned to TV and movies in the early sixties.

RITA COSBY: Husky-voiced, Brooklyn-born, Connecticut-raised TV cable news host and interviewer.

HOWARD COSELL: Born in Winston-Salem, North Carolina, raised in Brooklyn, became a television and radio sports reporter and commentator. Best remembered for his calls of many of Muhammad Ali's greatest fights.

PETER CRISS: Born George Peter Criscuola in Brooklyn. Best known as the drummer for the seventies rock band Kiss.

BILLY CUNNINGHAM: Brooklyn-born, played basketball for Erasmus High School, won the MVP in the Brooklyn League in 1961. Played for North Carolina and the Philadelphia 76ers, later coaching them to the 1983 NBA championship.

ANN, JOAN, AND JOHN CUSACK: Brooklyn-born siblings, movie and TV actors.

CHAPTER FOUR

DEM BUMS AND OTHER ASSORTED SPORTS

I was on a ship in the South Pacific coming back from Navy service in Guam. It was late in October of 1945. They had dropped the big one at Hiroshima, and I was finally on my way home after two years . . . when a sailor came up to me on the ship. He was all excited. He had heard something on the radio he thought might be of interest to me. "Hey, Pee Wee, the Dodgers just signed a nigger ball player!"

—PEE WEE REESE, CAPTAIN OF THE
BROOKLYN DODGERS

Bob Gans: Everything in Brooklyn was always sports-oriented. When we were growing up, politics was hardly ever discussed in the streets, but every baseball, hockey, or basketball game was analyzed from the second it ended until the next one began.

Mel Brooks: We'd hang out as kids on the back of a trolley and somehow get to Ebbets Field and sneak in. There was always a way—we'd walk backwards when the crowd was coming out or sneak under a fence. We'd cheer guys like Ducky Wucky Medwick of the St. Louis Cardinals, from the bleachers or left field. We'd chant, "Ducky Wucky, Ducky Wucky," and he'd look up and smile. It was all good-natured. No one ever threw beer cans or anything like that.

Pete Hamill: Basically, our neighborhood was blue-collar, Irish, Italian, and Jewish, either immigrants or their children. Everyone got along because we had one major thing that held everyone in Brooklyn and throughout the city that made all the ethnic and religious groups come together: the emergence of big-time sports that happened after World War I. You could be an Irishman, an Italian, and a Jew and you could all be in Ebbets Field, sitting together, rooting for the Dodgers. It was the kind of neighborhood where you could walk through the streets in the summertime and never miss a pitch because in the years before television, radios were on everywhere, playing loudly through the open windows.

There were not many cars around, because during the war they didn't make any, which is why stickball flourished. You could actually play it in the streets and not worry about getting run over. If a car happened to come by and park, we'd use it for third base.

FRANK LOGRIPPO: There was a lot of sports played in the neighborhood, even though there were almost no ball fields. Our only field was the street, with all the buildings and cars, not just the parked ones but the ones coming up and down the avenue. Our game was stickball. There was a main street that came perpendicular to Twelfth Street, where we played. If someone hit a fly ball, it was your obligation to catch it, even if you had to run into moving traffic to do so. It was a bad block because there was a full stop sign on our side but none on the main cross street. I can remember about fifteen car crashes and three deaths on that corner. With all the buses and traffic, if you didn't know the traffic, or if you were on a visiting team that wasn't familiar with the pattern, you'd chase a ball and could get killed if you weren't very careful.

The older guys had their stickball games, the younger guys had theirs, and they were completely different games in every way. The older guys used to come from other neighborhoods, and teams would import guys for games, the difference being among the older guys there was always a lot of heavy betting going on. Arguments over foul balls, was it fair or foul, were constant. I never saw a real fight break out over it, but they came close. Real fights were reserved for the next age group, the guys who played hockey. That was a very serious league.

They used to play in Prospect Park on the basketball courts, wearing roller skates instead of ice skates. And these guys could fight. Sometimes things got so intense, one team would send for a guy from South Brooklyn just so he could throw the first punch. Then everyone would throw their gloves down and start whacking away. Some of these guys were actually pretty good athletes, but they'd get hurt a lot, not because of the games, because of the fights.

There was always something to do. We used to play these games like "Buck buck how many horns are up," "Three feet off the German line." Inevitably, somebody always got hurt. One guy would lean against the wall and stand up straight, and the other guy would put his shoulder into his stomach. Four or five after would put their heads in between his legs, so it looked like the back end of a circus human horse. Other guys would then come and run and leap and jump where the head was, to get the others to cave in. If you caved in, you lost. Part of the strategy was to get the heaviest guy on your team, because when he ran and jumped, no one could come down any heavier.

In the summer we also played a lot of boxball, a game played on the natural squares of the sidewalk. Three squares were divided into an entire ball field, and a "spaldeen," a pink rubber ball with a soft powder on it that had a high bounce level, was pitched and slapped to various designated parts of the boxes. Stickball was played with a broom handle and a spaldeen, and distances were measured in sewers. Some guys played stoopball against the stairs of a building, throwing a spaldeen against the edge of the steps and letting it arc back as if it were hit by a bat. The rules were as sophisticated as actual baseball. We put a basket under a corner streetlight, by where the elevated subway ran, the "El," and because the street was a dead end against a right-corner turn, there was less traffic. We'd make a backboard and put it under the light so we could play late into the night.

HERB COHEN: At Ebbets Field we'd sometimes get free tickets from the Police Athletic League and get to sit in the left field upper deck, but usually we'd just find a way to crawl over the divider and get down into the lower seats closer to the field. We were there so much they thought we actually *had* those season boxes. At Yankee Stadium we couldn't get PAL tickets, of course–these were the *Yankees*–but they also didn't have an admissions gate like Ebbets Field did, where one person went through at a time. There would always be a mob of kids waiting to get in, and whenever they'd hand out unsold seats they'd let five of us in a row come in.

Every summer we'd see about sixty or seventy games. There was no TV, naturally, so we'd either have to listen on the radio or go in person. All summer we'd argue over who's better, and not just the ballplayers, but the announcers, which was just as important to us. Was Red Barber, who announced for the Dodgers in those days, better than Mel Allen, who was better only if you were a Yankee fan? Those arguments took all night.

Long before the Brooklyn Dodgers, the New York Yankees, and the New York baseball Giants became synonymous with team sports in New York City, there were other games that filled the people's leisure time. As early as 1665, the British and the Dutch introduced lawn bowling, ice skating, and horse racing to the colonies. The British and the Dutch played the Indians every year for a "bowl" game championship. The prize: 102 beans.

Billiards became popular in the city around 1730. Chess was played in the colonies in the early 1700s; Ben Franklin was an aficionado. In 1857 the first tournament in the United States, the American Chess Congress, was held in New York City. In 1866 the Atlantic Yacht Club was organized in Brooklyn; by 1894 it had its own clubhouse at Sea Gate.

While baseball had been played in New York in the mid-nineteenth century—Candy Cummings, for instance, who in the 1860s and 1870s played with the Brooklyn team in the old National Association, is credited with throwing the first curve ball in the game's history—in 1883 the game came to the original Manhattan's Polo Grounds, so named because polo had been played there during the 1870s. This park was just north of Central Park at 110th Street between Fifth and Sixth Avenues. There were two fields there; the New York Gothams (later the Giants) played on one, while the New York Metropolitans used the other. Only a canvas barrier separated the two outfields, which meant that sometimes a player from one team would crawl under the canvas to retrieve a ball from the other field (the ball would still be in play). The second Polo Grounds opened in 1889 at Coogan's Hollow, between 155th and 157th Streets; two years later, the Giants moved their park to the north end of Coogan's Hollow, two blocks up, and despite a fire in 1911, which necessitated the building of a new stadium from the ground up on that site, the team stayed there until its departure for San Francisco.

In 1883, the same year that both teams that eventually would become the Giants and the Dodgers played their first games, there were seven trotting tracks all over the New York City region, outdoor tennis was all the rage, and boxing was considered the all-American sport.

By the early twentieth century, baseball's popularity had surpassed that of boxing and made the city a one-sport, three-team town. Regarded as the national pastime even in an era when the game was still only played at the major league level no farther west than St. Louis, New York baseball fans could choose between the New York Yankees, the New York Giants, and the Brooklyn Dodgers. Streetcorner variations of the game included stickball, punchball, and many others where city kids calling themselves after their favorite pro player tried to hit a spaldeen past two or even three sewer openings, the ultimate broomstick blast.

Of those three major-league teams, only one remains: the New York Yankees. The New York Giants, in hindsight the least mythical of the big three, were actually the most successful baseball team in New York around the turn of the twentieth century, a standing that lasted until the arrival of Babe Ruth and the rise of the Yankees' dynasty.

After World War II, the New York Giants won only one World Series (four straight against Cleveland in 1954) and boasted few players for the ages besides Willie Mays. It was the other National League team, the Brooklyn Dodgers, that captured the outer-borough imagination of New York City.

The Dodgers came to be known affectionately to their fans as "dem bums" after making it into two World Series, in 1916 and 1920, losing both, and then not making it to the big dance again until 1941.* The pennant-winning celebration that year was pure Brooklyn.

PETE HAMILL: There was great excitement everywhere: car horns blowing, bells ringing in a hundred church steeples, sirens screaming from firehouses. The Dodgers had won the pennant! I wasn't sure what a pennant was, but it must have been a glorious thing to win, for we were given the day off from school and my mother took us on another long walk, to Grand Army Plaza. There we stood, among thousands of joyful strangers, on the new steps of the gleaming white Brooklyn Public Library and watched the Dodgers parade in triumph up Flatbush Avenue on their way to Ebbets Field. The ballplayers were huge tanned men with great smiles and enormous arms, sitting on the backs of convertibles, waving at us all. . . .

Just remember one thing, McGee, [my father] said to me, in a grave voice. The Dodgers are the greatest thing on earth. . . .

. . . But then a Dodger catcher named Mickey Owen dropped a third strike, the Yankees won the World Series, and we all had to wonder if God was a Yankee fan. That couldn't be possible. God was a Catholic, wasn't he? And since the Dodgers were from Brooklyn, they must be Catholics too. Or so we thought.

* The Dodgers and the Yankees have met in the World Series seven times, with Brooklyn winning only once, in 1955.

The story is a bit more secular than that. The Brooklyn Trolley Dodgers were established in 1883 as an independent baseball team, and the next year they joined the American Association. In 1889 they changed their name to the Brooklyn Bridegrooms, and in 1890 they switched to the National League, where they struggled to stay alive. After a stretch when they were known as the Superbas, the team settled on the name Dodgers in 1911.

Charley Ebbets had risen through the Brooklyn Trolley Dodgers management ranks, beginning as a scorecard vendor and eventually becoming personal assistant to Joe Doyle, one of the owners of the struggling local Brooklyn ball club, who also ran a gambling house. Slowly but steadily, Ebbets bought shares in the Trolley Dodgers until, by the time of Doyle's death, he owned a full 40 percent of the team, enough to get him elected to run it by a couldn't-care-less board of directors who shunned the money-losing property at every opportunity.

The team's original playing field was located in Washington Park, a mosquito-infested dump that Ebbets figured would cost more to upgrade than to build an entirely new stadium, especially with the extra revenue more seats and a better location would produce. For the next four years, Ebbets bought up land in Brooklyn's Crow Hill section (known informally, and somewhat disdainfully, as "Pigtown"). Ebbets took on partners, and on April 9, 1913, the brand-new Ebbets Field opened. The field was designed by renowned architect Clarence Van Buskirk, who added its distinctive Colosseum-like touches—the classic stadium archways and decorative terra cotta—and was completed at what was then the whopping cost of $750,000. Its rotunda was an eighty-foot circle enclosed in Italian marble with a floor representationally tiled in the likeness of stitches of a baseball and complemented above by a chandelier with twelve baseball-bat arms topped by twelve baseball-shaped globes.

Still, for all its hokey grandeur, Ebbets Field had its share of problems, beginning with the fact that it was the smallest park in the majors; when completed in 1913, it had a seating capacity of only 25,000, which was increased to 32,000 in 1932.* As time passed, the fans had to put up with the stench of perennially backed-up toilets and a serious lack of ventilation that made the field and seating areas feel at least ten degrees warmer than the surrounding air.

Still, Ebbets Field had a unique populist appeal that kept it full of fans. The outfield walls were always crowded with visually screaming advertisements and billboards, most memorably Abe Stark's "Hit Sign Win Suit" ad that, to players making an average of $4,000 a year in salary, added a bit more meaning to getting a hit.

The famous sign, which was under the scoreboard, was actually the second sign. An earlier, bigger sign had been on the right-field wall, and a lot of balls hit that sign—so many that some evenings the store altered more suits for ballplayers than for paying customers. The second sign was much harder to hit with a fly ball, being at the base of the wall and only three feet high by thirty feet in length. Mel Ott was the first player to hit the second sign, winning two suits in 1931. But Carl Furillo was such a good fielder that not many other players wound up getting the free suit.

Pitcher Carl Erskine—known as "Oisk" to fans, "Oilskin" to detractors—played with Carl Furillo during those years.

CARL ERSKINE: I often get mail from young fans who say, "I didn't see you pitch, but my grandfather did." Then they ask where I got my nickname, "Oisk." Of course, that's a foreign language—"Brooklynese." The Brooklyn faithful pronounced Carl Erskine "Cal Oyskin," eventually shortened with yells from the very close Ebbets Field stands to "Hey, Oisk, I'm witcha babe, trow it tru his head," or, on a bad day, "Trade 'im to the Jints."

Ebbets died in 1926 and several of his partners soon followed him to the great field beyond, leaving being the team hopelessly in debt

---

* By comparison, Yankee Stadium's seating capacity was approximately 54,000.

and without real leadership until 1942, a year after the Dodgers had won the pennant for the first time in twenty-one years and the team was finally able to attract new investors. Among them were Branch Rickey, former part owner of the long-standing National League champion St. Louis Cardinals, and an unknown lawyer by the name of Walter O'Malley. If together Rickey's and O'Malley's infusion of cash saved the franchise from going under, their partnership nevertheless was a contentious one—they hated each other's guts. Unfortunately, each was legally prohibited from selling out his interest without the other's permission. The egalitarian Rickey considered O'Malley a drunken boor, while the street-savvy O'Malley thought Rickey an effete snob.

Nevertheless, after World War II the Brooklyn Dodgers came to represent to their die-hard fans the ultimate in American democracy, a true and clear reflection of just what exactly that hard-fought freedom the country had won was all about—the right to live, work, and play alongside fellow Americans regardless of race, color, or creed. Despite their differences, O'Malley and Rickey agreed to take on the then-daunting task of ending the long-standing unwritten ban against African American players by signing a Negro to join the club.

His name, of course, was Jackie Robinson. When in 1947 the former UCLA football and basketball star agreed to become a Dodger, he joined the ranks of a team filled with immortal players whose names ring like the bells of an East River ferry passing under the great Brooklyn Bridge on a timeless summer day: Pee Wee Reese, Duke Snider, Gil Hodges, Carl Furillo, Ralph Branca, Eddie Stanky.

CARL ERSKINE: Mr. Rickey was a genius in reading not only the talent of baseball prospects, but also their attitude and aptitude. This genius is what led Mr. Rickey to his greatest achievement—finding Jackie Robinson and coaching him so that he could hurdle the color barrier in baseball and ultimately be elected to baseball's Hall of Fame. However, even that accomplishment pales in comparison to Jackie's impact on America in its struggle to allow every citizen the same civil rights. Jackie proved he belonged, and he helped to open hearts and minds.

Now, how did Branch Rickey single out this hot-blooded, gifted athlete? As a four-sport letterman at UCLA, Robinson showed everyone he could play, but so could dozens of other black players. Branch Rickey came at it from a different direction. As a farm boy in southern Ohio, he was raised by a strong Christian mother who made her son promise he wouldn't abandon his faith when he went into this roughshod business of pro baseball. His research told him that Jackie, too, had been raised by a strong Christian mother who instilled in Jackie the virtues of discipline and respect for every individual. Also, Jackie was educated, a college man at a time when baseball had few college men. His intelligence would help him understand the significance of Rickey's attempt to break from tradition.

One thing Branch Rickey desired of his players was that they be married. When Mr. Rickey met Rachel, Jackie's wife, a beautiful, intelligent college nursing graduate, he must have thought, "This is my man."

The foundation for this momentous move was laid when, during a private meeting with Jackie, Mr. Rickey gave him a word picture of the physical and mental abuse he would face. Then Rickey pulled from his desk drawer a volume, Pepini's *Life of Christ*, and read to Jackie the parable of "turning the other cheek."

"The bully is done," Mr. Rickey said, "when your only retaliation is a nonviolent response." As history would show, Mr. Rickey picked the right man.

MAURY ALLEN: After an early season slump and a slow start, Robinson got into high gear. He was running bases with abandon and would lead the league in stolen bases with 29 . . . he broke a record for sacrifice hits with 28. The flair, bravado, brazen style of his running could truly be said to have revolutionized play in the National League. He hit 12 homers, had 5 triples and 31 doubles, scored 125 runs to lead the team in that significant department and batted .297 after spending most of the second half of the season over .300. The Dodgers won the 1947 pennant by five games and the team outdrew every other club in the league. On and off the field people were beginning to notice him not as a black but as one fine player.

There were still incidents, some significant, some trifling, in almost every first visit of the Dodgers to a town. Some of these incidents brought out the best in people. In Pittsburgh, the crowd was on him early with racial slurs. Hank Greenberg, the Jewish star who had come over from Detroit to finish his brilliant career, chatted amiably with Robinson after he drew a walk. "Hang in there, Jackie, you'll be all right . . . I know what you're going through."

Pee Wee Reese, a Louisville, Kentucky, native who was the Dodgers' shortstop and team captain, and whom many Dodgers of the late 1940s and early 1950s looked to for leadership, was credited with doing more to break down the racial barriers than anyone else playing in the majors in Robinson's first year when, in full view of a hostile, nasty crowd, Reese walked over from his position at shortstop to comfort his teammate.

MICHAEL SHAPIRO: The fans were taunting Robinson mercilessly and Reese walked over, and in full view of the jeering masses, draped an arm over Robinson's shoulder. (Carl Erskine, who was close to Reese, was convinced that as the two men stood together on the field, Reese said, "If you think this is bad, wait 'til we get to New York," because that was just the sort of thing he would say. Whatever Reese did say remained a mystery.) . . . The sportswriters wrote glowingly of that moment in Cincinnati, of how remarkable a gesture this was, a white man from Louisville displaying great courage by extending himself to a black man in such dire and public need.

SPIKE LEE: Historically, it seemed that the Yankees didn't want any black or Latin players, so they represented an elitist, country-club mentality and were not of the working classes, although they would make an exception for a DiMaggio, a Rizzuto, or a Berra. The Yankees had the same chances to sign the Mayses, the Dobys, the Hank Aarons, the Ernie Bankses, and the Roberto Clementes as the National League teams had, but it never happened . . . then in 1954 they grudgingly got the catcher Elston Howard, and then they brought him in to back up the guy who outside of Mickey Mantle was their best player, Yogi Berra.

I saw Jackie Robinson play at Ebbets Field, and that was one of the earliest and greatest thrills of my life. I was there for about twenty-five games his first year, sitting in the 55 cent seats, which were the best because they looked right down at the stadium. To see this black man at second base, it was mesmerizing. His skin color, the way he played the game—he did it a whole new way—and his guts.

The people in the seats never disliked Jackie. It was the other ballplayers, the rednecks and the crackers from the South, the Dixie Walkers and the like, that was the hard thing for him to overcome, to resist belting them one—he had a coat of fucking armor on him—but the fans in Brooklyn loved him. By his fourth year in the league, he was the boss, telling the other guys what to do out there. He was the kingpin. He was just plain-ass tough. He was a God to me.

Most of the Dodgers played together through the postwar years thanks to baseball's restrictive reserve clause, right up until the shocking day the team moved to Los Angeles. For Brooklyn baby boomers whose earliest memories of childhood were of the Brooklyn Dodgers and who felt as close to the boys in blue as they did their own families, that amounted to an utter abandonment, reaching its way into some very treacherous psychic ground. For many, the last game played in Ebbets Field, on September 24, 1957, marks the exact moment the social, economic, and financial devaluation of Brooklyn began.*

---

* The Dodgers came in third in the National League their final season in New York, going 84-70, finishing eleven games behind the Milwaukee Braves, who beat the New York Yankees in seven games.

MARVIN AND WALTER ROSEN:* When we lost baseball, we lost the one single culture that every hardworking immigrant from who-knows-where had created and shared with one another. It had been a culture of trial, hope, and exhilaration ever since the team first banded together. . . . On that last day at Ebbets Field, an entire way of life was eradicated. O'Malley would receive hate mail for decades. In the window of the Dodger Café across the street from Junior's that day, one fan taped up a sign listing three names—O'MALLEY, HITLER, STALIN—in that order. In 1960, Ebbets Field was demolished. Most of the brick and rubble was used as landfill for new real estate ventures, but [Junior's has] a small piece of brick from the famous ballpark. It's beautifully mounted on a color rendering of Ebbets Field . . . a big reminder of the days when Brooklyn housed a stadium where ordinary bums became heroes.

It was indeed Brooklyn's darkest hour, the grand disillusion. Time didn't stand still after all. Like the music of Glenn Miller, Mom's homemade apple pie, and Dad having one job his whole life, summers spent listening and watching the Brooklyn Dodgers had become a fondly remembered relic of an American past.

The team was, in fact, one of the last holdouts. By the time the owners began to talk out loud about moving, old Abe Stark had moved up from clothier to borough president, a position some believed to be more powerful and influential than that of the mayor of the City of New York. Alongside the notorious "master builder" Robert Moses, appointed in 1946 by Mayor William O'Dwyer as the city's construction coordinator during the postwar boom, Stark became a key player in the off-field fifties sport that pitted city-backed financial and political clout against private ownership and the people's wishes.

Moses, who had already destroyed much of the streets in old New York neighborhoods and the street life that went with it in his obses-

---

* Taken from a written transcript of a conversation in which the individual speakers are not differentiated.

sive desire to accommodate the new middle class and its own obsession with the automobile, intended to turn a city that had come to rely on public transportation into one long, uninterrupted series of looping highways that led directly to the suburbs. In other words, he wanted to turn it into Los Angeles.

Much of the Bronx had already been plowed under, and more of it would go down to accommodate the Cross-Bronx Expressway. Thousands of blocks of Brooklyn neighborhoods were slated to go down, too, under Moses. Most notably, the amusement park area of Coney Island was not allowed to expand and modernize; instead, low-income public housing was built that would have devastating effects on that neighborhood and every other neighborhood in the city where it was introduced.

The end of the Brooklyn Dodgers came on the heels of the greatest success story in the team's history: After five failed attempts at beating their uptown rivals, the New York Yankees, they won the National League pennant by thirteen and a half games and won the World Series in 1955, beating the Bombers in seven. The Dodgers lost the first two from the Yankees at the Stadium, then took three in a row at Ebbets Field, lost the sixth game at Yankee Stadium, and then won the Series' seventh and deciding game. In that one, left-hander Johnny Podres pitched a 2-0 shutout that ended with a ground-out by black Yankee rookie Elston Howard.

SPIKE LEE: But the Yankees never did receive the benefit of the doubt in Brooklyn, even after Howard hit that home run in his first World Series at-bat in 1955. It was the year Brooklyn finally beat the Yanks in the World Series. Ellie's fault, is what the Yankee fans probably said. Never should have signed him. In Brooklyn we'd had Roy Campanella. Three-time MVP. The Italians in the 'hoods rooted hard for Campy. When he got a hit, he was a *paisan*. But when he whiffed–*moolan yan*.

JOHNNY PODRES: I never knew how important that was to the people of Brooklyn until I got back to my hotel that night and they were gathered out there, thousands of them to welcome me back. They carried on all night, and there was just no sleep. It was wonderful.

BEN VEREEN: Dad was so proud of the Dodgers. He used to take his car and park it by Ebbets Field and wait for a ball to be hit over the wall. All of us were proud. There were certain days when the blacks could come to the ballpark without any trouble, and most of us would sit in the same section. When the Dodgers won the World Series, wow, what a night it was. I'll never forget that night. People were banging cans and dancing in the streets. And then they left us and broke our hearts. Those Brooklyn bums.

CARL ERSKINE: The 1955 World Series was the ultimate highlight for Brooklyn Dodgers fans everywhere. To this day, Brooklyn baseball fans have an annual countdown at the exact hour and minute when Elston Howard grounded out to Pee Wee Reese for the final out of the seventh-game 2-0 victory.

The following year, the 1956 season, a tough pennant race resulted in the Dodgers winning it by a single game over the Milwaukee Braves, only to meet their arch-enemies once more, the surging New York Yankees, who took the American League pennant by nine games, and whose center fielder, Mickey Mantle, had won baseball's coveted Triple Crown with a league-leading 52 home runs, 130 runs batted in, and a .353 batting average. So important was this series that no less a personage than the president of the United States, Dwight D. Eisenhower, came to Ebbets Field to throw out the first pitch of the first game. With Sal Maglie on the mound, the Dodgers drew first blood, winning 6-3. Game two saw an even greater come-from-behind victory for the visiting Dodgers, a 13-8 extravaganza that left them two games up going to Yankee Stadium for games three and four—which they promptly lost, 5-3 and 6-2.

The fifth game became the stuff of legend, the only perfect game ever pitched in a World Series. The hard-living Don Larsen, the "imperfect man who pitched a perfect game," according to *Daily News* sportswriter Joe Trimble, had done the impossible. For the second time in five years, the Dodgers had been on the losing end of baseball history. The first time was at the Polo Grounds in 1951, when New York Giant Bobby Thomson hit the ninth-inning "shot heard 'round the world" in the one-game playoff that eliminated the Dodgers from going to the Series that year.

WOODY ALLEN: I was a delivery boy for a Wall Street stationery firm. I used to lug stationery, you know, bottles of ink—cases of ink, actually—and cartons of stationery up to these Wall Street firms. I was on the street that day. I had a good bet on that game. I had gotten tremendous odds. I was a Giants fan, right in the heart of Brooklyn, and had taken the Giants just on a lark when they were 18½ games out or something. I couldn't pass up the odds. Then they started closing the gap. I was standing near a newsstand at a corner. Must have been a hundred people around me listening to the radio, and when [Thomson] hit it, we just exploded. We went crazy. That was the single greatest moment probably in sports in my lifetime.

BOBBY THOMSON: When Don Mueller singled and Lockman sent him to third base with a double, Don made a half-slide into third, and pulled the ligaments on both sides of his ankle. When Don was in pain, on the ground, I walked down there from home plate to see what was the matter with him. Oddly, that broke the tension for me, and I didn't even realize that Branca was coming in from the bullpen to pitch to me. . . . It changed my whole mind-set. I even blocked out the noise of the crowd [and kept telling myself,] "Wait for your pitch. Get a good pitch to hit. Do a good job." Usually I never psyched myself up when I went to the plate. But this time I did.

GERALD HOWARD: I grew up in Bay Ridge, Brooklyn. My father grew up in Brooklyn as well, and like everyone else in Brooklyn was a loyal and rabid Brooklyn Dodger fan, all through the twenties, thirties, forties, and fifties. He lived and died with the team and suffered the excruciating disappointments they offered to their fans. I was all of one year old when the infamous shot heard 'round the world was fired, but the story he tells about it remains vivid for me. He was out in the alleyway, in my grandmother's house in Flatbush, washing our car, a big black Dodge, and listening to the game on the radio. It was the ninth inning and the Giants were at bat. There were a couple of men on base, and Sal "the Barber" Maglie was pitching, got into a jam, and then they brought in Ralph Branca. As my father tells it, he yelled out, "Oh, no, not Branca," because the day before, he, Branca, had thrown a big fat home-run pitch to one of the Giants. My father therefore had a real bad feeling about bringing him in. Sure enough, he served up the home-run pitch to Bobby Thomson, exactly as my father feared, and the Giants won the pennant. I believe that was close to if not the worst day in my father's life. That moment was seared into his memory and the memory of all Brooklyn Dodgers fan. Nobody ever got over it, really.

SELWYN RAAB: I've never lived in Brooklyn and have no desire to move there. The largest influence it had in my life was traveling to Ebbets Field as a New York Giants baseball fan and defying the hateful Dodgers by stretching in the top of the seventh inning in defiance of insults from their rabid fans. One of the most cherished moments of my younger days was Bobby Thomson's 1951 play-off homer that confirmed my belief that the myths about the Dodgers' unique mystique and noble character were naive fairy tales.

BRUCE WULWICK: The Dodgers emphasized the great camaraderie and communal feelings in Park Slope. I remember when my neighbors across the street, Mr. and Mrs. Finkelstein, got the first television on the block. We were all big Brooklyn Dodger fans, and everyone on the block would congregate on the weekends in their home to watch the Dodgers play baseball on TV. I'm sure that scene was played out all across the borough. One of the greatest memories of my life is when the Brooklyn Dodgers won the World Series, when Sandy Amaros made that incredible catch in left field and threw the ball to Pee Wee Reese, who relayed it to Gil Hodges to double up the Yankees and win it all. And one of the worst was when Bobby Thomson hit the so-called shot heard 'round the world in '51.

HERB COHEN: I remember in 1951 when the Dodgers were way out in front, the "miracle" year that was ruined by the shot heard 'round the world by Bobby Thomson against Ralph Branca in the third game of the playoffs that won the pennant come-from-behind style. Larry King drove not just his friends but his friends' parents crazy. He would argue with them, make fun of them if they were Giants fans, and then when the Giants won that game you didn't see him for three days. He went into hibernation. He came out only when the Giants lost to the Yankees in the Series.

The perfect-game loss to Don Larsen took the heart out of the Dodgers, and some feel it was the turning point in moving the team out of Brooklyn. The Dodgers won game six 1-0 in ten innings, thanks to an error by Enos Slaughter, but in the seventh and final game the Yankees pounded the Dodgers with home runs—Yogi Berra hit two, Bill "Moose" Skowron hit a grand slam—and when it was all over, the Yankees had won the game, 10-0, and taken the World Series.

The next day the entire team left without fanfare to play promotional baseball for five weeks in Japan. Later, several of the regulars agreed to appear with Jerry Lewis, a big Dodger fan, in a movie that was filming in Hollywood. It was the beginning of the grand West Coast seduction that would soon result in even more unthinkable disaster for Brooklyn Dodger fans.

CARL ERSKINE: After visiting Japan in 1956, the Dodgers were a natural to be invited by Jerry Lewis to be in his movie *Geisha Boy*. We filmed it in Hollywood at the old ballpark used in the Pacific Coast League days.

We made $300 each in a deal I negotiated with Jerry Lewis since I was player representative. Although he used only certain Dodgers, Lewis agreed to pay everyone on the roster the same.*

By then it was already too late to save the Brooklyn Dodgers, even though Walter O'Malley had received a verbal promise from Mayor Robert F. Wagner before the 1956 Series had begun, assuring him that real progress had been made on the notion of building the Dodgers a new stadium in downtown Brooklyn.

Talk of a new stadium had started in 1950, the result of the lingering bad feelings between Rickey and O'Malley. O'Malley had secretly decided to try to take over sole ownership of the team from the aging Rickey, a move the crafty sixty-nine-year-old Rickey had already anticipated and countered by agreeing to sell his shares in the team to real estate developer William Zeckendorf for a flat $1 million. The only problem for Rickey was that according to the terms of his original deal with O'Malley, technically he had to give him a chance to match the offer, something he believed O'Malley would not do. O'Malley managed to raise the money with the help of his principal financial partner, May Smith (the widow of John L. Smith, who had also held shares in the Dodgers), and agreed to an additional $50,000 to compensate Rickey for the 5 percent down payment Zeckendorf had already paid. Having exercised his option, O'Malley now became the sole majority owner of the Brooklyn Dodgers.

The team he bought himself into, and Rickey out of, despite a colorful roster of players and a rabidly loyal following, was not making a lot of money. Postwar attendance was down, and television money was still being renegotiated. O'Malley wanted big money for the TV rights to all future Dodger games.

* Carl Erskine, Gino Cimoli, Pee Wee Reese, manager Walt Alston, Charlie Dresden, Johnny Podres, John Roseboro, Gil Hodges, Carl Furillo, Duke Snider, Jim Gilliam, and Charlie Neal all appeared in the film.

Carl Erskine: Baseball was traditionally a day game. Lights were first used in Cincinnati and Brooklyn in the mid-1930s. Baseball had always been a bus and train game. The Dodgers introduced flying by using a DC-3 to fly the team around Florida during spring training in the early 1950s. . . . Eventually, the jet plane keyed baseball's expansion to the West Coast.

Baseball had also been a radio game. In the late 1940s, television was introduced, and baseball thus became a sport that could be watched as well as heard from afar.

Don K. Reed: I'll never forget when I went to Ebbets Field for the first time. In the fifties, we all had black-and-white TVs. I remember walking through the walkway down to the seats and the color of that grass hit me right between the eyes. I couldn't get over how green it was. Kids like me who grew up in Brooklyn watching TV thought grass was as gray as the concrete beneath our feet.

Even with the famous "Brooklyn Sym-Phony"—a group of friends from Williamsburg who regularly came to games and played musical instruments from their seats in section 8, row A—when O'Malley took over, the average game at Ebbets Field was attracting only about fourteen thousand fans a game, less than half the park's capacity. Despite its cultural significance, the team was a financial loser.

While O'Malley sat in his office trying to figure out how to turn a profit with his franchise, the imperious Robert Moses continued to redraw the map of New York City, setting his sights this time on a super-highway that would join the Brooklyn-Queens Expressway with the Belt Parkway. To do so, he would have to condemn whole tracts of neighborhoods in Midwood, Canarsie, Flatlands, and East New York. While this was not an easy task, Moses certainly had the authority to do so. He was by now the head of the Triborough Bridge and Tunnel Authority, the New York parks commissioner, the construction commissioner, and the slum clearance commissioner. He had power and he liked using it.

By 1956 he had built seven bridges, sixteen expressways and highways, a thousand housing project buildings, and hundreds of playgrounds, and had even had a hand in the siting and construction of the United Nations (outmaneuvering Nelson Rockefeller, who'd wanted it to be located in Rockefeller Center). In public, no one dared criticize him. In private, he was routinely referred to, by both politicians and those lower-to-middle-class citizens of the city whose lives he had uprooted forever, as New York's Albert Speer, even though Moses was Jewish.

Moses believed it was his responsibility to aid those without money or power or property. He would do so by ruthlessly imposing on New York City his vision of what the world should be like. It was a vision that O'Malley liked and encouraged. He believed that Moses would get behind a new stadium for the Dodgers, and as early as 1952 O'Malley formally approached him about the idea. Moses listened and seemed encouraging but would make no commitment. A year later, O'Malley announced plans for a new Dodger Stadium, with seven thousand parking spaces (Ebbets Field only had seven hundred) and fifty-two thousand seats, nearly a third more than the current Dodger home. The only thing missing from the plan was a site. Affordability was something O'Malley knew he could achieve only with Moses' help. Moses had power under Title I of the Federal Housing Act of 1949 to condemn and tear down what he called slums (what others called neighborhoods) for the greater good of the public, replacing private property with parks, libraries, schools, hospitals, and roadways. O'Malley figured that a ballpark would certainly fit the definition of what was the greater good for the citizenry of Brooklyn. That same year, he began what amounted to a courtship for the favors of Robert Moses.

O'Malley wanted a site at Flatbush and Atlantic Avenues in downtown Brooklyn, but Moses had his own ideas for the area. He wanted to build a civic center there, complete with a new courthouse, a new home for Long Island University (for that he had his eye on the legendary Brooklyn Paramount, whose rowdy and racially mixed rock-

and-roll shows personally offended him), a greatly expanded and redesigned Brooklyn Hospital, and, of course, new highways.

Moses and O'Malley engaged in a series of moves and countermoves, but the fact was that time was running out. The team had owned the stadium but not the land beneath it any longer, and the land's owner, real estate developer Marvin Kratter, was going to exercise his option to force the team out.

At the same time, Los Angeles and San Francisco were looking for existing teams whose franchise owners would be willing to move them west, thereby expanding major league baseball into a coast-to-coast sport. With support from the city's second major newspaper, the *Los Angeles Herald-Examiner*, Los Angeles County supervisor Kenneth Hahn had sent overtures to O'Malley, who had initially rejected any such notion. O'Malley wanted a new ballpark, but only across town, not across the country.

However, with Moses embroiled in a battle to save his Brooklyn-Queens Expressway from being irretrievably stalled by the strong-willed citizens' committee of Brooklyn Heights, O'Malley began to lose patience with both Moses and the city, which seemed indifferent at best as to whether the Dodgers remained in Brooklyn. While in Los Angeles with his team, some of whom were appearing in the Jerry Lewis film, O'Malley met secretly with Hahn to discuss the possibility of actually moving the team west. It was during this meeting that O'Malley was told he could have the property known as Chavez Ravine near downtown Los Angeles for free (including the rights to anything that might be below the ground—such as oil, for instance) and that the city would help him build a brand-new stadium for the Dodgers.

In December 1956, the New York City Board of Estimate rejected a new ballpark for the Dodgers, citing cost, and denying O'Malley's request that the city offer a bond issue to cover the cost of construction of just the parking lot. Instead, the board announced, Moses was intending to build a housing development on the very site O'Malley had wanted for his new stadium.

Then, just as the failure to find a new site was made public, O'Malley sold Jackie Robinson to Horace Stoneham, the millionaire owner of the New York Giants, in a move that horrified Brooklynites.

O'Malley still continued to equivocate. He would keep the Dodgers in town, he said, if the city would agree to condemn the land he'd long wanted, on Flatbush and Atlantic. He was now in a position to fund the construction of the stadium and parking facilities himself, as his new backer was none other than Nelson Rockefeller, a rabid Dodger fan, who was willing to single-handedly build the new stadium (in return for part ownership of the team) if it meant keeping the Dodgers in town.

Late in 1957, a last-ditch effort was made to keep the Dodgers in New York, at a site in Flushing Meadow, Queens. Moses had gotten the city to supply all the necessary funding for it, including the cost of a new parking lot. The deal killer was that the Parks Commission would own it and lease it back, at a hefty profit, to the Dodgers. Thanks but no thanks, said O'Malley. The burgeoning West Coast cable TV company Skiatron offered the Giants and the Dodgers $2 million dollars apiece in cash for broadcast rights to home games if the teams moved west. The combination of obstacles in New York and lures in California tipped the balance, and on the heels of Stoneham's shocking announcement that the New York Giants were moving to San Francisco, O'Malley let it be known that he had reached agreement in principle with the City of Los Angeles to move the Dodgers there for the 1958 season.

GERALD HOWARD: After 1957, my father would refer to Walter O'Malley invariably in one of two ways: "that son of a bitch O'Malley" or "that no-good bastard O'Malley."

Although hard-core Dodger fans were crushed, the public outcry was surprisingly minimal. Most of the legendary Dodgers from the teams earlier in the decade were already gone, and the team's enormous base of boyhood followers with them. Campanella's hands were shot (and soon he would be permanently paralyzed in a tragic auto accident); Reese had turned forty, and his huffing and puffing were hard to watch and impossible to miss; and the sale of Robinson (who would never play a day for the Giants) represented in very real terms the end of the glory days of Brooklyn baseball.

The general feeling among those who still cared about baseball in Brooklyn was that the Dodgers' move made them feel like housewives who had put their husbands through college, only to find themselves having grown older while their devoted man had run off with a younger, better-looking woman.

In one final and highly ironic coda, while campaigning for the borough presidency in 1991, Marty Markowitz loudly proclaimed his intention to bring an NBA team to Brooklyn (he also hinted at a major push toward secession, something that quickly fell by the wayside after his election). But he had another wild idea, too. One of his very first official acts after taking over Borough Hall was to call Peter O'Malley, the son of Walter O'Malley.

MARTY MARKOWITZ: I heard that the team was up for sale and I said, "Mr. O'Malley, it would be great for your family name and everything if you would consider moving the L.A. Dodgers back to Brooklyn." I must tell you, that conversation was very brief.*

RICHARD RADUTZKY: "We were betrayed, plain and simple."

With baseball gone, Brooklynites scrambled to find another sport (rather than another baseball team) to fulfill their competitive needs, with, at times, some unexpected results.

CHA-CHA CIARCIA: I was the first guy that brought boxing back to Brooklyn, after thirty-something years. I was a promoter for a while and

---

* The Los Angeles Dodgers were eventually sold to Rupert Murdoch.

brought boxing back to the Rollerama on Eighty-sixth Street in Ben-sonhurst. It was originally a bowling alley upstairs and downstairs it was a skating rink and also a bingo game. I decided to bring profes-sional boxing matches in. I had some good fighters, like Tony Danza, when he was still pursuing it before he became a TV star, Gerry Cooney, Vito Antuofermo, I mean top-notch fighters. Danza was a great puncher.

I remember we got very popular, and I had all these things going on to bring in more people. We needed a round-card girl, and one day I told my friend Skinny, I said, "Hey, you're good at talking to the girls. Go upstairs to the bowling alley and get me a round-card girl." He says, "How much do I wanna pay her?" I says, "Not more than twenty-five dollars. I don't care what she looks like, as long as she shows up and she doesn't cost more than twenty-five dollars."

He comes back about an a half later. "I got the round-card girl," he says. "Let me talk to you about her." "All I want to know," I says, "does it cost twenty-five dollars?" "She's twenty-five dollars," he says, "but let me tell you the story." "I don't wanna hear nothin'," I say, "I'm busy."

At the time I had managed to make a deal to put the fights on cable TV. Manhattan cable had just opened up and was looking for some orig-inal programming, so I bought my own time to promote my own fights. We showed the fights and suddenly everybody is going crazy about the round-card girl. Whistlin', goin' berserk. I go to my cameraman and I say, "How do you like my new round-card girl?" "She's got a great body," he says, "but she ain't too hot in the face." I said, "Yeah, but lookit, the guys are goin' crazy."

Now, it's the last match of the evening and it's the last round, and she walks around for the last time, and at the end she takes off her wig and throws it into the ring and everybody starts screamin', "It's a guy, it's a guy!"

The commissioner of boxing at the time, Marvin Cohen, wanted to get my license revoked for that. He wrote a letter to Governor Cuomo complaining I used a transvestite round-card girl. I hear about this and I grab Skinny. "What the hell did you do to me? You got a guy?" "I went upstairs like you said," he says, "and said, 'Where's all the girls?' 'There ain't none around,' he says, 'why you need girls?' I tell him I'm looking for a round-card girl. 'How much does it pay?' he asks. 'Twenty-five dollars.' 'My sister will do it,' he says. Then he goes home, his sister ain't home, so he dressed up in his mother's clothes, and came back walking in high heels."

Skinny sees him and the guy says, "I couldn't get my sister but I could sure use the twenty-five dollars." So that's how that happened.

I promoted the first title fight held in Brooklyn in modern times—Manuel Melon against Milton "Black Widow" Owens, who was an undefeated middleweight from Orlando, Florida. It was for the WBC Continental America's Middleweight Championship. We did it in Prospect Hall on Prospect Avenue. We sold the place out in about five minutes. The fights were always popular in Brooklyn.

I promoted wrestling too, in Abe Stark Arena in Coney Island, St. Thomas Aquinas Church, Prospect Hall, Rollerama. I worked with Vince McMahon Sr., Arnie Skolin, Angelo Sovoka, Gorilla Monsoon. We promoted a tag-team championship in Coney Island, and the night before the reigning champs lost their title on television. There was a riot the next day!

However, to a new post-Dodger generation of street kids, a different sport would dominate, one that required only a hoop and a ball rather than a whole field to play.

DARCY FREY: Even in Coney Island there is a use to which a young man's talent, ambition, and desire to stay out of harm's way may be put: there is basketball. Hidden behind the projects are dozens of courts, and every night they fill with restless teenagers, who remain there for hours until exhaustion or the hoodlums take over.

One of the most celebrated native Brooklyn basketball fans was and still is Spike Lee.

Spike Lee: I followed the Knicks. They had gotten good by the time I was twelve in the fall of 1969. . . . My siblings and friends did everything together. Hoop was a part of it. There were Catholic schools around. St. Peter's and St. Paul's parish school down the street from us. We didn't go to Catholic schools; we went to the public school around the corner, P.S. 29, which we called 29s. We played ball in the school yard at 29s—punchball, boxball, softball, stickball, two-handed touch football, and always stoop. My brothers and I played stoopball in front of our house; then we went around to 29s. People chose up sides, and we went half-court for hours, both spring and fall. I never played any organized sports, just choose up sides in the school yard. I was on the small side, so I tried to use my speed to get around people and for defense. We didn't travel around Brooklyn to play. We weren't that good. . . . We were all sports fanatics, and every block had a team, and that's what we would do. . . . Like me, Woody Allen is a true-blue Knick fan. Big games, little games, he's usually there. He and his beloved sit opposite [my wife] Tonya and me at the Garden; they sit behind the scorer's table. When the game is over and we head out, or while waiting for the elevator in the bowels of the Garden, we may say "Good game" or "Bad game" to each other sometimes, as the case may be. . . .

We have some things in common. Hoop, cinema, and Brooklyn, of course. Woody grew up over in Flatbush. He is a writer and a filmmaker, in that order, he might say; I may be just the opposite.

Opposites can attract. I wanted to find out more, so I looked Woody up, over at his cutting room. "In Flatbush? *Sure* I played," he said. "I played punchball, stickball, boxball, stoopball, all the Spaldeen ball games, two-handed touch, two-man basketball, three-man basketball and baseball. I was a very good athlete. For a while I wanted to pursue a career in baseball. I played second base for the 70th Precinct Police Athletic League team. I was a good ballplayer. I played all the time, night and day. That's all we ever thought about then. Mostly it was baseball. Then when I got to be sixteen or seventeen, I started writing. Drifted into that. But a *Giants* fan? In Flatbush? That was an extreme polarity, inside New York City." Woody Allen is provincial about Manhattan, as reflected in his work; and I am provincial about Brooklyn in mine. Maybe one's fandom was part of it–maybe the start of it. Sensibilities must start somewhere.

LENNY WILKENS: I was born in 1937 in Bedford-Stuyvesant. Growing up, I was a Brooklyn Dodger fan. Baseball was everyone's first love, at least everyone I knew. We all watched it during the summer and played it all year round, if we could, or street versions of it, like stickball. Some friends of mine started playing basketball as well; one of them was Tommy Davis, who would go on to become a great baseball player for the L.A. Dodgers. He kept asking me to play some basketball with his friends, then eventually I went on to CYO [Catholic Youth Organization] basketball for Holy Rosary, which was the elementary school that I went to. I liked it so much I'd continue playing at the playgrounds in my neighborhood whenever I got the chance. During gym periods at Boys High School I realized I was getting better and decided to go out for the freshman team. Mickey Fisher was the coach. He had about fifteen guys he wanted on the team, and I think I was the fifteenth.

They only played the first six guys so I didn't really see all that much court time, plus I was busy trying to keep my grades up. I continued with CYO and PAL [Police Athletic League]. Finally, in my senior year I put on a real run for the team and made the starting five. That was exciting, but back in those days in Brooklyn, we'd play on weekends in the schoolyards and there would be huge crowds coming out to watch us. It was very competitive and a lot of fun, and rough. If you couldn't play, they wouldn't even let you on the court. A lot of toughening up took place in those days. School yard basketball in those days was much rougher than it was at school.

The two schools that were really good for basketball were Boys High and Jefferson. They were competitive with such big basketball teams as DeWitt Clinton in the Bronx and Westinghouse. Basketball really took off after the Dodgers left. It was great playing for Boys. I only played for a half year, but I could tell that it made us really somebody special in the neighborhood. We were like stars. We were as big as the guys who went to NYU, before the fixing scandal hit there, CCNY. Names like Ed Roman were legends to us, Sherman White, and there was another church like Holy Rose called St. Peter Claver and they used to have games every Sunday night that everyone came out to see. A lot of the older guys played in those, even after they'd left school. That was neighborhood basketball at its absolute finest. There were several playgrounds where the competition was something everyone talked about on the corners, in the candy stores, everywhere.

A friend of mine who was a priest at Holy Rosary wrote to Joe Mullaney, the athletic director of Providence College, on my behalf and told him about me. I had already graduated midyear, which was why I only played a half season as a senior, and because of it I wasn't eligible to play college ball that year. I did play for the post-season PSAL championship team. Joe Mullaney actually came down to see me play that summer, during the post-season tournaments. I played in the Flushing Y series. The two big teams were Dan Palmer's All Stars and the Gems. These were teams made up of all the high school all-Americans from the entire city. I thought I was going to play on the Gems, but I was cut. So we organized another team from all the players who didn't make it and we wound up not only winning the tournament, but I was named the MVP. Joe Mullaney's dad was at the final game and saw me play.

Life in Brooklyn in those days was great. The Dodgers were still there and they were everything for us. If you were an athlete and played on the playgrounds, no matter what color you were you could go anywhere in the borough and no one would bother you. Bed-Stuy was a rough place, don't get me wrong. There were a lot of gangs, of course, but they never seemed to bother the kids on the playgrounds. It was like sacred turf, so to speak.

STEPHON MARBURY: For me, following in the great tradition, adding to the legacy of basketball players, baseball players, actors, actresses, writers, all of whom come from Brooklyn is a real privilege. The mix is so great, and the statements they've made so bold. Having a chance to do that, having come off the streets of Coney Island, never fails to take my breath away. I take whatever success I have as a form of tribute to all those who came before me. You know, I'm a born-and-bred Brooklyn kid, I love the city, Coney Island, where I was born, is where my heart is at. No matter where I go, when people hear I'm from Brooklyn, they react as if they know it—"Oh yeah, Coney Island, I know that place. Where the Cyclone is!"—like that. We called Astroland and all of that "the rides," "Let's go to the rides."

I never really saw any place else in the world as a kid except Brooklyn, so to me Brooklyn was the world. Every avenue was like another country. It was a rough place, to be sure. You could say the wrong thing, make the wrong turn and be robbed, or killed, and I guess I was lucky because I had a talent that enabled me to get out. Getting out is a funny thing, because my heart, my soul, and a lot of my family still lives in Brooklyn. A part of me will always be that kid shooting hoops, with a dream in my hand as much as a basketball. Going through the rough years, the rough streets, drugs, shootings, the everyday living on the dark side, but strangely enough not a lot of racism. There were too many different kinds of people, and we all kind of grew up and went through everything together, black, white, Chinese, Puerto Rican, Asian, Russian, Jamaican, it was very diverse.

All my older brothers played basketball, so I started playing with them, as early as when I was two years old, in our backyard. I played in the Coney Island courts, near the handball courts, the basketball courts next to the boardwalk near the aquarium, on West Twelfth Street. I never played all that much on those courts, but I watched other guys and saw a different style of basketball than what I saw on TV. It was real rough and competitive. A lot of guys realized that if they were good enough, it might get them out of their neighborhoods and into another world. The NBA was that to us, some other world where there was only one way to get there. For me, I always knew that basketball was going to be my thing, my life's work. It was the only thing I did, and I did it well, even as a little boy. My dream, like everyone else, was to make it to the NBA, but by the time I was a sophomore at Lincoln High School, I began to think that I was good enough that I could really achieve the dream. Going to Lincoln was great, there's the legacy, right up on the wall in the main hallway. I dreamed of having my name up there.

I was a Knick fan as a kid, so that's the only team I ever really wanted to play for in the NBA. Baseball was something that really didn't mean anything to us. I was born long after the Dodgers left, so to me, Brooklyn is and always was a basketball town. As a kid, basketball was the game. Baseball was my father's game. It's been the best experience for me, playing in New York. That's my dream. The journey from Brooklyn to Manhattan took a long time, via the Gauchos, a city team that played up in the Bronx, on 149th and the Grand Concourse, all over the city, anywhere there was a game. That led me eventually to Georgia Tech, where I played college ball. I loved it there and got great preparation for the NBA.

Brooklyn is special. It's a tough place to live, and it's a beautiful place to live as well. It's the medium between those two ends that makes it so. Everyone from Brooklyn understands that instinctively. You tell somebody else that, it doesn't sound right to them. To live in Brooklyn, growing up there, seeing how everyone is raised, it's a real education.

Brooklyn to me is a place that molds and grows you. A lot of people have heroes when they grow up. Mine wasn't a sports figure. Mine was my mother. She was the only one I ever idolized.

Not everyone who plays basketball on the streets of Brooklyn gets to play in the NBA. David Tawil is fifty-four years old and still plays basketball hard and on a regular basis with the boys, now men, he grew up with. They've been playing together for nearly half a century. Today he runs a day camp in the summer at the Bayside, Queens, Jewish Center and runs various sports programs for kids. He believes that basketball is the perfect metaphor for life, and that the better a youngster learns the game, the better he will be in life at taking risks, working hard, breaking a sweat, and developing his life's skills.

DAVID TAWIL: My nickname is Ditto. I grew up in Bensonhurst, the Sephardic Jewish community—mostly Jewish guys and Italian guys. My father, my four brothers and me—Isaac, Harry, David, Ezra—can sing *pizmonim* the way kids do rap music today. *Pizmonim* are tunes that are related to celebration, childbirth, weddings.

They were elegant guys, without a lot of money but culturally rich. They conducted their lives with such civility and ritual around the synagogue. I grew up around all that. Five brothers in two bedrooms. That made all the difference. One's an engineer. One's an accountant. One's a manufacturer. There's Ph.D.s all over the family. All from this stuff, this root of Brooklyn living, eating around the table, the rice and the meatballs. We had to scrimp on the dishes we ate, but the music was rich and gave us a wealth of cultural nourishment. We ate Jewish food, and when I'd go to my Italian friend Johnny's house I'd have the *pasta e fagioli*. Stepping over the cultural lines was as easy as a waltz.

There were three kinds of Jews where we lived—Sephardic, from Spain and the Middle East; Ashkenazi Jews, from the East, Russia; and Italians, who we considered just like Jews. But the thing that bound us together most of all, everything you needed to know, came from playing basketball. Everything you ever needed to learn about life you could find out in Seth Low Playground. Now, there are certain parks in Brooklyn which were enclaves; they were where you got all of your life lessons. You found out who the scumbags were, you found out who the good guys were, you found out who you wanted to be like, who you didn't want to be like, what it was like to be bullied, that you didn't want to be a bully, you found out that you had to stand up for yourself, how to take risks as a result of just getting in and out of the park. Playing the game of basketball on concrete, it was a brilliant piece of time in all of our lives. The heart-to-heart stuff you learn in the streets of your neighborhood. You quickly are able to distinguish the bullshitters from the real people. You're able to see that right there in the park.

From the age of nine to about seventeen, every day after school and all weekend we would dash to the park with a sandwich in our pocket to play basketball. Or we'd go with a group of our friends on the stoop and play punchball and stickball in the streets. Or we'd go to the JCS [Jewish Community House of Bensonhurst], where we first met and fell in love with the women we married and had our children with. The JCS really housed us, in the sense that it gave us a place to go. We had these little jackets that we wore that defined what group we were in, that we had named ourselves; little Jewish nonviolent gangs—the Imperials, the Saracens. And there was always music at night on the roof of the JCS that gave us a place to dance with our girls.

When someone came around and pretended to be something he wasn't, who was mean-spirited to others, who cheated when he played, you could sense that. You knew who the guys were who would stand up for you when you needed them, who wouldn't let people bully you or anybody else.

I went to Lafayette High School, where five thousand kids were running through the hallways. A great institution. I still play basketball there now. I go back every Saturday morning, playing with the same guys I've been playing with for forty, fifty years. Woody Harrelson, the actor, is one of them; Gary Goldberg, the playwright; Pete Schneider, another great writer; Ed Mazria, who's now lecturing around the world on global warming; and some less-well known guys, like Louie Shor, sixty-five, a brilliant coach; Freddy Grasso, another one; Nick Gaetani, who works for the NBA today; my pal Gilley, fifty-nine. Some guys, of course, didn't make it. Some got caught up in the bad stuff the streets offer and gave up their lives to it. Two guys I grew up with died from drug overdoses. That's painful. It's a part of life. Fouling out, I guess you could say. That happens anywhere.

My grandkids come to the games. So it's three generations that gather every Saturday morning. Gilley plays with his son and his grandson.

I play with my three sons, and now my grandson is getting to enroll. They come from Jersey, Westchester, Long Island. Some of them have to drive an hour and a half to get to the gym. We have all kinds of rules for the games. No crashing through screens, no back picks, no rough stuff. The game is designed so that no one ever gets hurt. Twelve guys, four on four, two games and you're out. I'm the commissioner of the league, I watch over the games, make sure the violence is curbed, and make sure we're just having fun. Right now I'm trying to remove scoring from the game so that the whole experience becomes a purely Zen moment. The game becomes just about playing, for the sheer fun, without any competitiveness to get in the way. Let's just play, what's the difference. We've been keeping score our whole fucking life in Brooklyn—cars, houses, women, everything has a score that's kept. I'm trying to make it beautiful, a look back to the innocence and beauty of our early lives. Other games the guys curse, foul each other, like on the handball courts, where a disputed call almost always leads to some kind of fight. We won't have that in the gym.

This game gave us a life. We have lasting friendships that came out of it. We get together and we talk about our joys together. Black, white, Jewish, Italian, Arab, Haitian, it doesn't make any difference. Who you are comes out during the course of the game.

Friendship and support is everything. In Brooklyn you can still go to a public school and get a great free education. The lesson? Work at something, bend over, get dirty so you smell like Brooklyn. When someone smells Brooklyn on you, you've done a good day's work for yourself. Feel it. Be passionate about your life, no matter what you do—waitress, gambler, brain surgeon, bus driver. Brooklyn teaches you how to do that. It puts it in your face and never lets you look away, or into one of the mirrors of distortion like at the fun house. Brooklyn is reality up close. I had opportunities to live and work in other places, but I had no choice.

Brooklyn is the big court.

✖ ✖ ✖

MORE FAMOUS BROOKLYNITES

VINCENT D'ONOFRIO: Born in Brooklyn in 1959, raised in Hawaii, Florida, and Colorado, D'Onofrio returned to New York City to study acting. His breakthrough movie, Stanley Kubrick's *Full Metal Jacket,* made him a bankable star. Currently the star of TV's *Law and Order: Criminal Intent.*

ALAN DALE: Pop crooner born Aldo Sigismondi in Brooklyn in 1925. Began as a comic in the New York Italian-language theater, eventually hosting his own TV show on the early Dumont network, which drove his recordings onto the charts. Biggest hits came in the fifties, including "Cherry Pink and Apple Blossom White," "Sweet and Gentle," and "Heart of My Heart."

TONY DANZA: Born Antonio Salvatore Iadanza in Brooklyn, lived with his Sicilian American family until his teen years, then moved with them to Malverne, New York. Began his professional life as a boxer in the 1970s and later switched to acting. Breakthrough role was Tony in the TV sitcom *Taxi.*

LARRY DAVID: Born in the Sheepshead Bay section of Brooklyn in 1947. Was a struggling stand-up comic before writing for *Saturday Night Live.* In 1989 created *Seinfeld* with comedian Jerry Seinfeld, perhaps the most popular sitcom of all time. In 1999 created *Curb Your Enthusiasm* for HBO.

MARION DAVIES: Born Marion Cecilia Douras in Brooklyn in 1897. Joined the Ziegfeld Follies in 1916, which led her to Hollywood, where she became an early silent film screen star. Best remembered as William Randolph Hearst's paramour during his years building and living at San Simeon. Orson Welles based part of his 1941 film *Citizen Kane* on their relationship.

CLIVE DAVIS: Born in 1932 in Brooklyn to working-class Jewish parents, became a lawyer for the firm that represented CBS Records, which then hired him as a staff corporate lawyer. Eventually became president of the label, and is credited with helping to discover and record Janis Joplin; Santana; Bruce Springsteen; Chicago; Billy Joel; Blood, Sweat, and Tears; Earth, Wind, and Fire; and Pink Floyd. Founded his own label, Arista, in 1974, with a roster of artists that has included Barry Manilow, Dionne Warwick, Whitney Houston, Sarah McLachlan, Kenny G, the Notorious B.I.G., Sean "Puffy" Combs, Aretha Franklin, Toni Braxton, Air Supply, the Grateful Dead, and dozens more of the biggest names in music.

TOMMY DAVIS: Born Thomas Davis Jr. in Brooklyn in 1939. Was a power hitter who played for the Los Angeles Dodgers and the New York Mets, among other major league teams. Originally signed by the Brooklyn Dodgers at the urging of Jackie Robinson; the team moved to Los Angeles before Davis was called up from the minors.

CALVERT DEFOREST: Brooklyn-born actor and comedian, best known for the character of Larry "Bud" Melman, which he played on and off for nearly twenty years on David Letterman's late-night TV talk shows.

DOM DELUISE: Born Dominick DeLuise in Brooklyn in 1933 to Italian parents. Well-known film and TV comic actor.

ROY DEMEO: Born Roy Albert DeMeo in Brooklyn in 1941 to working-class Italian immigrant parents. Became a ranking, or "made," member of the Brooklyn-based Gambino crime family. The DeMeo "crew" was heavily involved with pornography, murder, auto theft, loan sharking, drug distribution, and prostitution. DeMeo's favored site for disposing of dead bodies was the Fountain Avenue garbage dump, where the sheer volume of trash delivered daily made it all but impossible to discover the bodies buried underneath. Was murdered mob style during an investigation of the Gambino family, via a hit ordered by Paul Castellano, who would himself be murdered at the order of John Gotti. It is widely believed that DeMeo was the model for Tony Soprano of the popular TV series *The Sopranos*.

CHAPTER FIVE

THE WAY WE WERE . . .
AND WEREN'T

Yesterday somehow slipped by me

It died like an old forgotten friend

Didn't I just turn sixteen in May

Now thirty-five's just around the bend

I throw the dice in all of the alleys

C'mon baby, let 'em roll

And boys, if you weren't from Flatbush,

Jack, you didn't have any soul.

—"(I USED TO BE) A BROOKLYN DODGER"

MEL BROOKS: My mother's maiden name was Brookman. That's how I got Brooks as my stage name. We lived in Williamsburg, on South Fourth Street. My mother moved us into the top floor of a five-story building at 365 South Third Street, close to the corner of Hooper and Keith.

I went to P.S. 19 until I was ten and then started what was called in those days junior high school. I went to J.H.S. 50 in Williamsburg, in '35. I was ten, and I remember we had a test about the signers of the Declaration of Independence. I was struggling with it. My brother Irving, who was ten years older than I am, had just returned that night from Brooklyn College, where he went for eight years to get his degree in pharmacy and chemistry, working at a ten-hour job during the day to help pay the rent, so he could go somewhere with his life. My other brother Lenny worked at the Colony record shop, where he came to know Artie Shaw and Glenn Miller. His buddy was Woody Herman. He was in World War II and flew forty missions; he was a prisoner of war, all of it.

Anyway, Irving came home from his nightly stint at Brooklyn College and saw me struggling to remember the names of the signers of the Declaration of Independence. I didn't have the book to study from because I wasn't allowed to take the book home from school. "What's the problem?" he asked. When I told him my dilemma, that about the only name I could remember was Benjamin Franklin, and maybe George Washington. He said, "Well . . . I don't know if George Washington signed . . . but where do you play roller hockey?"

I said, "Rodney Street."

"Rodney," he said. "There's a signer. What's your favorite movie theater?"

I said, "The Marcy."

"Well, where's the Marcy?"

"On Marcy Avenue."

"Well, there's a signer. Where do you play stickball?"

"Rutledge Avenue."

"Well, there's a signer! And where do we live?"

"We live between Hooper and Keith!"

"Two more signers!"

I said, "Irving, I'm beginning to get it! Franklin Avenue! Hancock Avenue!"

"Why do you think it's called Williamsburg and not Greenpoint? Because all the streets are named after signers of the Declaration of Independence!"

This was a great discovery to me! I got an A on the exam, remembering all the streets' names in Williamsburg.

HERB COHEN: I tend to have good feelings about my years in Brooklyn. What I know for certain was there weren't that many private homes where I grew up in the forties. Mostly people lived in apartment houses or homes that had four families living in it.

As kids we'd play ball all night, in the streets, even after it got dark, which in the summer was usually not till around nine-thirty. What we'd do is throw the ball up and someone would have to catch it under the lamppost, the only light, and it really tested our reflexes. By the time it came down we had maybe a second to see where it was before we either caught it, dropped it, or it hit us in the face.

JOAN RIVERS: When I grew up in Brooklyn, the first half of my life there, it was fabulous. My playground was the Botanic Garden, where I used to play under the cherry blossom trees. Even as a little girl in Brooklyn I could sense how spectacular nature was.

My dad was doctor with a huge practice. His office was on 417 Pennsylvania Avenue. First we lived on Eastern Parkway, before my parents bought a house on New York Avenue on a street that was known as "Doctors' Row." My dad had his office in the bottom of the house, which was a converted brownstone.

I knew every inch of my block, right up to the little movie theater at the end of it, the Bellow. In those days, it was very "neighborhood": there was a fish store, a grocery store, and as a little girl I could walk by myself without any sense of danger. I could get on my bike and ride all over the place. I never worried, nor did my mother.

But Manhattan was where everyone wanted to live, no matter what they say today about how great everything was. That was the big time. My aunt lived on Park Avenue and we would drive to her place for Sunday musicales. Isaac Stern would come, and a lot of his friends and associates from the world of classical music. Crossing the Manhattan Bridge felt magical. I knew that I wanted to live in Manhattan, in a penthouse, on Park or Fifth Avenue, because that was sophistication.

What's so fascinating to me was how my mother was always defending Brooklyn. We'd go to parties in Manhattan and people would be putting Brooklyn down, and she'd say, "Well, you don't know it." That's all changed now. People are trying to get back *into* Brooklyn, those who have left or those who have heard about how great it is. And you know something? They're right. The housing is glorious, the neighborhoods are lovely, and there are trees everywhere. It buries Manhattan for coziness.

HERB COHEN: Brooklyn was a special place and way for me to grow up. Without realizing it at the time, in that decade and a half following the end of World War II, it was ideal, my childhood a Mark Twain saga urbanized to fit the environment.

I grew up in Bensonhurst, which had a fabulous ethnic mix. Ninety-eight percent were from southern Italy or Eastern Europe, which meant that everyone spoke with their hands to communicate. When we went to school we were told never to gesture with our hands. Today I speak for a living and make big bucks speaking all over the world, and I use my hands all the time. Those teachers obviously didn't know what they were talking about.

I remember Bensonhurst as a very touchy-feely place. Other neighborhoods had their distinctions, but when I was there we did things our own way. For instance, no one ever "dressed for success." We dressed the way we dressed—our parents put clothes on our back. And no one ever changed their names. You knew who was Italian, who was Jewish, who was Irish by their names as much as anything else.

MARIA BARTIROMO: I was born and raised in Bay Ridge. I loved growing up there so much; in fact I go back a lot because my parents still live there. It was just the perfect mix of suburbia, yet with city concrete, streets, street corners. My playground was the street itself, on Eighty-fourth Street. "Manhunt" was a street game we made up with the other kids on the block. When I got a little older and wanted to go out to the big city, I didn't have to leave home forever to do it. All I had to do was take a train or get into somebody's car and I was there, in Manhattan, the center of the universe, but at the end of the day I could go home, to my parents' home. It was really the best of both worlds. My parents owned an Italian restaurant, the Rex Manor, on Sixtieth and Eleventh, and to make extra money, I checked coats on weekends when I was growing up.

Bay Ridge was a neighborhood that was always changing. It was part of the great outer-borough "melting pot" as people like to call it, which is a kind of microcosm of what America itself is. When I was growing up in Brooklyn there were Middle Easterners, Lebanese, Italian, Polish, Jewish, Spanish, so many ethnicities that made all of our lives that much richer. Being in that melting pot is an attractive thing for anyone who enjoys diversity, and you don't know if you enjoy it until you're in it. So those of us who were born in Brooklyn and who grew up side by side with immigrants I think were better off for it. As were they. Learning how to get along with everybody was something that would serve me well when I went into television, where everyday you meet different people and deal with them on various levels, from the matter-of-fact to the most-important. It makes you cool!

I was a little too young to have experienced the whole "Saturday Night Fever" phenomenon that took place but even though that left, the heat remained. Brooklyn was always "hot" in that sense. Something was always coming up from the street, radiating the culture. It was one of the best things about the outer boroughs. So much of what later becomes the mainstream starts there and then finds its way to Manhattan, if it has any staying power.

In fact, Brooklyn is getting hotter and hotter. That has its good and bad points. One of the reasons Brooklyn was so vital was because it was filled with neighborhoods that people were born into, in homes or apartments their parents could afford. Now, with the prices going up, it's a different kind of heat. It's not radiating so much as becoming a place where people want to go for other reasons, mainly I think economic. But that's changing. Many places in Brooklyn are now at least as expensive to live as they are in New York City, if not more.

I really fell into television and finance. I went to NYU because it was easy to get to from Brooklyn and it was considered a very good business school, which is what I wanted to major in—business. Plus there was the added advantage that NYU was what we called "in the city," Manhattan, where, as we all got a little older, we went into more and more. That gave me a unique opportunity of being able to experience the allure of "the big city" but still retain my life in the neighborhood back in Brooklyn. I couldn't have done that if I had been from anywhere else. Quite literally, the best of both worlds. You're either an émigré to the big city or you stay home where you were born.

I had always done well in business classes. I had an affinity for it, so I thought I would just stay with it and see where it would take me. I then kind of fell into television when, in the early nineties, I got an internship at CNN while I was still at NYU. Because of my business background they put me in business news, which at the time was really in its infancy; "Business Television" did not really exist at the time. I began at a very entry-level position, as a production assistant at CNN, and rose up the ladder as a writer, a producer, until I became Lou Dobbs' producer. I moved over to CNBC in 1993 because I had the opportunity to go on camera.

I had extraordinary luck. Most people who go into broadcasting, especially if they're from the outer boroughs, have to leave the city and start in small markets, and spend years working their way back to the city, which is the number one market for any type of broadcasting–radio, TV news, entertainment, anything. New York is number one, Los Angeles is number two, Chicago is number three. Most of the time you start in a small market, maybe number 503, and try to make the jumps that bring you closer and closer to New York. I did it by crossing one bridge. Climbing the business TV ladder gave me a literal step up because it was a relatively new field and nobody was really doing it anywhere else but here.

It's no accident, I think, that I came from Brooklyn, because of the strong work ethic that I learned from my father, combined with a naturally aggressive, competitive thing that you get from growing up around so many other people, where you compete for everything from a spot on the local team to a seat on the local subway. As a kid I remember going into the kitchen of the restaurant and seeing my father, with a bandana around his head, sweating. My image of my mom is her walking up 84th Street with a million bags in her hands, after having gone shopping for the family. Both my parents were hard, hands-on workers, and that was the foundation of everything for me. Their work ethic was just over the top and as a result of that I always worked hard no matter what level of job I had in the media. I was that tough Brooklyn girl pushing my way to the front, which eventually *became* the top. I was never afraid of hard work; I was always a go-getter, and that was something that came directly out of being born in Brooklyn. I cherish that as I cherish my entire upbringing in Brooklyn. It taught me street-smarts, hard-work smarts, and at the end of the day it is a combination of those two things, the Brooklyn "genes," that are the foundation of who I am and why I've been successful. We all can use a little luck once in a while, but luck will only take you so far. You've got to have the ability to seize on opportunity, and that was something I was primed to do from my earliest years.

I still love Brooklyn. As I say, my parents still live there, a lot of my best friends still live in Brooklyn, I go there all the time, I cherish it. And always will.

FRANK LoGRIPPO: My baptized name was Francis. It's now Frank because I used to get into too many fights being called Francis by the other guys. Frank, middle initial J., which stands for Joseph, after my dad. In those days we stuck family lineage into our names to make sure everyone knew who we were and where we came from.

I was born in Jewish Hospital in 1940 in the Borough Park section. We lived in an apartment house, the same one I lived in until I got married when I was twenty-five, in 1965. We moved once, when I was nine, from three rooms on the first floor to four rooms on the second floor, when my sister was born and we needed more room. I was nine at the time.

The thing that was so special about Brooklyn was the collage of the social fabric that existed. My biggest fear when I was a kid was that my mom and dad would one day move away from the block! I mean, if we went one block down, up, or over, it meant moving to a completely different neighborhood, and that would have been a strange and different world to me. We *never* hung out with guys who didn't live on the same block. Because of it, you could come out almost any time of the day or night, in the summer especially, but even in the winter, and feel completely safe. These were not just your friends but your neighbors. If you lived in the same building you were like family.

The building I lived in was sixteen families and the doors to every apartment were always open during the day. They were locked only at night. You'd hear a knock, someone would come in with a plate of pasta they'd want you to try.

The smells throughout the building were fantastic. The cooking, the sausages, it was almost like a European commune. Every Thursday night was macaroni night, so I knew that I was going to get some kind of spaghetti or macaroni, even if someone else's family made it. Everyone made enough for everybody. On Sunday someone would knock on the door and come in with a piece of pastry, come in and have a drink with my dad.

PETE HAMILL: In [public] school the first year [at the age of six], I learned two things that began to give me some sense of self. One, I was Irish. At school, kids kept asking: What are you? I thought I was American, but in those days in Brooklyn, when you were asked what you were, you answered with a nationality other than your own.

"LITTLE" ANTHONY GOURDINE: When we were kids, the streets of Brooklyn were tough, but a different type of rough than today. I grew up in the Fort Greene projects and could generally get around Brooklyn safely, even though I was black. I would never walk those same streets now. It's too rough out there. It's changed. Yeah, Brooklyn has gotten a lot better, there's a lot of new money coming in, that's a good thing. If you have money, okay, you can live in those new high-rise condos. If you don't, nobody cares about you, what happens to you, and that generates a lot of dangerous anger among the street-life people, especially the disenfranchised youth. The poor people have no place to go. When I was a kid we were poor, but we had homes.

Certainly you could tell the difference between, say, the streets of the Bronx and the streets of Brooklyn. It was a different kind of life. The Bronx was scary. There was no sense of closeness there, no street kind of life that didn't come along with a lot of danger. We never went up there. It was like a different planet.

Which is not to say we didn't have our own gangs. We had a lot right in our neighborhood. The Saint Street Angels, the Chaplains, the Bishops. You can see where the link was! There was a fair amount of it, but you know how they say there was honor among thieves? There was a code of street life that, if respected, kept you out of harm's way. Meaning their way.

HERB COHEN: Growing up in Bensonhurst taught me how to relate to people, how to humanize myself and admit my flaws. Perfection made us uneasy, so don't try to be something that you're not. Better to be human, which is the personification of imperfection. I learned that how I said something was more important than what I was actually saying. That was the thing about Bensonhurst; its people had great style and demeanor that was instantly recognizable to a Brooklynite anywhere else in the world.

I attended P.S. 128, and then Bensonhurst Junior High School, which was actually physically attached to P.S. 128. I then went to Lafayette High School for my sophomore year–in those days junior high school included the first year of senior high school. My best friend was and still is Larry King, the talk-show host. We grew up and went to school together. Both of us did well in junior high and thought high school was going to be a breeze, so we didn't work all that hard. Because of it we got lousy grades, so bad that we were moved from the academic program to the general program. I remember the day it happened, Larry thought it was funny. "Hey," he said, laughing, "we made the FBI." By that he meant "forever born ignorant."

I didn't think it was that funny. I knew my parents were going to kill me because I was expected to go to college. So I tried to keep it secret from them. The general class was like being in the penitentiary. We were treated like criminals. Mr. Starz was our teacher, or maybe I should say our warden. Being in general meant we couldn't take biology. Instead we were given earth science, where we studied rocks. And we took a lot of shop classes, woodworking, electrical wiring, sheet metal, while other people were taking normal subjects. Geometry wasn't for us. We got arithmetic. What is four and eight . . . it was horrible.

And there was not a lot of girl-chasing in it for us. We were heterosexuals beyond question, but our thing was always sports, not girls. When it came to the opposite sex, we were slightly retarded. We had no money, so we used to do something we called "house dating." That meant when you had a date with a girl you went over to her parents' house. They would have Pepsis or Cokes, the lights would stay on, and we would do bits and shticks to try to make the girls laugh.

There were things in Brooklyn we never understood. Signs, for instance. We used to see signs that said "Post No Bills" right up there on a wall. Or "Kilroy was here." What did that mean? None of us knew. It just became part of the street iconography of our neighborhoods.

The big drink of our generation was the egg cream, made, as everybody knows by now, without eggs and without cream. Everyone drank them. And we had no TV, so we always listened to the radio. Sometimes we'd stare at the radio as if it had a screen. It was a magical device. By looking at it, you could see what was happening on the broadcast. When TV finally did arrive, it seemed like a big letdown to us. One of the biggest celebrities in Brooklyn to us was a local kid by the name of Dennis James, who somehow showed up on television every night even though he seemed for all the world to us like a mama's boy. He was always saying, "Okay, mother" to the television screen. We didn't like that. So we watched a lot of wrestling, which was on all the time.

Every kitchen table in Brooklyn had a bowl filled with wax fruit. Why, no one knows. And the living room had a couch covered with a skintight clear plastic cover that never came off unless some special guest came. In my lifetime, no special guest ever came to our house who was worthy of having the plastic removed.

In my youth, cab drivers were different than they are today, especially those who drove through Brooklyn. They were nothing less than sages, philosophers, and psychiatrists. Driving a cab was a profession, not a job. You'd get in a cab, you had a problem, by the time you got to your destination the driver had figured it out and solved it for you. And all you had to do was pay him what was on the meter. Unfortunately, there are no real cab drivers anywhere in NYC anymore. Certainly no people who are careerists, only actors between jobs, novelists doing research, Vietnamese refugees saving up to buy a restaurant, people from the Middle East practicing their English and/or map-reading skills. It's altogether different today. Worst of all, the drivers don't know where anything is. They're not even sure what city they're in.

Eventually I went to law school, graduated while my wife was going to college, and at one point realized that we had no money because we were both full-time students. One of us had to switch over to night school. That was me. I went from day law to night law and finished up that way, and got a job as a claims adjuster, and that's how I learned as an adult how to deal with people from Brooklyn. How you deal with people in Bed-Stuy is not that different from how you deal with people on Park Avenue. You respect them, you give them a sense they're human beings, you acknowledge their dignity. I was so good I was asked to teach the other claim settlers how to do it.

In 1963, I started teaching a three-week course in negotiation for attorneys, where I began using terms like "win-win," "win-lose," et cetera. Only I didn't have the brains to copyright that stuff. Where did I learn it from? From Brooklyn, from my parents. They were immigrants. They were happy to be in America. They appreciated all that it had to offer. They not only paid retail, but they would overpay. They had insurance on which they never made a single claim because they didn't want the company to raise their rates. That was the state of mind, the Brooklyn psyche that helped to make me who I am today.

MEL BROOKS: I guess Williamsburg is gentrified today. Big rents. When we lived on Third Street we paid $16 a month. I remember my mother called a family meeting one night. She said she couldn't stand it anymore, she wanted the excitement of having an apartment that was open, that looked down from the front side of the building. An apartment had become available that faced the street, where the action was, but it was $18 a month. However, you could see the guys selling ice and watermelon from the window and all the Jewish women sitting on the stoop gabbing. All she could see from the old apartment were clotheslines. She wanted *life*! But she didn't know if we could afford it. My dad had died years earlier, in 1929–he was only thirty-four–of tuberculosis; my mother was only thirty-one. And after that we had moved around to a couple of apartments until we found the place on Third Street. [My brother] Irving told her to take it, that he would contribute.

I did too. I ran telephone calls, got a nickel from the people I called down to Dr. Hirshstein's pharmacy. Bernie delivered the New York *Daily News* out of the back of a truck. Working together, we all managed to make up those extra two dollars.

I grew up on those same stoops. We played stoopball. We'd spread the Jewish newspapers, the *Daily Forward*, which was like the Jewish *New York Times*, or the more progressive *Freiheit*. If someone was going to the grocery, they'd always knock on their neighbor's door and say, "I'm going, what do you need?" That was my neighborhood. So great and wonderful and close and loving. That's why it never occurred to any of us that we were poor, because in every way except monetarily, we were very, very wealthy. Money was different in those days. For fifty cents you could get a meal at the local deli, you could go to the movies and then to an ice cream parlor with your pals and still have a dime left over.

BRUCE "COUSIN BRUCIE" MORROW: I was born in Brooklyn and grew up in the Flatbush section, on East Twenty-sixth, until my dad got rich and we moved to East Twenty-ninth. It was an easy move. We carried everything. I went to P.S. 206 and then to James Madison High School. These two public schools were the greatest experience I had growing up. I was mixed in with an amazing, eclectic batch of people, all different religions, unfortunately not too much racial mix. Unfortunate because without it you lose a lot of cultural enrichment, which in so many ways is the ultimate contribution Brooklyn gave to America and the world.

The after-school activities were great. We used to go to the lots. I grew up on the lots. Nobody outside of Brooklyn knows what that means. At one time, Brooklyn, like most urban areas, had open dirt fields, unde-veloped real estate with hills and dales. Acres and acres. This was our playground after school. We always knew if there was a spy in town. We'd say, "Are you coming to our block? Let's go to the stoop, or let's go to the lot." If they didn't know what that meant, they were banished from the neighborhood.

On Saturday morning, my mom would pack up a cream cheese and jelly sandwich for me on Silvercup white bread, wrap it in wax paper, give me an empty Hellman's mayonnaise jar that she'd filled with tap water, and say, "Go with your friends." The East Twenty-sixth Street guys would go to "our" lot and "our" hill. Across the field, about an acre away, were the hated and feared guys from East Twenty-eighth Street. This amounted to a color war between us. We'd go out with a white flag, we'd meet, and we'd say, "Let the games begins!" The idea was to somehow capture the other guys' hill. This was done by running up, tackling them, and throwing dirt bombs–dried mud with rocks in them. When they hit the ground they'd explode in a cloud of dust in your opponents' eyes and then you could tackle them. Once we had them conquered, we'd plant the East Twenty-sixth Street flag on their side of the lot. That was always a great day.

MEL BROOKS: People loved each other and cared about each other and shared a wonderful communal spirit that pervaded Williamsburg. My mother, my grandmother, my brothers, and me, we were all part of that very great spirit.

There were many movie houses on Broadway, and you could see three features for ten cents, or a double feature and a "chapter" and Fox Movietone News, the races, where if you chose the right one you got a stick of gum for free. My mother was a great heroine. She'd be in the kitchen all day, put out three milk bottles on Friday night, get nine cents back, and then borrow a penny from somewhere so she could give me ten cents to go to the movies.

Later on I tried to take care of her. I bought her a house in Florida and took care of her until she died at the age of ninety-three, but for all the money I made writing the Sid Caesar show, and then becoming Mel Brooks on my own, it was a smidgen, a scintilla, of what she had given to me with her love and her time and her great sacrifice. And that includes the life she provided and let me live in Brooklyn. She was always so proud of me, she and her sister, Sadie, I don't know if they ever watched anything more than the credits on the Sid Caesar show when it came on. As soon as my name came on, they'd jump up and down and shout.

We didn't have any trees. The good earth to me was cement. It was so hard we didn't play hardball because if you hit the ball hard enough it might go into another county. Or into the East River. I still remember all my early friends. The peregrinations are fascinating. Most of the people who came out of there went to a few places when they "made it," meaning more than a hundred dollars a week, either Queens, Forest Hills, or Rego Park, or Long Island, or Staten Island, or New Jersey, but never farther away. That was a big mistake for one reason; once you had a house you had a fence and that was the end of the neighborhood. The immeasurable thing called friendship was irrevocably lost and that was the essence of what urban life was on the streets. All the kids poured out of their tenement apartments, into their hallways, down those marble stairs (the marble always came from Naples, it was so cheap in those days), to the slate steps of the stoop, into the asphalt of the gutter, which is what we called the street, and that was the life.

Yeah, the schools were overcrowded, thirty or forty to a class, but it was okay, we didn't mind, we loved each other. It was a great life. The only thing that really turned it all bad, that negatively impacted my life, was when they introduced a thing called homework at school.

That and World War II.

I had to leave Williamsburg and go to Fort Phillip, where they did crazy things like putting cheese on meat, and eventually was shipped overseas to send artillery shells into the sky. I saw about four months of combat before the war ended. I was lucky. Had I been one year older I never would have come back. When I did, I met up with Sid Caesar, and that began my exit from Brooklyn. Howard Morris, another writer on the show, got me my first Manhattan apartment, on Horatio Street in the Village, near the Hudson River.

I brought a lot of grace and cachet with me that I had grown up with in Brooklyn to a more commercial world when I began writing for Sid. When we were kids we'd walk across the Williamsburg Bridge to the Lower East Side and that was okay, there were a lot of Jews there. However, when we'd go any farther uptown it became very scary and very exciting at the same time. That feeling held over into my writing, I think, that combination that attracted me to the city and people to my work.

I first met Sid in the mountains, after the war, where everyone from Brooklyn either went to or worked. We were both musicians. I played drums in the Borscht Belt and Sid played the saxophone. Then Sid hit it big and gave me a call to come and work for him. I gave him a few jokes when he played the Roxy and we became real pals. He told me he was going to do the *Admiral Broadway Revue,* which later became *Your Show of Shows,* and wanted me to write for it. I got paid $50 a week and I was off. I moved to Manhattan but took with me all that I had learned growing up. Eventually I moved to Los Angeles, but I retained the part of Brooklyn that sharpened my senses and my sensibilities. When we made the movie version of the stage version of *The Producers,* we shot it in Brooklyn, at the Navy Yard, which has been converted into a movie studio. So, in a way, it was a homecoming of sorts. I could hardly recognize Williamsburg; it was different but in a way it was still the same. I'm a Brooklyn guy, it's in my bones and it's there in Brooklyn. There's a certain rhythm you get growing up there. Every Brooklyn kid has it. Always on the right beat. The Bronx, no; Queens, you were out of it; but Brooklyn, that was *it*!

FRANK LOGRIPPO: I went to New Utrecht High School. Buddy Hackett went there. So did the comedian Jack Carter. It was a huge institution, as big as a prison, and mostly Jewish and Italian, and some blacks but not many. We always had to wear a shirt and tie every day. The teachers all wore suits, ties, dresses.

We had enormous respect for our teachers. You studied hard, behaved yourself, and ate lunch in the school lunchroom. They served great hot meals then, roast beef with gravy, a slice of bread with a mound of mashed potatoes. One friend of mine who lived in my building, "Crazy Joe" we called him, had a tremendous appetite. He'd take a whole loaf of bread and put it on his tray, and two roast beef servings.

I remember getting beat up once in that lunchroom. There were these two guys from the Hawks who went over to this little kid and said, "We want your lunch." "But I'm eating my lunch," he said. So they just took his sandwich. I got up and said, "Give him his sandwich back." I never thought about the dangers. I was just very righteous, which I attribute to this day to growing up in Brooklyn. Anyway, these guys looked at me like I was crazy. I said, "Give him the fuckin' sandwich back!" I remember getting punched in the head from behind and going down, and a guy leaning over in front of me and kicking me in the side of the head, right in the temple. Who knows what would have happened if the gym teacher, a little Irish guy with this wonderful brogue who was built like a bull, appeared out of nowhere and started pulling these guys off me. Then he picked me up and said, "Hey, laddie, how are you?" "I'm okay, I'm okay," I said, just before one of those guys from the group came over to me and said, right in front of the gym teacher, "You're fucked, because this guy you tried to stop? He fights *men*! He kicks the shit out of *men*! We're going to be waiting for you outside later." I remember going to my next class, and there was a test, and as I tried to look at the blackboard, I started blacking out. I had to tell the teacher about the fight, and she let me take the test the next day. I went out, met these guys, and had my head handed to me. I paid the price, but I went home happy because I didn't like bullies, and still don't, and in my neighborhood you didn't let them pick on smaller guys and get away with it.

I remember the big polio scare of the fifties. When the first vaccines were ready, all the kids in the neighborhood had to go to the police station, where there were lines waiting to get the shot. In those days we all wore pieces of camphor pinned to our shirts, because our parents believed it helped keep the polio away, at least as much as if not more than any vaccine.

We all hung out at Bianco's candy store, which sometimes drove the owner, Mr. Bianco, a little crazy. If there were too many of us in there at the same time, Mr. Bianco would get pissed off and throw everyone out for a while. Mr. Bianco and his wife came from Italy and opened a candy store. Usually, the wife was the money person, watching all the cash, ordering the inventory, paying all the bills, while the husband was like a glorified super, fixing everything, making everything, doing all the physical work while he ran the store. Mrs. Bianco knew how to stock their place. You could always bank on an assortment of Mallomars, jelly rolls, whatever, on the counter, while Mr. Bianco made egg creams like no one else in the world. He also featured homemade lemon ice that was the best I've ever had to this day. When his wife died, he sold off whatever candy stock he had, and because he didn't know how to order more, he used to give me a couple of bucks to go buy whatever Stella's candy store, a block down, had on their counter.

Bianco's eventually disintegrated and became a total hangout. Mr. Bianco would just sit there all day and say nothing while he smoked his cigars, Italian stinkers we used to call them. If you got too close he'd blow smoke in your face until you couldn't take it anymore and run outside.

At the same time, he knew he could trust the guys from the block. For instance, if he had to go in the back for a while, he'd ask whichever one of us happened to be there to mind the front until he came back and think nothing of it. Neither did we.

DON K. REED: We used to hang out at a place called Mitchell's, over in Bay Ridge. It was a cheap hamburger and malt place, but it gave us an excuse to drive our souped-up cars there–a fierce competition all to itself–and pretend not to be trying to pick up girls.

The tough guys really hung out at the corner candy store. In Brooklyn, the candy store was the center of the teenage social universe. Mine was called ABC, and I got everything I needed there–egg creams, school supplies, comic books, two-cent candy, spaldeens. It also had a phone booth with split doors with windows so you could close out the rest of the universe in your desire for absolute privacy when you were calling up a girl. That was crucial.

Everyone knew everyone else at the candy store, and the owners were like our surrogate parents. If we wanted a soda but didn't have any money they'd mark it down in a little book and our parents would pay for it at the end of the week.

On any given summer night, everyone would be outside, or downstairs, as we called it. Older folks would take folding bridge chairs down and sit on the sidewalk, while the kids would hang out at the candy store, either with transistor radios or listening to jukeboxes, which most candy stores had at the time.

FRANK LoGRIPPO: The guys on my block palled off according to age. If you were three to five years' difference, maybe even two, you were in a different group. Each group did different things, and each group's personality was different. The older guys gambled, they played horses and hung out in bars. Every Friday, Saturday, and Sunday night they drank, and for a break they'd step outside of whatever bar they were in and tell each other incredible stories of what happened to them. The younger guys, like me, would stand as close as we could, say nothing and hold our breath as we listened to these wild tales.

I hung out with two groups, which was unusual. My age group used to collect baseball cards and flip them for money. Flipping means you hold a card in your hand and let it fall to the ground, calling face up or face down before it hits. These were very serious games that sometimes went on for hours on end. Whenever we heard that some candy store on another block had gotten a shipment of cards with different players, we'd walk, sometimes for miles, to buy them.

Yo-yos were big too. For a while we all had yo-yos. There were different grades of the best-balanced yo-yo, the Duncan. The best of these was the platinum with the little diamond on the sides. Now, my mother had a marble table in our apartment that she didn't want stained, so my father put a glass top on it. And he always warned me not to play with the yo-yo inside the house. So one day I was standing in the living room practicing my around-the-worlds when I did hit the table and broke the glass top. My father, who had a terrible temper, went crazy. My mom was able to stop him short of killing me.

Me and my guys went to the movies, usually the Garden, on Saturday mornings. We'd go in droves, maybe thirty kids. There was always a line when they'd show three cowboy movies, maybe a Tarzan. Once inside the screaming that would go on during the film was amazing. Most of the time the yelling was so loud you couldn't hear the film. The matrons were a pain in the ass, they'd always kick us out at three o'clock, even if it was in the middle of a movie we hadn't seen. They were tough, they'd shine a searchlight right in your eyes, and if you talked back, they'd pull you out of your seat, drag you to the exit, and throw you right out into the bright sunlight while you were temporarily blinded. If we did get to stay until the end, the exit doors would open and everyone would spill out, like a fire. If it was a cowboy or a war movie, we'd come out shooting finger guns and punching each other, imitating our heroes on the screen.

A couple of blocks away from where I lived was the Jewish area. The main shopping area there was Thirteenth Avenue. It's still a great place to shop, but now instead of the immigrant Jews who lived there when I was growing up, it's mostly Hasidic today. Those shops had everything–great delis, bakeries, dairy, appetizers, all of it. Butter was cut from a big piece. Fish were bought live. Also chickens. They used to be bought and have their necks slit into a V-shaped cone by Mr. English, the shop owner, to bleed out before being plucked and wrapped. I hated being sent there by my mother because the smell was so overwhelmingly disgusting.

In the summer, the older men would get a milk box and put them out under a streetlight and play "Brisk," an Italian card game. The women used to take their folding chairs out in front of the apartment house and just sit out and talk. You'd see this line of women and they were just talking, about kids, what happened at shopping, whatever. This was the social fabric of Brooklyn.

My mom always worked. I had to go to a lady when I was small to be minded. My mother worked for the phone company. My dad didn't really make enough to support the family. I remember that we paid cash all the time for everything. When something had to be charged, the local store owner would just write in pencil in a little book, in columns, the names and amounts of people that owed money. It was a very trusting system. The pencils they used were hand-sharpened by a knife. Nobody ever used such fancy machinery as a pencil sharpener.

There were no gangs in my neighborhood. There were gangs at school, like the Hawks. Occasionally if someone from our neighborhood got in trouble with a girlfriend who happened to have a brother in a gang, one of the guys from it would come around to threaten him. One time two hundred guys from a gang showed up to beat one of my friends up because he went out with this beautiful girl he wasn't supposed to. To this day I don't know how he managed it. Her ex-boyfriend came around with the rest of the gang and a general brawl broke out. I still remember punches being thrown. That was the closest I ever came to actually being in a real gang fight.

When I got a little older, I started hanging out in one of the neighborhood bars, like all the other guys, and talk to my friends, sometimes for hours. As we'd talk, we'd each shift our feet a half step or so, that's very Borough Park. After an hour, without knowing how the hell we got there, we'd be out on the street. It always happened gradually. Like global warming.

Every now and then you'd get someone complaining if it was two or three on a summer night and a bunch of us were on the corner. I always tried to get everyone to keep their voices down, but nobody listened and sooner or later someone would call the cops. Brooklyn cops, there was no fucking around with them. They'd come around, they'd tell you once, and if anyone said anything that sounded even half snotty, let alone arrogant, the cops, they were all big guys, if you stood close enough because you were stupid enough, you'd get a real kick in the ass and that was how they enforced the law.

Across the street from Bianco's was this guy Carmello, who had a bakery. A couple of friends of mine worked there every night until three in the morning baking bread. A couple of us would hang out with them for a while until Carmello would show up and kick us out. Now, these guys were degenerate gamblers. They'd bet on how many drips of rain would come from this side of the awning versus the other. Or if they saw a couple of roaches, how long it would take them to reach a certain spot on the ground.

Willie the druggist had the corner drugstore and he treated everybody. No matter what was wrong, you went to see Willie. If you had something in your eye, whatever, Willie. His diagnosis was always the same. We called him the hooch. It didn't matter what was wrong with you, he gave you a bottle of something that cured you. Only drastic situations brought you to the doctor. I had my tonsils taken out in the doctor's office, with ice cream after. There were a whole bunch of kids they did at the same time, on a cot, all waiting for it to be over so they could get the free ice cream.

Guys of all ages used to go to the confraternities but I never did. Either I was shy or I thought it was stupid. Confraternity was the Catholic church-run dances in the basement of the churches. Everyone got dressed up in suits and the women in dresses, men slapped on Palmolive after-shave. My friend Sammy used to come into Bianco's and stink out the whole place until we couldn't stand to be there anymore. I mean, he used to use the whole bottle for just one night in confraternity. After, guys would come out and, if they'd manage to rub up against the girl they danced with enough they'd always come in their pants and that wet circle was a highly public sign of a very good night. Sammy started working in his father's butcher shop, so he had money way before all of us. He bought a powder-blue Pontiac convertible, beautiful, and because of it went out with a different girl every week. His claim to fame was to pull up, jump out of the car, and show off his stained pants. He wouldn't say anything, just grin while his head bobbed up and down.

No one ever went to Manhattan, or even thought about it very much. To us, that was the city. There was too much going on right where we were. We didn't need the city. On the weekend, it could be one in the morning, someone would say he felt like having watermelon and we'd all jump in the car and go down to Phil Pepper's in Coney Island and get these huge slices. Sometimes we'd go on the rides, the Steeplechase, or the best wooden roller coaster in the world, the Cyclone. My friend Joey used to always get in the first car with his girlfriend, Annette, and stand up for the whole ride.

In the summer if we didn't have wheels and it was a really hot day we'd take the train to Coney for a nickel. We'd go on the rides, or go to Sunset Pool, which was for the public. Eventually we graduated to the Steeplechase pool, an upper grade of people and a cleaner pool. One of the older guys was more or less the leader. He always had a comb in his pocket and was always combing his hair straight back. He'd wear a shirt with a pack of cigarettes in his front pocket or rolled up in the sleeve. We threw him into the pool one time, and that led to a big fight. All these guys were ever looking for was an excuse to kill each other.

The end of the day we'd grab a couple of hot dogs at Nathan's and french fries to eat on the subway on the way home. What can I say? It was the greatest.

Whenever anyone from the neighborhood got married, the whole block was invited. Not formally, with invitations or anything like that. You just knew about it and you showed up that Saturday night, for Frankie and Marie's wedding, or whoever it was. Whether you were six years old or eighty years old, you went to the basement of the church after the wedding. There was always a live band, and you just spilled in and ran for a seat at these round tables. In the middle were sandwiches, wrapped, with titles on them–salami, capicola, cheese, cold cuts–so you knew exactly what you were getting. On one table if they ran low on one, like salami, someone would yell over to the next one, "Hey, you got any salami?" "Well, what do you got?" "I got a couple of capicolas here," and they would toss them from one table to another. That's why we called them football weddings. At least four hundred people would always show up.

I myself married a girl who lived just two houses down from us. And I was the only guy I knew from the neighborhood who had gone to a real college. By then, I could see the changes beginning. In my aunt's building, she lived on Twenty-first Avenue and Seventy-eighth Street, the Pakistanis were starting to move in. Today, in the building where I lived as a kid, there's nothing but Chinese and Pakistanis. When I got married and moved to Jersey, and would come in to see my mom, I would say to myself, where are the kids playing stickball? Where are the games? It was a gradual fall-off of the street life of the neighborhood until it was nothing. It was a heartbreaking thing for me to see. As young folks like me got jobs and moved away, we took the old culture with us.

JOHN KARLEN: I was born on Fortieth Street between Fifth and Sixth Avenue, in the Bay Ridge section of Brooklyn across the street from Sunset Park, which is, by the way, the highest elevation point in the city– 237 feet. As a kid I'd go with Mikey Spiro, my friend, and we'd sit in the park and look out at the Statue of Liberty.

Brooklyn was tough to live in for my family. When I was a child we moved around, six or seven different places. How could I love walking around with paper in my shoe where the bottom has worn through, no fucking coat in the freezing winter, the sleet and rain in my face? But what do I remember most? *Rats!* Rats counted in Brooklyn. Everyone talked about them, if you had them, on what floor they were on this week. For some reason they never went above the second floor. Did you ever hear of the Norwegian brown rat? It's the largest fucking rat in the world. They first came into Brooklyn on the French ships that docked at the Brooklyn seaport. They'd creep through the streets and into the buildings. Before I'd open my door, I'd always shuffle my feet loud on the hallway floor and listen for the scurry.

Some of them really didn't give a fuck, they were that brazen and aggressive. One time the old man and I were coming home from the racetrack and we open the door, put the lights on and there are two of them in the rat trap, dead. I can still remember how ugly they looked. A year or two later I'm in the army and stationed in Korea and I'm washing my hands in the bowl, and before I can get my hands out I see there's a big fat rat in it. I had to go all the way to Korea to find the same son of a bitch in my bowl. Only there you could shoot them, which I did.

The real unspoken truth of Brooklyn is that it's a shit-fuckin'-hole of roaches and rats. It's got the greatest food, great parks, all of that candy store nostalgia and egg cream crap, but the truth of the matter is it's a disgusting, fucking, miserable shithole.

I can remember as a kid, one December, it was damp and cold, and my father says, "We're going to go to Manhattan, to the Roxy [movie theatre] to see *Arabian Nights*." So what happens? We went down into the subway, out of this black, eerie piece of shit called Brooklyn, rode on the subway for forty-five minutes, crossed the bridge, got off at Forty-second Street, and walked out into wonderland!

It's 1943, I'm nine years old, there are a million soldiers and sailors walking around, and it looks like ten million nightclubs to keep them busy. The atmosphere was beautiful. We're fighting a real war that *counts,* for our *lives,* and suddenly I realize there is life beyond my neighborhood, there is a real difference between the desolate darkness of Brooklyn and the bright lights of the crossroads of the world!

How could I like Brooklyn? I'm a Polish kid who grew up in an Italian neighborhood, I had to work my ass off just to stay alive. I had to speak louder and tougher than the others. I had three sisters, which didn't help, seeing how sad it was for girls growing up there. They really couldn't be "girls" in Brooklyn, with all its filth and dirt and shit. That was how I saw 80 or 90 percent of Brooklyn. There may have been a nice side to it, but I never saw it.

One time I fought Pete Hamill and his brother, Brian, at P.S. 10. I know it was them. There is a vague remembrance of it by Pete in one of his books when he's talking about him and his brother. We were playing for corks or something and then all of a sudden there's two guys beatin' the shit out of me. I got in my punches, but I can remember this beautiful shirt I had and the fucking thing was ripped to pieces and I walked home bleedin' and busted up and I never said anything to my mother and father about it, if they were even there; maybe they weren't, it doesn't fuckin' count. My sister says, "What happened?" and I say, "What the fuck ya mean, what happened? *Shaddup!*"

But there is awesomely good stuff in Brooklyn. Taking a walk in Prospect Park, that is awesome. It's about a third the size of Manhattan's Central Park and twice as beautiful, but it's also a walk through the jungle. I would go there with my sister Tilly. If you walked another ten blocks you would be in an entirely different, elite group. You never went there. You had your own little pieces of turf. Everyone in Brooklyn was always separated by all this supposed "togetherness." Accidentally walk into that Tigers' neighborhood where Pete Hamill came from and you had to walk on eggshells, with your head down, not making any noise. If you made it to the Garfield section, where the Italian guys hung out, you always felt the air of murder around your head, the kind that would make the front pages.

PETE HAMILL: There were immense black gangs in Bedford-Stuyvesant called the Bishops and the Robins; the Navy Street Boys from the waterfront in Fort Greene; tough Jewish gangs from Brownsville and Coney Island. And there were street gangs right in the neighborhood.

The gang at our end of the neighborhood was called the Tigers, most of them Irish. Their great rivals were the South Brooklyn Boys, most of them Italian. They all wore variations on the zoot suit, brightly colored trousers with a three-or-four-inch rise above the belt, ballooning knees, tight thirteen-inch pegged ankles. The rear pockets were covered with gun-shaped flaps of a different color, called pistol pockets; sometimes a bright saddle stitch would run down the side of the trouser leg. . . . The colors and combinations were drastic, radical, personal, at once an affirmation of their owner's uniqueness and a calculated affront to those locked in the gray dark memory of the Depression. In summer, the gang members wore T-shirts with the sleeves rolled high on the shoulder and a cigarette pack folded into the roll. . . .

On the street, we learned their names and their histories and heard the legends of their wars. Tigers and South Brooklyn Boys lived by primitive codes, most of them outlined in what became their catechism: *The Amboy Dukes* by Irving Shulman, published in 1947, probably the best-read novel in the history of Brooklyn. The codes demanded that all loyalty go to the gang, ahead of family, church, city, or country. Every guy had to drink hard and fight to the death; the women had to "put out" for the men. Although they supported themselves with burglaries and other minor crimes, they despised the mugger, they would never hurt old people, they would not ambush drunks in the dark or roll lushes in bars . . . dozens of South Brooklyn Boys ended up in the Mob. . . .

The basic template of my life was cut in Brooklyn. I was ten when World War II ended. Most of what I knew, what I remember at least, what happens around 1941, 1942 onward. We lived in several places in Brooklyn, but the main place was 378 Seventh Avenue, top floor right. That was hard because my father only had one leg. He lost the other playing soccer in the immigrant leagues in the 1920s. No penicillin, gangrene, amputation. So it was hard for him going up and down those stairs, but he worked most of the time in a factory across the street, catty-corner from where we lived. 378, for people who live in Park Slope now, is between Eleventh and Twelfth Streets and the factory was on Twelfth. It made fluorescent lights. Not surprisingly, the kitchen in our apartment had a fluorescent light that made all of us look pale blue. My brother and I used to run out to play to make sure we hadn't turned permanently blue.

This was a period in Brooklyn when the Depression was still on. In ours and many neighborhoods like ours, our families didn't profit from the war, we fought it. We had our share of flags in the windows denoting a kid was in the service, and there was a big sign on Thirteenth and Eighth Avenue that listed everybody who was serving plus the ones who'd died. The war itself was unlike this preposterous thing we're involved in now; it was literally shared by everybody. We had to deal with rationing. A lot of women worked because the men were gone. Young men above all were gone. The Depression was over, for them, because they were able to have more than $11 in the banks–the ones that trusted the banks, that is.

JOHN KARLEN: In Brooklyn, guys jumped from the rooftops of six-story buildings, across alleys, just to prove how tough they were. Not even on a dare. Just on an existential level, just to do it. If they didn't make it and they fell to the ground, they were dead. That meant in retrospect they were not tough enough to live in Brooklyn. I did it three or four times. Macho bullshit made me, and luckily I was fast and could jump, or I'd be dead now.

When I was eighteen my best buddy went into the air force. He was stationed in Denver, Colorado, and sent me a letter telling me about how great the food and the women were. That was it for me. I joined the next day. Before that I had been out of Brooklyn once in my life, for one week, in Ronkonkoma, Long Island, with two friends while I was a teenager. I got on the Long Island Railroad and went there and I couldn't believe it. The smell of the country, being able to catch a fish–I caught a turtle on a hook. And yet, when all was said and done, I couldn't wait to go home. At the end of the day, it was Brooklyn, not Ronkonkoma, that gave me life.

I got out of the air force in 1955 and went back to Brooklyn. Fucked around for a year and a half, met Judy Schoenberg, who finally convinced me to go to the American Academy of Dramatic Arts on the GI Bill. When guys used to "get angry" as actors in a workshop, I'd say to myself, what the fuck, they don't even know what anger is! In Brooklyn, I was angry all the time! And it was acting led me out of it, and my experiences as a kid growing up in Brooklyn made me good at knowing how to "play angry."

Acting became my real ticket out of hell. I always drew 100 percent on my upbringing in Brooklyn. I did a lifetime worth of roles before I landed the part as Harvey on *Cagney and Lacey*. We had a seven-year run; that's a lifetime if you're not a horse player.

The comedic side of me took a little longer to come out, I guess, because it was all bullshit to me, all that TV canned laughter and unfunny writing. I used to see guys who came out of my class making $300,000 an episode on some dopey show who couldn't act a lick. And Brooklyn, that became some sort of airwaves Shangri-la of laughter, family, harmony, racial equality, and I don't know what else. It certainly wasn't the Brooklyn I grew up with. Even though it might look like Brooklyn—which, incidentally, to me it never does—it isn't Brooklyn.

Despite everything, I remember going with my father to Nathan's, having a hot dog, maybe two, making sure the roll was soggy, that made it ten times better, drinking an orange soda or a root beer and sitting on a park bench. I would tell them without hesitation that I was proud to be from Brooklyn.

BEN VEREEN: I grew up in Williamsburg. I remember Fulton Street as a kid, and Chauncey. I remember the United Baptist Church, and the Tip-Tap-and-Toe shoeshine parlor there. I remember having Dixie cups of ice cream on Sunday. Because of the blue laws, the deacons would all get their shoes shined at Tip-Tap-and-Toe and fill empty Dixie cups with liquor before they went to church. The shoe shiners would tap-dance as they did their work and sing and snap their rags. When they were finished, they'd bring out their own Dixie cups!

Some people called where we lived a ghetto. I called it home. Sometimes we would rent out a room in our apartment to help pay the rent. Mom would divide the refrigerator between the boarder and us, their food and our food. Sometimes late at night when I'd come home I'd eat all the stuff that was on the other side, because it looked so good.

My father worked at the Gypsy paint factory; my mother worked as a maid, a seamstress, and a maintenance woman at the Loew's Kings on Flatbush Avenue. I was about ten years old. When everyone would go home and she was cleaning up, I'd get on the empty stage with the house lights all up and put on shows just for her. At one point my father wanted to be a floor waxer, so he saved up and bought himself some equipment. He'd put it in the back of his car, I'd go along with him and we'd go up to Canarsie, the Italian neighborhood, the Jewish neighborhood, and wax everyone's floors, until he decided it was too much work.

IVAN KRONENFELD: I was born and raised in Brooklyn, I went to school at Winthrop Junior High School 235 in Brownsville, lived on Albany Avenue in Flatbush with my first wife, and did not move out of Brooklyn until I was twenty-seven years old. Our parents were immigrants. When I was seven years old I was hanging out on the stoop, and I wanted to meet other kids. This kid comes down the block and says to me, "Come on, let's take a walk." He was also seven but we were like little adults. Two girls walking in front of us must have been twelve. The kid says, "Watch this." "Ey," he says to one of them, "you wanna fuck?" I said, "Wooowwwwwwww!" And he and I became friends for life. When we would cut school with another kid, Slipovitz, we'd all go to the penny arcades in Times Square and wind up running from the truant officers. A few years later, there was a pool hall we hung out at across Utica Avenue, which was Abe's on Fifty-first Street and Church Avenue. I guess my world went from Flatbush Avenue to Utica Avenue—that was the border of the map of our neighborhood.

We all worked after school. There was a guy, Yogi, I first met in Mr. Morgiello's junior high school history class. One day Mr. Morgiello called on Yogi and said, "What did Magellan do?" and Yogi said, "You think I don't know, right? Magellan, he circumcised the world!"

Brooklyn is smart and faced-paced and always has been. I think at least part of the reason may be traced back to immigration. After World War II, most of the immigration was Jewish, and most of them concentration camp survivors. And in typical Brooklyn fashion, they arrived with no sympathy, no caring by those already here, or by anyone. They were simply referred to as "refs," short for refugees. As in "A couple of refs moved in next door."

One day I'm still a kid and we're all standing on the corner, and a lot of refs are moving into the neighborhood. One of them, an Italian kid, just got off the boat, came up to Slipovitz and says in broken English, "How do I mail a letter?" Slipovitz says, "I'll be happy to take care of you." He takes him over to the fire alarm box and says, "You pull this lever and you wait for the postman, who will come to pick up the letter." He pulled it, the fire engines came screaming up to the corner, and he hands one of the firemen the letter. They took him away. He was nine.

I remember Abie was a ref who delivered orders for the Associated Supermarket. He was pretty good with his hands. And Sonny started a fight one day with Billy, and Billy was pounding him pretty good, until five or six of Sonny's guys held him down and Sonny bit off his ear. I remember thinking that day, hey, this isn't like in the movies at all. In *Bad Day at Black Rock* one guy, Spencer Tracy, *with one arm,* was able to take on a whole barroom full of tough guys *and win!*

But it wasn't only toughness they brought. Those who managed to survive the concentration camps and leave the shtetl to go to Brooklyn were not the local weaklings or Joe the Moron. So you have people who are clever and quick and willing to take risks and have those kind of genes. The same is true from Jamaica or Haiti: let's all go get in a leaky boat and if we're lucky we'll all wind up in Brooklyn.

I went to Erasmus Hall High School. Barbra Streisand had just left when I entered. Billy Cunningham, the basketball star, and Bobby Fischer, the chess champion, all went there. It's funny, my crowd wasn't exactly into chess, but they would always point him out and say, "See that weird kid? He's a chess champion." "Yeah, who gives a fuck?" was the usual answer.

Flatbush in the fifties was predominantly Italian and Jewish but there was plenty of everything-else-white as well. When I was a kid it was all white. Now it's almost all black. My first wife, a lovely woman with whom I'm still very friendly, Jeanette, was from Bensonhurst. We got married when I was twenty-six, in 1972. I was still living in East Flatbush, which had seen a dramatic shift in population. We were both teachers. When we first got married, her sister came over to help put my terrible bachelor apartment in better shape. I remember she was crying bitterly. I said, "What's wrong?" and she said, "My sister"–meaning Jeanette–"is living with the niggers," meaning in the neighborhood. That was Brooklyn in the midst of what is often euphemistically called "the turn."

Although I was still young, I was there for the post–World War II immigrant-influenced gang era. The Egyptian Lords was the gang in my neighborhood. Here's the kind of stupid thing that went on. The gangs would rent basements in these four-family houses for next to nothing and they'd gamble down there and have parties. In the house next to the one I lived in on East Forty-second Street the Chessmen opened up a clubhouse. First thing, they demanded to be invited to our local dances and we said no, they couldn't come. What do you do when the Chessmen tried to muscle in? You have to kill Jackie Himmel, the president, warlord, whatever his title was. There's no other way to do it. They had a war council in Sherman's candy store, where much of the profits came from bookmaking, not from two-cent candies. Blackie ran the book in the back, with Lummy. It wasn't even a separate room, it was the back table.

I knew the night it was going to happen. They came in and Billy C. stabs Jackie Himmel. They get to the corner and Tommy L. says, "Where's my knife?" Billy says, "I left it in Jackie Himmel!" "That's my best knife!" "Okay," Billy says, "let's go back and get it!" So they get there just as the cops get there to take the knife out of Jackie Himmel's lung.

The church was St. Catherine's of Genoa, and they had a confraternity every Thursday night. On one particular Thursday night a "spic" had the nerve to try to go to it. What do you when a "spic," nobody at the time would think of calling him anything else, like a Puerto Rican, comes to confraternity? Kill him! What else would a reasonable man do? The young Puerto Rican fellow happens not to want to get killed so easily, so he stabs Anthony D. pretty good in the liver. The rest of the guys chased the spic fourteen or fifteen blocks to Nostrand Avenue, leaving D. bleeding on the sidewalk. The kid runs into a cab and the guys jump on the cab. Somehow he gets away. They go back to D., who's been bleeding to death in the street. Now, we were two blocks from Kings County Hospital and there were pay phones on every corner to call an ambulance, but no, they walk him to Bobby B.'s house on the corner of Albany and Lenox. Bobby's mother says, "He's not going to bleed all over my floor." So they finally walk him to the hospital. Amazing he lived, not that it was any great boon to mankind.

In fact, he almost killed *me* one day. We lived in the schoolyard. You got there eight-thirty in the morning and left at midnight. No grass, of course, all concrete. The schoolyard doubled as our Madison Square Garden, the backyard, Las Vegas, the cultural center of our youth. The rules were, if you were playing on one of the stickball courts and the hooligans came, you left the court. There was no debate. Fair is fair is one thing; we were there first, we knew life was not the movies.

One day I'm playing stickball with a guy called George Wechstein. So me and George are playing and Anthony D. and the hooligans come over and say, "Get the fuck off the court." So we were going but I guess we didn't go fast enough. That's a mistake. A failure of etiquette! Our backs were to them and we can hear them yelling, "You Jew cocksuckers," just as the baseball bat comes sailing from 150 feet behind me and goes right over my head and misses me by an inch or so. It hits, that's called dead.

The Egyptian Lords were kind of universal in that they were interdenominational. They were certain Italians and Irish gangs, all from the neighborhood, so in that sense it was about race. The Bishops were the black gang, the Fort Greene Avenue Chaplains were the Puerto Rican gang, then there were smaller gangs like the Chessmen. There was a federation of gangs in New York called Pigtown. You know the two crooked cops that were hit men for the mob, the ones they extradited from Las Vegas, and then the judge decided the statute of limitations had run out? One of them, Lou Eppolito, comes from East Flatbush, from Pigtown. Eppolito is a Brooklyn–East Flatbush–Pigtown guy. Sonny Sevino, may God rest his soul, was, like Arthur Miller says in the beginning of *A View from the Bridge*, cut in half, right in front of Blackie the book, two, three o'clock in the morning. Guys from Pigtown rode by and did it.

Now, my understanding is that, technically, Pigtown was not East Flatbush, it was East New York, but I read that Eppolito came from East Flatbush and was involved in Pigtown.

There was also pure crime, like the Lupo brothers, who made the front pages of all the papers at the time: "Four Lupo Brothers Found Dead in a Car in Kennedy Airport."

You can't grow up in Brooklyn and not like the tough guy image because you grew up intimidated by the real tough guys. I think it's why writers like Pete Hamill and Norman Mailer were so attracted to fighting. They saw it as a metaphor, to be sure, but they were also attracted to the sheer stance, the almost preening macho charm that always came along with it. Even Arthur Miller had some of that in his writing.

I don't know where I fit into Brooklyn anymore. Borough Park is Orthodox; in spirit I'm Orthodox, but not in practice, so that's out. Brooklyn Heights is for people who are spectacularly wealthy, which I'm not. Boerum Hill, Cobble Hill, that's for young kids. Williamsburg is artistic. Greenpoint is Polish, so I don't think I have a place there anymore. And you know what? I think Brooklyn is supposed to be that way, a way station, a one-way station, someplace you're raised before you move on.

Woody Allen is someone I'd say traveled that route. No matter that he lives in Manhattan, he's very much Brooklyn. It's not like you'd have to figure out he was from Brooklyn. You could probably even figure out that he came from Kings Highway, he's that specific.* He's got a certain

---

* His first residence was his parents' three-story frame house at 968 East Fourteenth Street, three houses in from Avenue J, in the Midwood area of Flatbush, not far from Kings Highway.

smart way. I don't know if it's something in the water, because whether its Woody, or Rabbi Schneerson, there's something there.

RABBI SIMON JACOBSON: As far as Jews go, Woody Allen is a Jew, therefore he represents Judaism by definition, and he has made his career out of being a Brooklyn Jew. He's a rabbi, with a cathedral all his own. Actually, I think he represents a big segment of Judaism, which are the cynical Jews, the ones that have seen all the baloney. He laughs at it. It resonates for a lot of Jews, and it resonates for me too, because I know those type of rabbis. The sad part is that Woody Allen only paints half a picture. There's another half. Not all Jews are hypocrites, or neurotic. So I think he got one-half of the picture quite well, but not the other half. And because of it, he reinforces the stereotype, and frankly, I would have felt the same way had I not met other real Jews. Judaism is not here for four thousand years because people were dogmatic, neurotic, and hypocritical. How could they have survived the Holocaust with a power beyond? It's what makes us Jewish, what people feel when they go to Israel, or on Yom Kippur.

But even Woody Allen, in his films, he is conflicted; the Jewish conflict is always there. He senses there is more but doesn't know that you have to build synagogues in your own heart and soul, where there's no consumer fund-raising or politics.

WOODY ALLEN: My biggest regret in retrospect is that my parents didn't live in Manhattan. It's such a regret of mine. They thought they were doing the right thing and probably thought that they couldn't afford to move. In a certain sense, given who my parents were and how much money they had, it was fine to live in Brooklyn. But the truth is, if they were a little more enlightened, I could have grown up in Manhattan in the late thirties and forties. I would have loved that. Now, of course, the city is much more of, you'll forgive the expression, a shithole than it was then. I love it now like a boy loves a father who is, say, an alcoholic or a thief. But when I think that there were kids who grew up on Park

Avenue and Fifth Avenue in the thirties and forties and had their child-hood there and there was no crime to speak of, what a paradise! . . .

My mother always said I was a happy kid for my early years and then when I was around five, something happened, she always felt, that made me turn sour. I have no memory of any such event or anything trau-matic, nor could anyone offer up any traumatic event. So I don't know. I *was* a loner from an early time on. I remember other kids in class psy-choanalyzing me amateurishly when I was in the sixth grade and say-ing, "Well, do you notice that when he walks to school, he walks through the back alleys?" which I did. I often went down the block and hung a left to make a shortcut. They said, "It's because he doesn't want to be around people." And you know, that couldn't have been more true, though I wasn't totally conscious of it at the time. And my family was not like that. They were loud and demonstrative, but I definitely have never been social. It's a paradox.

Bruce Wulwick: I was born August 11, 1942, at Brooklyn Jewish Hospi-tal. I attended yeshiva in Borough Park, which I hated because I believed the teachers were very cruel. I was glad to get out and finish high school at New Utrecht. It's funny, these big high schools were very similar throughout the borough. More than similar. Jefferson and New Utrecht were exact duplicates of each other. Anyway, having been at an all-boys school, then going into this huge coeducational place, I couldn't help but notice the one overwhelming thing that had been missing from my education and my life: *girls.*

I remember things I did as a youngster that remain vivid in my mem-ories to this day, like the trolleys or cable cars that rose with the huge arm above them to get electricity from the cables, or buying lemon ices at the Savarese pastry shop, where a small cost six cents, a large cost twelve.

Sunset Park, on Fiftieth Street, the borderline with Bensonhurst, was where I grew up. Our neighborhood had neat, organized homes—mother/daughter homes, they called them, with the owners living upstairs and the downstairs rented out to newlyweds. Everyone took care of their own space.

We were one of four Jewish families on the block. The rest was all Italian. Everyone got along well, but there was a palpable tension among the Italians against the Jewish families. The only overt anti-Semitism I encountered when I was growing up was on the way home from the yeshiva. Coming home from school, we'd all take our yarmulkes off, because we didn't want to let the neighborhood guys know we were Jewish. Guys would harass us if they found out. It wasn't terrible, it came with the territory, but it was there. Interestingly, Fifty-ninth Street today is the largest Hasidic community in the world. I lived on Fifty-ninth Street in Brooklyn for thirty-five of the thirty-seven years I lived in Brooklyn. When I got married and started my own family, we decided to move to Valley Stream, the suburbs, because we thought it would be better for the children.

I think part of the reason I remember Brooklyn so fondly was because of the social atmosphere. It's hard for younger people to understand what the world was like before the Internet, cell phones, not a lot of phones, period, and, when I was a boy, no television. In order to occupy yourself you had to associate with other people, and that became a crucial part of our lives. Little games like hit the penny, played with a spaldeen and a penny placed between two cement squares on the sidewalk; boxball, where you could approximate an entire major league baseball game with a single spaldeen and those cement squares, slapping the ball in a certain designated area for a single, double, triple, et cetera. Or we'd just get together, the guys, and sit on the stoop and talk.

Sometimes we'd play an Italian card game called Brisk. It's played with three cards in your hand, take out all the eight, nines, and tens, and in order to win you have to get 120 points. Some of the words used in the game were "reach" and "drop a load," double-entendres that made it fun. We'd play for money, maybe just a dime, but that dime made the whole thing worthwhile.

The neighborhood I grew up in had a lot of gambling. No matter what you did, money came into it. If you played softball in the schoolyard, it was for money. I started gambling in Brooklyn, from the little Brisk game to going to the trotters up in Yonkers. I used to go to the track every Friday night, either Yonkers Raceway or Roosevelt Raceway in Queens. These were the twin-double years. You had to pick the fifth- and sixth-race winners, and then the eighth and ninth. This one particular Friday night, my friends were going, but for one reason or another I couldn't. I got a call from one of the boys, who wanted to know what my bet was. I said, "Put two dollars on eight and seven, and seven and four." "You sure?" he says to me, and I hesitated and then said, "Aah, forget it." I didn't want to spend the two dollars. That evening, sure enough, eight and seven and seven and four came in and paid $187,000! There was only one winner that night, and he got the whole thing. Had I put my two dollars down, I would have walked away with ninety thousand dollars! That became the story of my life!

Every night we used to go to Eighteenth Avenue and Sixty-third Street to get the next morning's paper as soon as it came off the truck, for that day's track results, and to find out the next day's daily number. We'd get there around nine, and maybe thirty guys would be looking toward the lower streets for that *Daily News* truck to arrive. As soon as someone spotted it they'd say, "I see it!" and everyone would line up. Not one person opened the paper from the front. It was always from the back, to the track pages, for the numbers, the results of that day's races and the sheets for the following day.

There was a gang in every neighborhood. Ours used to congregate on Eighteenth Avenue and Fifty-sixth Street in a park. We all had a D.A., or duck's ass haircut—a high pompadour and the sides combed back until it looked literally like a duck's ass. I used to put Vaseline in my hair and comb the sides for hours to try to get one. Anyway, this guy with the D.A. always dressed the same, a white T-shirt with the sleeves rolled up with a pack of cigarettes on one side. I was in awe of him. He was my hero.

Sometimes we'd go down to Brighton Beach, to the bathhouse. The first time I went I'd never seen naked men before and I couldn't believe it. The older men, mostly refugees, had the biggest balls in the world! Or sometimes we'd go down to Coney Island for the rides. I always wanted to go on the Parachute but never did, because I was too chicken.

Bob Gans: I was born in 1943 in Brooklyn, East New York, another part of the great borough of Brooklyn. East New York was a mixture of Jewish, Italian, Polish, Irish, and there was one black family, who happened to live around the corner from us. They were what everyone referred to as the Shabbos goy. The father came around on Friday nights and every Jewish family paid him a dime to turn on their lights, if they were so inclined, because on Shabbos you couldn't do that yourself.

We lived on Schenck Avenue, between New Lots and Hegeman Avenue. Some pronounce it "shank," but we all called it "skank." Hegeman Avenue and Hendrix Street and Van Siclen Avenue, they were the home of the dairy farms–Hegeman Farms, Sheffield Farms. Hegeman Avenue was actually unpaved when I was growing up. From Van Siclen Avenue going east, towards Jerome Street and further down, a dirt road for walking the cows on their way to be hand-milked. There were chickens everywhere, ducks, geese, maybe a half dozen blocks in East New York that catered to these farms. Aside from the farmers, the Italian people in the neighborhood had pigeon coops on the roofs. They also had chickens. They would raise and feed on both.

Schenck Avenue seemed to be just by the luck of the draw the dividing line between an all-Jewish community, going west, and a mixed, mostly Italian one, going east. We were all moderately to very poor, but in those days we didn't know it because everybody was poor. There were a few people on the block who were business types, and we considered them to be wealthy–they had a new car every four or five years and seemed to dress a little better than we did. Other than that we all went to the same local grocery store, with the soda box out front filled with ice. When we wanted that cold soda we had to go real deep to get to that root beer or orange bottle.

The neighborhood was homogeneous in the sense that the people who lived there did not fight among themselves. Nevertheless, we were all very territorial. Periodically, the younger kids, sixteen to twenty-three, would go into other neighborhoods, or the kids from other neighborhoods would come into ours to settle an argument. Our neighborhood was the one that the characters in the movie *Goodfellas* came from.* Growing up, I had no idea how tough these guys really were. They were just tough young guys, but later on, most of them became more than local thugs. They were future members of organized crime, of the Mafia, although that word never ever was uttered by anyone.

I went to P.S. 213, on Hegeman Avenue, and from there I went to J.H.S. 149. Every school in New York City had a number. I remember my first encounter, going from an all-white, mostly Jewish public school to perhaps a 60 percent black junior high school. Every day my mother gave me a quarter to go to school, in case I wanted a soda or a container of milk during lunch. My first day at junior high there were five guys, four black guys and one white guy, standing in the hallway. This very, very tall guy, his name was Leroy Ellis, and who ultimately became a basketball player in the NBA, was a really harmless nice black kid. Except he was about seven feet tall and weighed about 155 pounds. So as I'm walking in the hall that first day, this bunch of guys get in front of me, and Leroy says to me, "You got any money?" I was afraid to tell him no, so I said, "Yeah, I got a quarter." "Give it to me," he said, and the others chimed in, "Give him the quarter, give him the quarter!" I did, to save my own neck. It didn't take that long to get used to it and understand the drill.

From there I went to Thomas Jefferson High School. By that time I was a fully integrated teenager in Brooklyn, and wasn't afraid of anything. For instance, at night, I, and no one else I knew, was never fear-

---

* Martin Scorsese's *Goodfellas* (1999) was based on Nicholas Pileggi's nonfiction book about Brooklyn's local organized crime scene, *Wiseguy*, which told the story of the famous TWA terminal robbery.

ful of going out at night, or coming home, no matter what the time. It was like walking in your backyard. We were never accosted by anybody, and we knew the areas where we could go and not to go. We knew everybody, who the nice guys were, who the wiseguys were, but nobody started in with you just for sake of starting a fight. In other words, no one ever came after us for our sneakers. It was a different time.

The reason the mob became so rooted in Brooklyn was because it was, at its core, a very ethnic thing. It was a form of protection for the powerless immigrants who trusted only their own. Using that, mob guys could take hold of a turf quite easily, and the most concentrated place for immigrants was Brooklyn. And it wasn't just Italians. There was the Jewish contingent, and really every ethnicity had their own.

Another part of it was the legal system, I think. Maybe the law enforcement was more liberal in Brooklyn, or maybe it was more pliable, so to speak, but Brooklyn is where organized crime took root. And it was everywhere, or so it seemed. Everybody knew somebody who had an uncle or a cousin in the mob. It became a status thing.

Gambling was part of everything we did. There was a pool hall where everybody hung out; just guys, that is, no girls. The owner was also the local bookmaker. Across the street was a luncheonette. At the end of an evening out, whether it was to the movies, or on a date, or the track, no matter what time it was, twelve, one, two, everybody made their final stop at the luncheonette. Everybody discussed the events of the day and the evening, before going home. There were also guys who hung out there because they were hiding from bookmakers. Everybody held their hand over their mouth because they didn't want anybody to hear what they were saying except the person they were talking to.

As far as girls went, they were always local. Everybody in Brooklyn when and where I grew up married local girls, primarily because the neighborhood was your whole world, so the whole world was your neighborhood. The girls in your neighborhood were the only girls available. A major move in your life was considered from East New York to Canarsie.

Until you got a car, your wheels, you couldn't escape even if you wanted to. The people you grew up with remained your friends for the rest of your life. You partied in someone's finished basement. The only way you could get out of your own house, even just to have sex, was to get married. By the time you were twenty-four, the latest, you were married. I was married with two kids by the time I was that age. When you found some girl who allowed you to play around with her, or as we said in those days, dry-hump her, if you wanted to take it to the next level, so to speak, you married her. And then, more often than not, that's when sex stopped.

Everything came down to pride, and the people from Brooklyn's greatest asset was just that. For instance, there was one guy in the neighborhood who took a series of bets from one another guy, because he was going to the racetrack and wanted to save his friend, a tough Jewish guy, not a wiseguy, but tough enough, the trip. He was given a three-horse parley. When he gets to the track, however, he didn't place the bet. He figured the odds were so long, he could just as easily pocket the money. Sure enough, the three horses come in, and the payoff was something like $1,200, which in those days was a lot of money. The Jewish guy waited for the guy to return, and he never did. He started asking around where his friend was, and someone told him no one had seen him. He just disappeared, and no one knew anything.

What happened, was, the guy was so scared he caught a bus and went all the way down to Florida. For two and a half years he stayed down there. One night, everyone, as usual, is standing on the corner, about eleven in the evening, and a car pulls up. It's the guy who ran away to Florida. He gets out, walks up to the tough Jewish guy, and says to him, 'I got $1,200 for ya,' and starts counting it out in hundred-dollar bills. The issue wasn't money, it was honor. There was a sense of moral correctness that came with the territory. Doing what was right, whether it was paying off that bet or working hard to better yourself, you didn't do what was wrong because everybody would know and it simply wasn't worth it. Brooklyn-bred, the salt of the earth, and those who came from there know that instinctively. Others have to learn it by association.

IVAN KRONENFELD: It's funny, you go anywhere in the world and you say Brooklyn and everyone knows where you mean. There's someone from Brooklyn who responds on a personal level, with a certain pride. It's one of those places, maybe Dublin is another, that puts its mark on you forever. If you're a Brooklyn boy, you know the old cliché, you can take the boy out of Brooklyn, you can't take Brooklyn out of the boy. It's a rare combination. You either have grit or you have wisdom. Brooklyn kind of gives you both.

I work with a Haitian fellow today who is twenty-five years younger than me, who also grew up on Albany Avenue. His father had three boys and put them all through college driving a cab. All three of them. That's a lot of not being either a jerk or a cliché. It's astounding to me that his stories have such a familiar ring. Nothing has really changed.

✖ ✖ ✖

MORE FAMOUS BROOKLYNITES

ALBERT DEKKER: Brooklyn-born actor and politician who appeared on Broadway before heading for Hollywood and appearing in several major motion pictures, including Sam Peckinpah's *The Wild Bunch* (1969).

GABRIEL DELL: Born Gabriel Marcel Del Vecchio, gained fame as an original member of the East Side Kids, aka Dead End Kids, aka Bowery Boys, the youth group/gang introduced in Sidney Kingsley's play and subsequent 1937 movie *Dead End* (directed by William Wyler). As an adult, appeared in several motion pictures and was a supporting actor on Steve Allen's TV comedy show.

ALAN DERSHOWITZ: Became, at twenty-eight, the youngest full professor in the history of Harvard Law School. Gained fame for his defense of Claus von Bülow, on whose life the Hollywood film *Reversal of Fortune* (1990) was based. A noted First Amendment expert and strong civil rights proponent.

NEIL DIAMOND: Legendary singer-songwriter attended Erasmus and Lincoln High Schools; at Lincoln was in the same class as Barbra Streisand. Spent several years as a Brill Building songwriter, and as a singer had numerous hits of his own, including "Cherry, Cherry," "Solitary Man," and "Sweet Caroline," wrote "I'm a Believer" for the Monkees.

JANICE DICKINSON. Supermodel, fashion magazine cover girl, photographer, actress, reality-show star.

OWEN VINCENT DODSON: Poet, chairman of Howard University's School of Drama for thirty years.

HENRY DREYFUSS: An industrial designer noted for such innovative products as the desktop telephone, the Hoover vacuum cleaner, the Big Ben alarm clock, the New York Central's Twentieth Century Limited locomotive cars, and the City of the Future exhibit at the 1939 New York World's Fair.

RICHARD DREYFUSS: Grew up in Brooklyn and Bayside, Queens, before moving with his parents to Hollywood. He appeared in many important movies, including Steven Spielberg's *Jaws* (1975) and *Close Encounters of the Third Kind* (1977), won his Best Actor Oscar for the role of the perennially unemployed actor in *The Goodbye Girl* (1977, directed by Herbert Ross).

MARGARET DUMONT: Was a well-known stage and screen character actress when chosen by Groucho Marx to play his perennial foil in the legendary Marx Brothers series of film comedies throughout the twenties, thirties, and forties.

MIKE DUNLEAVY: Played basketball for the University of South Carolina. Was drafted in 1976 by the Philadelphia 76ers. Began his coaching career in 1990 with the Los Angeles Lakers and went on to coach the Milwaukee Bucks, Portland Trail Blazers, and Los Angeles Clippers.

ROBBIE DUPREE: Singer-songwriter best known for the 1980 hit single "Steal Away."

HERB EDELMAN: Attended Brooklyn College, where he studied to be a veterinarian before dropping out to become a hotel manager. Has appeared in several movies and TV shows, most notably as one of the supporting cast on *The Golden Girls*. Twice nominated for an Emmy.

VINCE EDWARDS: Vincent Edward Zoino attended Ohio State on an athletic scholarship before becoming a contract player for Paramount Pictures. Best remembered for his portrayal of the title character in the 1960s TV series *Ben Casey*.

BENJAMIN EISENSTADT: Operated a cafeteria for many years at the Brooklyn Navy Yard, before going into the tea-bag-making business. Invented the notion of single-serve sugar packets, failed to get a patent, and went on to invent a powdered form of saccharin. Sweet'n Low, in its famous pink packet, is still manufactured at its original factory near the Navy Yard.

Will Eisner: William Erwin Eisner was a legendary comic-book writer and illustrator, an early pioneer in the field of graphic comic novels.

CHAPTER SIX

LITERARY BROOKLYN

What thought you have of me now I had as much of you.
I laid in my stores in advance. I considered long and
seriously of you before you were born.

    —WALT WHITMAN

THE PUBLISHED JOURNALISTIC diaries of everyday life in Brooklyn are the chronicles of the borough's historical progress as well as its spirit and its soul. The first of these historical day-to-day loggings appeared in the legendary afternoon daily newspaper the *Brooklyn Eagle*, established in 1841 (as the *Brooklyn Eagle and Kings County Democrat*), a full decade before the arrival of the *New York Times*.

The *Eagle* was the brainchild of a group of Brooklyn's most ambitious young Democrats seeking a politically unified voice of advocacy and influence. The paper's first editor was Henry C. Murphy, who used his position to launch a successful 1840 run for mayor of the City of Brooklyn.

Five years later, in 1846, a young dreamer by the name of Walt Whitman took over as editor and turned the paper into a platform for his personal opposition to the expansion of slavery, via his support for the Free Soil Party and his belief that America was a place for the people "of all nations at any time upon the Earth."

Although forever linked with the borough, Whitman was actually born a few miles to the east of Brooklyn, on Long Island, New York. He was the son of Quakers descended from Dutch settlers and grew up on a farm where manual labor was done by slaves. While a young man he worked as a teacher and journeyman printer before entering the world of journalism at the relatively late (for the nineteenth century) age of twenty-seven, when he began at the downtown Fulton Street site of the *Brooklyn Eagle*. At the time the city was already a thriving metropolis, challenging Manhattan for the position of premier urban center for commerce, real estate, finance, manufacturing, shipping, and publishing.

Whitman reimagined the *Eagle* as a broadside with a distinct personality all its own, separate from what had become its chief competitor, the *New York Times*, whose Manhattan focus was, at least as far as he was concerned, turning increasingly national, its front pages frequently focused on state and federal issues. To Whitman, the politics and policies of Brooklyn were the real center of the New World universe. He was at once the progenitor of modern, personal urban journalism, with its emphasis on the politics of personality, and of the poetry of the urban everyman. Through his work at the *Eagle*, Whitman succeeded in establishing Brooklyn as the stronghold of Democratic political progressivism that it remains to this day. His political and social activism and new-style journalism laid the creative groundwork for the true form of his artistic expression: his monumental, revelatory, and in the truest sense, revolutionary collection of twelve poems, called *Leaves of Grass*.

The self-published *Leaves of Grass* eventually became the first great literary achievement to emerge from the streets of Brooklyn, and as such identified the muse as the city itself, setting the style and tone for the concrete passion that would once and forever define the borough's best writing. Such timeless names as Thomas Wolfe, Carson McCullers, Henry Miller, Betty Smith, Marianne Moore, Irwin Shaw, Isaac Bashevis Singer, Truman Capote, Hart Crane, Joseph Heller, John Dos Passos, Bernard Malamud, Arthur Miller, Hubert Selby Jr., and

Norman Mailer all were either born or lived in Brooklyn and produced much of their best material while living on—and often writing about—their beloved turf.

In an age when European Romanticism was in full literary bloom, Whitman's genre-bending (and gender-bending) *Leaves of Grass* was not immediately accepted as a work of peace and love. It did, in fact, manage to outrage a large part of the American populace. Its celebration of omnisexuality and its acknowledgment of the loneliness and frustration that were tied up with urbanization made his poetry among the most controversial of its time. The *New York Times* dismissed it as "thin" and "pretentious" and accused Whitman of an outsized ego for "styling himself the representative of America, the mouthpiece of free institutions, the personification of all that men had waited for."

Unfazed, Whitman continue to write of his beloved borough. *Leaves of Grass*, composed largely while walking the city streets, was a very specific yet universal broadside from his soul. It anticipated the coming wave of American naturalism by forging the link between the leaves of nature and the pages of his writing, making him the first Beat poet, lyrical melodist, and free-form journalist.

MICHAEL FRANK: It is important to remember that Whitman on heterosexual sex was strikingly explicit for serious literary writing in his or anyone's time. . . .

Whitman was unprecedented, too, in the way he portrayed women as erotic beings . . . , but he did not politicize heterosexuality the way he did homosexual "adhesiveness" . . .

Whitman the sly promoter of his own work and life surfaces in a manuscript titled "Analysis of Leaves of Grass," supposedly by Richard Maurice Bucke, who published a biography of Whitman . . . describing how British critics and readers appreciate Whitman's work better than their American counterparts, [it] is actually in Whitman's hand.

Across the river in Manhattan, while writing was increasingly becoming categorized and industrialized—journalists were journalists, reporters were reporters—Whitman helped establish the physical as well as cultural notion of the artist who stands outside the mainstream, who is the observer rather than the observed, whose vision is more warm reflection than cold fact. A powerful influence both stylistically and culturally (Whitman always said he preferred his works to be spoken aloud rather than read alone, a presentation the Beats would adapt a century later), his work's simplicity was a virtue born of the urban experience, the clear reflection of his own city life.

PETE HAMILL: Whitman taught us all how to look at New York City.

Indeed, his living legacy may be found in every modern urban American journalist, novelist, and poet, in the rhythms and feelings of every folk, pop, and rock lyricist from Woody Guthrie (a Brooklyn resident for many of his adult years) to Bob Dylan and John Lennon, in every outer-borough youth who ever kicked a stone across a concrete street while contemplating the ultimate direction of his own wandering soul.

Before the completion of construction on the Brooklyn Bridge in 1883, ferry service was the only practical way of crossing from Manhattan to Brooklyn. One of the first regular routes came as the result of the Pierponts, who lived in Brooklyn in the mid-nineteenth century and instituted regular ferry service to take them from Manhattan practically to their front door. They built a series of elegant row houses in a neighborhood that eventually came to be known as Brooklyn Heights.

Once the bridge opened, working-class access to the Heights disturbed the privileged isolation of many of its inhabitants, who moved deeper into Brooklyn, to Crown Heights, Clinton Hill, and Park Slope. By the 1940s, Brooklyn Heights had severely declined in status, and became a low-rent, high-risk neighborhood of little social distinction.

It was then that two major groups discovered the Heights. One was the Arabs. The immigrant Arab community of New York City had until then clustered itself mainly on Manhattan's lower West Side, one of the least residentially populated areas of the city, in an attempt to maintain the separatist way of life. When the ferry made Brooklyn Heights accessible, it seemed the perfect place for them to settle.

The Arabs quickly opened small retail shops on Atlantic Avenue, and soon the boulevard resembled nothing so much as the streets of Damascus or Beirut, with its open markets and crowded, noisy shops that are still in operation to this day.

The other group to find Brooklyn Heights was the writers and artists. During the early days of World War II, a dilapidated house at 7 Middagh Street, just on the other side of the Brooklyn Navy Yard and left in disrepair by the flight of the once-wealthy from the neighborhood, became the accidental home base for a group of twentieth-century literary and sexual rebels that included such mighty figures as W. H. Auden, Carson McCullers, Jane and Paul Bowles, Benjamin Britten, and, of all people, Gypsy Rose Lee.

The idea for this experimental home for wayward minds and hearts belonged to George Davis, the flamboyantly gay fiction editor of *Harper's Bazaar* during its 1940s heyday, when it routinely published (often when no one else in America would) Jean Cocteau, Colette, John Cheever, Dawn Powell, and Gertrude Stein. The magnificent vista of Manhattan on one side and the bars, brothels, and tattoo parlors that serviced the transient sailors stationed at the Navy Yard on the other made it a perfect location for Davis and company. He especially admired the neighborhood's off-center nature and saw his boardinghouse/salon as the legatee of Walt Whitman's life and writing style.

Other than opening his house to like-minded literati, Davis didn't have any great plan. His surrogate family included the soft-spoken, twisted southern girl Carson McCullers, whose *The Heart Is a Lonely Hunter* had made her a literary giant at the tender age of twenty-three, and the jaded gay poetic genius W. H. Auden, the British author with the face of a lizard who was, at the time, living in American limbo to avoid military service at home.

It was not long before the cozy threesome began to expand. On the heels of Auden's arrival came Chester Kallman, a onetime student of Auden's who had since become his lover. Benjamin Britten, involved with the production of a libretto for an opera with Auden, Britten's partner, the operatic tenor Peter Pears, and stripper Gypsy Rose Lee, who had moved to the Heights to soak up the literary atmosphere while struggling to finish her novel, completed the ménage.

Domestic life was problematic at best. The poet Louis MacNeice described the occupants as "so Bohemian, raiding the icebox at midnight and eating the catfood by mistake."

Tensions were inevitable. Once Auden's inner neat freak emerged, he began to complain loudly about the slovenliness of his housemates, while McCullers's obsessive cooking left aromas as thick as the smoke from Auden's flat, sour British cigarettes. Despite the factions that broke out along the crisscrossed sexual lines, a literate ongoing soap opera, some of the best work of their lives was produced by those living within the walls of what became known as "February House." Auden actually based much of his *The Age of Anxiety* on his experiences living on Middagh Street, Jane Bowles wrote *Two Serious Ladies*, and McCullers found a measure of inspiration in the local bar scene for several of the characters who would eventually show up in *The Ballad of the Sad Café*. Even Lee finished her novel, *The G-String Murders*. On the phone Davis once described the residence to journalist Janet Flanner as a "boardinghouse," which somehow came through the wires on her end as a "bawdy house." Today, neither description seems complete without the other.

What is poignant about the brief, turbulent years of February House is the opportunity it afforded a group of young, loose, and creative souls to live and work in a creative atmosphere that was, somehow, both on and off the beaten track. For them, Brooklyn was both a literary inspiration and a haven from Manhattan.

A sad ending for February House came in 1945, when city planning commissioner Robert Moses zoned it out of existence. Invoking eminent domain to condemn the area of Brooklyn Heights that included Middagh Street, he claimed it was a "vital and necessary link" to allow the Brooklyn-Queens Expressway to bypass the rest of the Heights.

The battle for the Heights wore on into the 1960s. The Brooklyn

Heights Association successfully fought Moses and won landmark status for the neighborhood that had spawned so much of the artistry of Brooklyn writers, ensuring that no more of it could ever be given away to the state for the sake of highways or high-rises. At least in this one stretch of Brooklyn, time, they promised, would indeed stand still.

IN POSTWAR BROOKLYN, a new generation of literary dreamers emerged. Norman Mailer, the crown prince of the Brooklyn literary elite, came out of a childhood background of Talmudic philosophy and modern street socialism. While still a boy, the street-smart Crown Heights sophisticate was telling friends that he hoped to follow in the footsteps of "great Jews like Moses, Maimonides, and Karl Marx."

FANNY SCHNEIDER MAILER: Barney [my husband] was still working in downtown Manhattan, and living in Brooklyn was cheaper and much easier than commuting from Long Branch . . . We moved to 555 Crown Street when Norman was nine. I wanted to move to Flatbush because I'd be able to have company more often if I was nearer to New York. Also, Crown Heights was more Jewish . . . One time Norman was bringing a magazine to Anne [a friend of mine] and when he got there Mrs. Smith [the landlady] said, "Oh, Norman, so now you'll be selling magazines." He said, "I won't sell them. I'll write them" . . . He was only six!

Mailer attended Harvard, graduated, entered the army, and after his discharge got married and moved into 49 Remsen Street, a two-room apartment in Brooklyn Heights that rented for $75 a month. It was on Remsen Street that he settled in to write his great American novel, *The Naked and the Dead*, while pursuing his other great interest, photography, something he had learned a bit about while studying aerial photographs during the war.

HILARY MILLS: Few who grew up in Brooklyn [as Norman Mailer did] have willingly returned to the borough after tasting the seduction of Manhattan, but Mailer created his own cultural outpost on the eastern edge of New York's harbor in Brooklyn Heights. Over the years hundreds of the famous have made the trek across the Brooklyn Bridge and mounted the four flights to Mailer's living room, where a spectacular view of Manhattan's skyline and the Statue of Liberty awaits them.

NORMAN MAILER: I doubt if ever again I will have a book which is so easy to write.

If Mailer had a literary ancestor, it was not Whitman, at least not directly. The lack of women in Whitman's life and in his work left something missing for the rough, tough, and lady-loving Mailer, who found energy and inspiration in the heaping passions of the great Brooklynite Henry Miller.

The literary, social, artistic, and geographic links to Miller, the obsession with sex as both inspiration and torment, and the devotion to objective realism as a lyrical focus that leads to social awareness are made clearest by Mailer himself.

NORMAN MAILER: Miller opens all the questions of literature–reopens the first question: What is the nature of that truth we find on a page? It is not that he bears no relation to the Henry Miller who is the protagonist of his books . . . he is more like a transparency laid over a drawing, copied and then skewed just a degree. He is just a little different from his work, but in that difference is all the mystery of his own personality and the paradoxes of a great artist. . . . He could be poetic about everything except fucking with love. While nobody can be more poetic than Miller about fucking itself . . . he still cannot write about fucking with love. . . . Miller bounces in the stink.

Henry Miller was born in Yorkville, Manhattan, but moved with his family to Williamsburg in his first year of life, where he grew up hearing in his head the creative turmoil that echoed off the hard streets.

Like all great novelists, his truest source of inspiration was the adventure of his own life, his best revelation the rough beauty of sex (as opposed to its companion piece, the refined beauty of love), and his greatest literary accomplishment floating in the lower depths or "stink" of sex in order to understand it enough to finally transcend it.

HENRY MILLER: I must have begun [writing] while I was working for the Western Union. That's certainly when I wrote the first book, at any rate . . . but the real thing happened after I quit the Western Union–in 1924–when I decided I would be a writer and give myself to it completely. . . .

In the year 1927 when my wife went to Europe and I was left alone, I had a job for a while in the Park Department in Queens. One day, at the end of the day, instead of going home I was seized with this idea of planning the book of my life, and I stayed up all night doing it . . . my whole work, from *Capricorn* on through *The Rosy Crucifixion*–except *Cancer,* which was a thing of the immediate present–is about the seven years that I had lived with this woman, from the time I met her until I left for Europe. I didn't know then when I was leaving, but I knew I was going sooner or later. That was the crucial period of my life as a writer, the period just before leaving America. . . .

But one becomes aware in France, after having lived in America, that sex pervades the air. It's there all around you, like a fluid. Now I don't doubt that Americans enter into sexual relations as strongly, deeply, and multifariously as any other people, but it's not in the atmosphere around you, somehow. Then, too, in France woman plays a bigger role in man's life . . . the Frenchman prefers to be in the company of women. In England and America, men seem to enjoy being among themselves. . . .

Well, it's very simple. The obscene would be the forthright, and pornography would be the roundabout. I believe in saying the truth, coming out with it cold, shocking if necessary, not disguising it. In other words, obscenity is a cleansing process, whereas pornography only adds to the muck. . . .

You know, I think I have written as much of what my hostile critics call "flapdoodle"–that is, metaphysical nonsense–as I have about sex. Only they choose to look at the sex . . . it's played a great part in my life. I've led a good, rich sexual life, and I don't see why it should be left out.

The third great voice of postwar Brooklyn literature belongs to Arthur Miller, whose play *A View from the Bridge* found in the great linking span a metaphor for artistic arrival in the mainstream of modern American theater, with the undertow of immigrant alienation one of the great American themes.

Harlem-born, immigrant-rooted, and raised in Brooklyn during the Depression, Miller learned early on that to be a writer from New York City was, by definition, to be a writer of artistic rebellion.

ARTHUR MILLER: Writing in more or less the language one spoke was a sign of poor education and vulgarity. Uplift was the inevitable purpose of writing at all, and propriety the aim of any written style.

This was a concept handed down by the public schools . . . we were not to read Whitman or Dreiser or Sinclair Lewis but Keats and Shelley and Wordsworth–writers who wrote English English. . . .

. . . When I was thirteen we moved to Brooklyn, and in James Madison High School . . . my first sight of kids leaving their stuff behind on their desks when they went to the blackboard was a powerful shock. Our P.S. 24 track team had all their street clothes stolen from lockers while they proudly ran in their shorts in a meet in Central Park. . . .

. . . [After the Depression began] For Rent signs were pasted across empty store windows, and there was hardly an apartment house with a permanent Vacancy sign on it. People were doubling up, married children returning to their parents with their own children. There were touch football games in the side streets between teams whose members were twenty or older, fellows with no jobs or even hopes for one anymore, playing the days away like kids and buying their Camels or Luckies one cigarette at a time, a penny apiece, from Rubin the candy store man on Avenue M. The normal rites of adolescent passage tended to be skipped over; when I graduated from Abraham Lincoln High School in 1932, mine was by no means the only family that failed to show up for the ceremony, nor did I expect them to attend. I knew that with my education at an end I was but another new young man on the long line waiting for work. Anyway, with a master's degree, as the saying went, you might get hired to sell ties at Macy's.

Thus were the seeds of fear and rage planted for Miller's greatest creation, the story of capitalism's (and Brooklyn's) iconic loser, the complete conformist Willie Loman, salesman ordinaire. If Miller's heroes loved to reach up and unhook a hot girl's skirt under the staircase as a gesture of inspired mutual heated disrespect, and if Mailer considered a woman's lips against his face a form of privileged anointment, Miller's Loman got his thrills behind the thin-walled privacy of the hotel rooms he stayed in as a traveling salesman, where a whiff of beauty was bribed to consent by a pair of cheap sample nylons.

All three men spent their youth in Brooklyn, from where they could see the skyline of the great metropolis as observers longing to be observed, worshipers longing to be worshiped, via their writing, as all-American as Fitzgerald and Hemingway. In that sense they were the epitome of the artistic outsider.

Ironically, the more successful they became, the more isolated they were by their success, exiled from the roots embedded in Brooklyn's concrete.

IVAN KRONENFELD: Whitman, Miller, Mailer. These I think are the giant literary figures of Brooklyn. What young boy can ever forget the first time he got his hands on *Tropic of Cancer*? A turning point.

PETE HAMILL: It's the time and the place on one level. Because there was no television, we went to the movies maybe once a week. There were little movie houses everywhere; I think there were six in my neighborhood I could walk to. Television came when the war ended. We'd been getting our entertainment through *words*, radio shows like *The Inner Sanctum* and *Mysterious Traveler.* The kind of writer I became was shaped by *hearing* words and *then* reading them. That's why I say that although there was poverty everywhere in our neighborhood we were not impoverished, because the radio gave us all kinds of things, including, besides entertainment, Franklin D. Roosevelt, Edward R. Murrow, Gabriel Heater, William L. Shirer, and a lot of others. I always thought I learned geography by looking at maps in the *Daily News* and the *Brooklyn Eagle* of the progress of the war.

We also had a library, that's still there, on Sixth Avenue and Ninth Street, that existed at all because of the generosity of Andrew Carnegie, one of sixteen hundred that he helped build. The library became a place where I also found entertainment as a kid, and information. I walked around Brooklyn with the Count of Monte Cristo. I went to Treasure Island with Jim Hawkins. I first read books not realizing that they had authors. I thought they were just there. So I didn't start out thinking, hey, I want to be an author. I had no idea what that even meant.

The other big influence on me was comics, in the newspaper and at the candy store. My mother was a big fan of *Terry and the Pirates,* a daily and Sunday strip that ran in the New York *Daily News* and was one of the greatest ever. It was done by Milton Caniff, one of the greatest. He also did, later on, *Steve Canyon,* which was not as good. *Terry and the Pirates* was as good as it gets. Caniff would have been a great movie director. Later on, I realized—after I had started drawing my own comics and writing them in composition books, when I began to do something with what was laughingly known in those days as my life—that I might be a painter, because I had discovered I could draw pretty well. What I didn't realize was that comics had also taught me about narrative. I wasn't good enough as a painter to understand that narrative was possible in a nonlinear way, so I turned to writing as my primary form of expression. It's what claimed me, finally, to be a writer. It came out of all those years in Brooklyn, and whether or not I write about Brooklyn, which I have and I haven't, is really a side issue. The need for a narrative in which things happen and mean something I learned there and I brought it to my journalism and to my novels. It made me an urban, New York, Brooklyn writer.

Later on when I got serious, I read the Studs Lonigan trilogy by James T. Farrell, I saw movies like *Marty,* written by Paddy Chayefsky, and realized I didn't have to go off to Barcelona and write about bullfighting–it was all right here, at home, in Brooklyn, if only I could find it and see it right.

I went into journalism in 1960 and never wanted to do anything else. I couldn't stand to go to sleep at night because I wanted to get up and do it again. I'd finally found something that made me think I could have a passion, that I could carry through a lifetime. I continued reading a lot of fiction, as I tried to learn that aspect of my writing as well.

I was inspired by various natural things, like the existence of Prospect Park, right in the heart of the borough, this beautiful park where Olmsted and Vaux corrected all the mistakes they'd made building Central Park, a place where you couldn't see the rest of Brooklyn, allowing your imagination to run wild. And the other thing was the beach. You could get into the subway and arrive at Coney Island. There was no beach in Manhattan, only Jacobs Beach outside of Madison Square Garden, not exactly the same thing. I think Brooklyn's beach had something to do with my writing. This, however, is not a universal thing, by any means.

This doesn't show up in someone like Mailer, although there were other things about Brooklyn that shaped him. However, the modern writer most affected, I think, by growing up in Brooklyn was Irwin Shaw. There's a sense in his work of beauty in the natural world, even in his story "Girls in Their Summer Dresses" as he walks through Washington Square Park. His writing sensibilities were put there by Brooklyn and stayed with him the rest of his life.

There's something else, too. So many people were either children of families who started in Manhattan, on the Lower East Side, or the West Side docks, where the Irish came from, and then moved to Brooklyn once the subways pushed all the way out. Brownsville, for example, was where Murder Incorporated began in that fashion, Mummy Davis and all those guys. But it also gave life to writers like Alfred Kazin, and, for better or worse, Norman Podhoretz.

Finally from the natural world is the light. The light was different in Brooklyn. You can see it in old photographs and you can see it today. The buildings were lower and the light bounced off the harbor, particularly in October, November, that you couldn't find in Manhattan because of the tall buildings. Cheever talks about the days when New York was filled with the river light. That Manhattan is almost impossible to find anymore. But it's still there in Brooklyn. For now.

I think there is a new Brooklyn literary scene, for sure, but I'm not part of it. There's a whole bunch of guys living there. The *Brooklyn Eagle*, which is now a weekly, has a feature called "Borough of Writers" or something like that, that interviews a lot of new writers from Brooklyn. I haven't read all of them; I've certainly read [Paul] Auster, Jonathan Lethem's *Fortress of Solitude* that I really liked. It's not *my* Brooklyn, but it's still, recognizably, Brooklyn.

Theirs.

One of the most difficult things to do is recognize a scene as it is unfolding. Without question, there are wonderful new writers emerging from Brooklyn, but even among themselves the feeling is divided as to whether or not they are at the forefront of a new literary horizon.

DAVID HAGLUND: I think it's just too expensive for there to be a Manhattan writing scene anymore, for young people trying to make it. Everyone I know who has come to New York to pursue their career has moved into Brooklyn. I just wonder if a few years from now they'll all be in Queens because Brooklyn itself is rapidly becoming just too expensive for creative working-class hopefuls to live.

But it's not just economic. There's a pace of life in Brooklyn that's dif-

ferent from Manhattan, that maybe allows a little more room for intro-
spection and reflection. I don't know how people in Manhattan can think.
Me, I'm from Boston, I live in Brooklyn, and it feels like a more interesting and bigger Boston, which felt nothing like Manhattan to me, ever.

BRIAN BERGNER: I was born in Elizabeth, New Jersey, in 1969 but I've lived
in south Brooklyn, Red Hook, for many years. My apartment is in Carroll Gardens or Gowanus, depending upon which window you look out
of, I guess. Carroll Gardens was a late sixties, early seventies real-estate-
based invention, but I don't think anybody knew how far the gentrification would go, both from the industrial part of Gowanus and the
industrial and projects areas of Red Hook. The difference is very little,
particularly when it comes to rent.

I'd been coming to Brooklyn as far back as I can remember, my whole
life, really. My father is from Rockaway, Queens, and my grandparents
live in Far Rockaway. I also had an aunt who lived in Coney Island, in
a development that Donald Trump's father built. Coming in from New
Jersey, we'd go over the Verrazano, along the Belt Parkway, to visit them
every couple of weeks. After college, I bounced around through Texas,
Iowa, living a kind of vagabond life, part-time writer, bookstore clerk,
that sort of thing.

One day in 1997 I got a chance to come to New York City, to work for
my uncle in the so-called rag trade. That lasted about five days before
we had a falling-out. By that time, I knew if I was going to stay in New
York City, it would have to be in Brooklyn. Manhattan, specifically the
Village, was no longer an option, financially or culturally. Brooklyn was
the only place I considered. My loci, I think, were Henry Miller, Hubert
Selby, Gilbert Sorrentino, and jazz music. And Mafia history. Brooklyn
had all of these elements I found fascinating.

Most people that I know who are "Brooklyn writers" are not part of
any movement or anything. They just happen to live here. For the most
part writing in Fort Greene or Park Slope or Carroll Gardens could just as
easily be on the Upper West Side of Manhattan, or Chelsea, or Astoria,

Queens, or Hoboken, New Jersey. They would be following the same creative drive they had when they were still in their writing workshops or in woody retreat in Vermont. I don't know if it's good or bad, but there definitely is this assumption of a typical creature, this so-called Brooklyn writer. If you look at the people's work, and I can't say that I've read *everything* out of Brooklyn, you'll find they're not dealing with Brooklyn in any substantial way. I think it's partly because they didn't grow up here. If you live in Park Slope, where I do, you tend to look toward Manhattan—which is very close by, and where most editors who live in Park Slope work, and where most writers aspire to be published—but not behind, where there are about two and a half million people with just as many stories.

PETE HAMILL: I don't think Park Slope attracts young writers who aren't rich! All those kids who used to get off the bus at Port Authority wanting to be writers, painters, dancers, whatever, might not be able to live in New York, anywhere in the city, including Brooklyn. You know, you can stick four airline hostesses in an apartment to share the rent but not four lyric poets.

AMY SOHN: I really don't think the Brooklyn literary scene is separate from the rest of New York's lit scene at all. A lot of writers I know live in Brooklyn but socialize both there and in Manhattan at least as much, if not more. A lot of the writing does tend to reflect Brooklyn, the surroundings, because there's a great affection that young writers have for living in Brooklyn. I'm thinking of Paul Auster and Jonathan Lethem. My second novel was a lot about Brooklyn, and my third is going to be even more about Brooklyn. It's so rich in material that I think writers who live here tend to build it into their work. I grew up in Brooklyn Heights, so I've been here my whole life, unlike other writers who come here looking for inspiration or atmosphere. I've also lived in the Heights, Cobble Hill, Park Slope, Boerum Hill. So I don't consider myself someone who "found" Brooklyn as an adult.

There is kind of a kinmanship between Brooklyn-based writers. It's generally supportive and friendly, not very backbiting, competitive, and all of that. But my literary heroes were certainly from Brooklyn. Henry Miller for sure. And I've been a fan of Paul Auster since I was a teenager. Carson McCullers if you can count her. Paula Fox. She wrote *Desperate Characters* and it's a great book. Bottom line, it's the talent of the writer rather than the Brooklyn element. I'm from Brooklyn, as I say. It used to be cheaper to live there, which is why so many young writers came, but it's not cheaper at all, really. Not at all.

BRIAN BERGNER: I don't know Amy Sohn personally, although I've read her stuff a lot in *New York* magazine. She grew up in Brooklyn Heights, which, okay, you can't take that away from her, but that's a very different upbringing than if you spent your childhood in, say, Bay Ridge, or Canarsie, or Bed-Stuy, or Bushwick, or any of these places. Now, someone like Paul Auster is interesting because he got to Brooklyn before it was the "cool" thing to do, sometime in the late seventies or early eighties, yet because of the type of work he does, you will find very little, if any, historic or anthropological material having to do with Brooklyn. There are other virtues, to be sure, in his writing, but getting a bead on Brooklyn as a thematic place is not one of them . . .

Jonathan Lethem is the one guy who stands apart. He's the exemplar, and one of the main reasons is that he's a native; he didn't move to Brooklyn to be a part of any scene. He has really made an effort to put a literary, physical parameter to define where he comes from. His recent book, *The Fortress of Solitude,* dealt with local history and culture.

JONATHAN LETHEM: The new Brooklyn literary movement, if there is one, has to do with people from elsewhere, who've come to the borough by choice, and good for them, there's plenty of room for all. But in a sense I'm the least relevant example. I had Brooklyn thrust upon me instead.

BRIAN BERGNER: Historically, for fiction there's three guys who are pretty much the exemplars when it comes to writing about the physical and emotional landscape of Brooklyn: Hubert Selby, Wallace Markfield, and Henry Miller. The Brooklyn sections of Miller's work are just so great. Selby's *Last Exit to Brooklyn,* even though it's Brooklyn circa 1964, I would still tell someone to read it before anything by Lethem to learn about South Brooklyn. That's not to put down Jonathan, but Selby was a visionary. Whitman was also great, but his Brooklyn is so far back and so different from anything anyone knows today except the name Brooklyn that it's not useful to use him for any kind of measurement. He's useful, of course, as a literary figure of greatness, but that's something else entirely.

Markfield is this cult sixties novelist who wrote *To an Early Grave* that was made into a film by Sidney Lumet called *Bye Bye Braverman.* I think Woody Allen borrowed a lot of his literary stylings from Markfield. Markfield also did a novel called *You Could Live if They Let You.* The protagonist is a stand-up comic who resembles a combination of Lenny Bruce and Don Rickles. A lot of it is in the form of interviews. Very much ahead of its time and very indicative of the Jewish Brooklyn of his day. Sorrentino is an exemplar of the Italian Brooklyn experience, not only brilliant and hilarious, and unlike Selby, who had a hard life that ultimately, I think, limited his output, Sorrentino did forty years of topnotch work right up until his death in 2006.

There's still a big lag between Brooklyn literature and Brooklyn reality.

DEBBIE BOSWELL: I was born in Brooklyn, in Crown Heights, of Caribbean heritage. I've lived there my whole life and have seen plenty of changes, mostly for the better. The quality of life is definitely going up. I think that people are putting their differences aside and learning how to live together in a better and more productive way. The Caribbean community, the African American community, and the Hasidic community have all learned how to make it work. Sure, there are skirmishes, but overall, it's so much better than it used to be. Everybody's just trying to live.

I've always loved writing. I do religious fiction, but I talk to the masses, even atheists. I like to write about real people going through real problems, and somewhere along the way finding God and getting their lives together. I don't feel a sense of any real literary community, but I do see so many people hanging out together and working by themselves, at independent bookstores, coffee shops. It's something I see in Brooklyn that I don't really see anywhere else, especially Manhattan.

I know my work would not be the same if I lived anywhere else. Whether or not that's part of a scene I can't say. There's racism everywhere, but the situation in Crown Heights has evolved so much, it's an amazing thing to see. It's the place to be if you're a writer, I think. Happening.

J. K. SAVOY: I emigrated from New Jersey, where I was born, to come to Brooklyn to be a writer, where I lived from 1974 to 1996. I had a moving business called Kenny the Mover. The sad thing is, the price of housing finally drove me from Brooklyn. Since my novel was published and sold quite a few copies, I guess you could say I was part of the new Brooklyn literary scene. I wouldn't say it's organized as such, but there is a group of young, creative thinkers. I used to own a coffeehouse in Brooklyn in the seventies, and I remember that everyone had their own perspective on everything, they liked to live it and to write it down. It was very similar to Greenwich Village of an earlier time, and then for a while SoHo, also in Manhattan, before the rents got too high in both places and drove the starving artists out, so to speak. People who are creative want to be around other creative types, so the abstract community of camaraderie followed itself over the river to cheap rents and stimulating environments. That's what helped make Park Slope and now Williamsburg hot literary neighborhoods. But as the rents get higher there as well, and co-ops and condos take over and help gentrify, the movement seems to be drifting over to Astoria, Queens, where it will settle for as long as possible until those writers are forced to find someplace else to live and work.

A writer doesn't start off successful enough, unless he or she is born rich enough to afford a brownstone where one can write. One writes where one can afford to live, and then one writes about his life.

ERICA TOWNSEND: I am from Brooklyn my whole life. I was born in Browns-ville, lived in East New York, Crown Heights, and I am a writer. I love to write about black men and black boys. I am part of the literary scene in Brooklyn today, the culture of creativity. All types of young writers are mixing and melting in Brooklyn and that stimulates me.

MAHOGANY L. BROWNE: I am the publisher of Penmanship Books, a group specifically created for performance artists. I was a performing artist myself. I came out of the Nuyorican Café, doing literary readings, strug-gling to find an agent and publisher for my own work. When I couldn't, I decided to put it out there myself. I was so successful at it that I decided to open it up to my friends. I am based in Brooklyn, right around the corner from the Brooklyn Museum.

I was drawn to Brooklyn because I wanted to be a writer and a per-former. I'd been living in California when I received an offer to come to work in New York City. I moved here and soon started writing on my own. I knew I was going to stay here because I had a strong sense of being cultivated by the creative atmosphere of Brooklyn. There's a pool of creativity bubbling in Brooklyn and I needed to be part of that. It's everywhere, in local coffeehouses, in independent bookstores, in rehab centers smack in the middle of residential areas. There's so much to write about but it always brings you back to yourself.

Brooklyn is totally different from Manhattan, where I spent some time when I first moved east. Brooklyn is the real thing. Manhattan is dirty and cute but Brooklyn is the soul of New York City. It is one of the few places that applauds its artists, that supports its artists, that celebrates its artists. That's the closest I can come to defining what it is about Brooklyn that makes it so special, so vibrant, that is the essence of the Brooklyn literary scene. It's a real community and nothing like that exists in Manhattan. There art is a hobby; here it's possible for it to be your life. There's always a workshop somewhere that will lead to a job, something related to your work, like curating, or small publishing, col-lege readings, there's even a Brooklyn Literary Festival. There's always something that helps you survive.

And you know what else? If you make it, if you get big and famous, you still have to wait at the back of the line at Junior's for your cheesecake.

✖ ✖ ✖

MORE FAMOUS BROOKLYNITES

EDIE FALCO (1963-): Brooklyn-born three-time Emmy Award–winning actress, best known for her role as Carmela on *The Sopranos*.

CY FEUER (1911-2006): Broadway producer and director who won multiple Tony Awards. Hit shows include *Guys and Dolls, How to Succeed in Business Without Really Trying, Where's Charley?, Can-Can, The Boy Friend, Silk Stockings,* and *Little Me*.

HARVEY FIERSTEIN (1954-): Award-winning actor, singer, and playwright, best known for *Torch Song Trilogy*.

BOBBY FISCHER (1943-2008): Born in Chicago and raised in Brooklyn, was a brilliant but eccentric chess prodigy, best remembered for his 1972 championship match against Boris Spassky, which Fischer won.

BILLY FISKE (1911-1940): Brooklyn-born member of the 1928 and 1932 Winter Olympic teams, won gold medals both times for the bobsled. When World War II broke out, he joined Britain's Royal Air Force and died as a result of injuries sustained during a battle in 1940.

JOHN FRANCO (1960-): Brooklyn-born pitcher who served as the Mets' closer for fourteen seasons.

DAVID GEFFEN (1943-): Dreamworks, Asylum, and Geffen Records media mogul. Born in Borough Park, mother owned Chic Corsets, attended New Utrecht High School.

JACK GILFORD (1908-1990): Best remembered for his many TV, stage, and movie performances, and several memorable Cracker Jack commercials.

RUTH JOAN BADER GINSBURG (1933-): Brooklyn-born associate justice of the U.S. Supreme Court.

JACKIE GLEASON (1916-1987): Starred in many motion pictures, best known for his portrayal of Brooklyn bus driver Ralph Kramden in the classic TV series *The Honeymooners*.

GERRY GOFFIN (1939-): Classic Brill Building songwriter (lyricist), composed dozens of hit pop tunes with wife Carole King.

GARY DAVID GOLDBERG (1944-): Writer and producer, created the TV series *Family Ties, Spin City,* and *Brooklyn Bridge.*

DORIS KEARNS GOODWIN (1943-): Pulitzer Prize–winning political biographer whose subjects have included the Kennedys, FDR, and Abraham Lincoln.

LOU GOSSETT JR. (1936-): Best known for his Academy Award–winning performance in the 1982 film *An Officer and a Gentleman.*

GILBERT GOTTFRIED (1955-): Nutty comic whose distinctive voice is heard in dozens of commercials and animated series.

JOHN GOTTI (1940-2002): So-called Teflon don of the Brooklyn-based Gambino crime family. Died in prison serving a life-without-parole sentence for the murder of rival gang member Paul Castellano. Liked to set off illegal fireworks every Fourth of July.

ELLIOTT GOULD (1938-): Best known for role in the movie *M*A*S*H.* Former husband of Barbra Streisand.

SALVATORE "SAMMY THE BULL" GRAVANO (1945-): Brooklyn-born mob hit man and stool pigeon, currently serving a nineteen-year prison term for drug trafficking.

ELLIE GREENWICH (1940-): Pop singer, songwriter, record producer, and Brill building alumna. Wrote and produced numerous hits with former husband Jeff Barry.

TERRY GROSS (1951-): Popular NPR radio host and co-executive producer of "Fresh Air."

BOB GUCCIONE (1930-): Founder and former publisher of *Penthouse* magazine.

BUDDY HACKETT (1924-2003): American comedian and actor. Gained fame on the "Borscht Belt" circuit of Catskill Mountain resorts he helped put on the cultural map.

RICHIE HAVENS (1941-): Folksinger associated with the 1960s Greenwich Village folk-pop scene. Best known for his open-tuned performance at the legendary 1969 Woodstock concert.

CONNIE HAWKINS (1942-): National Basketball Association Hall of Fame player. Born in Bed-Stuy, played with the Harlem Globetrotters, Phoenix Suns, Los Angeles Lakers, and Atlanta Hawks.

SUSAN HAYWARD (1917–1975): Feisty American movie star nominated several times for Academy Award, won Best Actress in 1958 for *I Want to Live*.

RITA HAYWORTH (1918–1987): Legendary Hollywood leading lady, the "Great American Love Goddess." Married five times; husbands include singer Dick Haymes, Orson Welles, Prince Aly Khan, and director James Hill.

JOSEPH HELLER (1923–1999): Novelist, graduate of Abraham Lincoln High School, best remembered for *Catch-22*.

SIDNEY HOOK (1902–1989): Achieved early prominence for his work interpreting the philosophy of Karl Marx. Became a leading member of the American Workers Party during the Great Depression. Changed his viewpoint dramatically, became anti-Communist in the early 1940s, and in later years championed pragmatism. Awarded the Presidential Medal of Freedom in 1985 by Ronald Reagan.

LENA HORNE (1917–): Popular African American singer, made several movies and had numerous hit records.

EDWARD EVERETT HORTON (1896–1970): American character actor who appeared in countless Hollywood movies, on TV, and on the legitimate stage. Narrated several animated characters for the Hanna-Barbera production company, and appeared as Chief Roaring Chicken in the sitcom *F Troop*.

CURLY HOWARD (1903–1952): Born Jerome Lester Horwitz, most famous as Curly, one of the Three Stooges. Brother of Moe and Shemp.

MOE HOWARD (1897–1975): Born Harry Moses Horwitz, another one of the Three Stooges.

SHEMP HOWARD (1895–1955): Born Samuel Howard, another of the Three Stooges.

MARTY INGELS (1936–): Comedian, actor, and voice-over specialist. Married to actress Shirley Jones.

DANNY KAYE (1913–1987): Born David Daniel Kaminsky, Ukrainian descent, attended Thomas Jefferson High School, served during his teens as Catskills resort tummler (all-around entertainment director). Broke into movies in 1935 and became an international stage, film, and television star. Appeared in several movie musicals, with much of his best material written by his wife, Sylvia Fine.

ALFRED KAZIN (1915–1998): Writer and literary critic. One of his primary themes was the immigrant experience in America during the early years of the twentieth century. Author of the classics *A Walker in the City* and *New York Jew*.

HARVEY KEITEL (1939–): Grew up in Brighton Beach, joined the marines, became a court reporter, studied acting with Stella Adler and Lee Strasberg, became a favorite actor of director Martin Scorsese. Has appeared in over fifty films, including Scorsese's 1973 *Mean Streets*, the film that made both him and Robert De Niro stars.

BERNARD KING (1956–): Played high school ball for Fort Hamilton High School, where his brother Albert also played. Spent fourteen years in professional basketball with the ABA and NBA, revolutionizing the role of the small forward in modern-day basketball. Played for the Knicks from 1983 to 1987.

CAROLE KING (1942–): Attended Madison High School, was a classmate of Neil Sedaka, and served as the inspiration for his hit single "Oh! Carol." Wrote dozens of hit songs with partner Gerry Goffin, and had a solo singing career highlighted by her legendary *Tapestry* album (1971).

CHAPTER SEVEN

THE NABES

We hooked a train and rode an hour to see the Bronx Park Zoo
And landed out in Brooklyn on Utica Avenue . . .
You got to change your subway train at every stop or two . . .
And every time you come wearing a different pair of shoes
—WOODY GUTHRIE, "THE NEW YORK TRAINS"

B ROOKLYN REMAINS THE historic entry site and first home for those willing to travel sometimes as much as halfway around the world to gain their freedom. Brooklyn's storied ethnic neighborhoods are vibrant, complex places that blend cultures in unexpected ways. Kenny Jones, a British East Ender who was the drummer for the classic rock band the Small Faces (later the Faces) and who replaced Keith Moon in the legendary band the Who, remembers Brooklyn more vividly than any other place he saw on his very first trip to America, when he was a homesick seventeen-year-old.

KENNY JONES: Being a baby-boomer East Ender made me quite passionate about neighborhoods. Where I grew up it was a turf issue, like Brooklyn is in America. The first thing I noticed about Brooklyn was how everyone I met was very proud of where their heart and soul came from, where the real people in their life were, the ones when you get in trouble you could run home to and know you'd be taken care of. When I began to understand what borough life in NYC was all about, I completely related to it. I was drawn to Brooklyn especially, much more than to any scene that was going on in Manhattan. Brooklyn just seemed more recognizable, and felt more like home. I'd never actually spent time in it, just saw bits and pieces on the way to gigs, but I could immediately pick out anyone who came to our shows or talked to us who was from Brooklyn. That great Brooklyn accent was unmistakable, and the deeper I looked into the soul of Brooklyn, the more I discovered there were real people in America who grew up dock-siders, like me.

RABBI SIMON JACOBSON: My paternal grandfather was originally from Georgia. I'm his namesake. He was Simon Yacobashvili. Today everybody is called -shvili, because in Georgian it means "son of." When he came to Toronto, in 1946, he Anglicized it to Jacobson. Three years later he came to the United States.

His father-in-law, Rebbe Schneerson, was almost killed in the Soviet Union. He moved to Europe. Then the Nazis invaded and he left the Continent through Lithuania, and came to America on one of the last ships able to leave Europe, in 1940. He already had some supporters in America from a visit he had made ten years earlier, in places like Chicago, St. Louis, Detroit, but he didn't have any supporters here. I never knew the exact reason, but I think the feeling in him was to relocate to New York City because it was centrally located, where most Jews were living. When he first arrived he stayed at the Greystone Hotel in Manhattan. In the mid-1940s they found a building in Brooklyn, and the whole family moved. They lived upstairs, the synagogue was downstairs, and Rebbe Schneerson lived on the second floor.

Rebbe Schneerson became one of the major forces in the revival of world Judaism. Everyone thought that after the Holocaust, Judaism would die out. In the twentieth century the combination of Stalin and Hitler killed millions of observant Jews. Six million by Hitler alone, which meant that a third of the culture was gone. No one knows how many Stalin killed, but a fair estimate would be another third. Even before, in the late nineteenth century, Jews fled Russia and Europe because of the pogroms that wiped out countless more, so there were relatively few Jews left by the end of the first half of the century. Most of those who did survive lost everything. It seemed as if in another ten or twenty years, those left would be so demoralized and without assistance or even sympathy they would all be dead and so would Judaism itself.

But then a miracle happened called Israel and the great revival of Judaism began. Was there one figure in America who helped to make the difference here? Rebbe Schneerson, who survived the hell of Russia and also the Nazis, basically rebuilt not just a community in Brooklyn but a philosophy that could speak to the Jews now living in the States, all over the country, and eventually Jews everywhere throughout the world.

For all its salvation, America was also a country where it was felt that in order to assimilate you had to lose your Judaism because there seemed to be no Jewish God in the new world. Everyone worked on the Sabbath, for instance. Rebbe Schneerson's message was essentially spiritual, and resonated with thousands upon thousands of immigrants who felt alienated and disoriented. He made it possible for American Jews to be deeply Jewish *and* American. Essentially, he believed we live in a hard dark world but one where it is possible to bring light. Beneath the dark surface of the world, personally, psychologically, emotionally, there is light, and that is the message. It's not even just a Jewish message, but a universal one. Jews have carried that message since the beginning of time, all the way back to Abraham, and Moses. To me, the Rebbe was like an Abraham and a Moses combined.

Paradoxically, although Crown Heights in Brooklyn was the center of the rebbe's movement, it is not the center of Judaism, because there is no center. Part of the message is that you have to go out and build Jewish centers everywhere. Crown Heights is, rather, the place from where American Jewish life *emanates,* the nucleus. The roots of the spiritual revolution were and are in Crown Heights.

My father, Gershen Jacobson, was a journalist who worked for the

New York Herald Tribune and was a correspondent for the largest Israeli newspaper. His work brought him to New York, where he decided to settle. He met my mother, they got married in 1955, and took a place to live in Crown Heights.

I was born in 1956 at Brooklyn Jewish Hospital, which no longer exists. We lived on St. Marks Place until about 1964. At the time the neighborhood was white and predominantly Jewish. They called the area around Eastern Parkway "Doctors' Row" because a lot of prominent physicians lived there. Eastern Parkway was a desirable place because as the first parkway ever built in the United States it was modeled after the Champs-Elysées in Paris. Eastern Parkway used to be called Crow Hill. Washington fought a Revolutionary battle here. On Eastern Parkway there are plaques commemorating the soldiers who fell during World War I. It's good to know who walked on the ground before we did, I believe.

Eastern Parkway is and always has been a very prominent community. It has the Grand Army Plaza, the Brooklyn Museum, the fifty-two-acre Botanic Garden that offers twelve thousand different plants, and Prospect Park. The garden was built next to the museum over rough meadowland once used by the Parks Department as an ash dump; today it blooms year-round. The subways were originally built by the people in control, naturally, and they wanted them to stop right where they lived. That's why, you can trust, wherever there are subway stops in Brooklyn, those were the areas where the most powerful people lived. Eastern Parkway was one such neighborhood.

When I grew up the neighborhood was completely white and mostly Jewish, a mix of secular and religious. The religious influx actually came after the secular one, after World War II. The survivors relocated here and built the largest Conservative synagogues in the country on Eastern Parkway. My father sent me to Lubavitch schools, so I grew up in an environment of spiritual thinkers and leaders.

As far back as I can remember, Rebbe Schneerson was a towering figure in my life. As I grew older and began to struggle with my own spirituality, I identified even more with his message, which to me was a true Jewish message, not dogmatic and not narrow-minded. It wasn't Woody Allen Jewish, but had to do with a more spiritual awakening, involving world change–that you must engage the world. We're here not just to survive, to eat and sleep and make money, but to transform this universe in some way on a personal and collective level, to make a home for the divine in this material world. To do so, according to the rebbe, we all have to recognize our brotherhood, Jew or non-Jew, black or white. *Everyone* is chosen by God to do that, to help each other by playing the spiritual music. That was very seductive to me, and I plunged in. I began to write, to teach, and thank God, I feel that I was in the right place at the right time.

Later on, in the sixties, a lot of blacks started moving into Eastern Parkway. It began in the early sixties and there were literally riots in the streets because of it. I remember the yeshiva I went to, on Bedford and Dean, just north of Eastern Parkway, which is now called Bedford-Stuyvesant, or Bed-Stuy. Anyway, one afternoon we went to lunch and were playing in the schoolyard, and I remember seeing hundreds of blacks throwing garbage cans everywhere. That was part of the seething unrest that was rippling through the entire city, the entire country, for that matter.

All the major cities–Cleveland, Chicago, Los Angeles–were in turmoil and quickly turned black, because the whites got scared and ran to the suburbs for safety. When it happened in Brooklyn it created a vacuum that was filled by blacks and other minorities. Brownsville, which had also been a very nice community, quickly turned into a slum once the so-called white flight began. It was like an epidemic of panic among white people.

MARTY ASHER: That's true. When I was ten, in the early sixties, my parents, who were middle-class Jews, wanted to flee from Williamsburg, where I was born, because the neighborhood was changing. We moved from Williamsburg to Canarsie, where the new public housing projects had been built, which were at least 75 percent white (the rest being mostly Puerto Rican and black). Howard Schultz also lived there as a kid. He eventually grew up and started a little chain of coffee shops called Starbucks.

Canarsie was kind of the Staten Island equivalent of its day, a frontier of sorts. It was all the way out there, away from the main drags, but had all the feel of a real neighborhood. There was a bread truck delivery guy, a milk guy, a cupcake guy, all of whom made regular stops in the project. I spent hours playing skelly, a game played on concrete, on a board drawn with street chalk and markers made of bottle caps filled with melted wax. I played it with the other kids in the designated playgrounds, a large part of the reason my parents moved there, so that I could be safe.

I went to Stuyvesant High School in Manhattan, one of the three "special" high schools in the city–the Bronx High School of Science and Brooklyn Tech are the other two–which you had to have great grades to get in. My parents used to warn me that if I didn't make it, I'd wind up at a "regular" high school, in this case Thomas Jefferson High, which sounded to me like the threat of a prison sentence. Meaning heavily mixed. Not that we were all that wealthy or anything. I remember visiting a friend of mine whose parents had moved out of the original neighborhood to Long Island and being stunned when I walked into his house. They had real money and they had made a real move. But it wasn't until I went to Stuyvesant that I began to understand that the world was not limited to Brooklyn. I remember I had this intense crush on my French teacher. I think that helped. She actually invited me to her house for dinner one time. It was the first time I'd ever had any wine other than Manischewitz. By the time I graduated from high school there was never any question in my mind that I was going to leave Brooklyn entirely and move to the city, meaning Manhattan, meaning the Village.

ANDREW MILLER: My parents moved to the Slope–Park Slope–in 1975, the year I was born. They had lived for many years in Eastern Parkway, near Crown Heights. One night, just before I was born, two girls were having a fistfight in the stairwell of the apartment building and their mothers were there. Instead of breaking them up they were egging them on. That's when my parents looked at each other and said, "We have to get out of here."

The two areas they looked at were Park Slope and Fort Greene. They would drive to Park Slope and just sit and park on the street and marvel at how quiet it was. The homes in Fort Greene were built for a high-class clientele, whereas the brownstones in Park Slope were aimed strictly at the middle class, which is where they wound up.

A week after they moved in some guy got shot across the street. My mother still talks about walking out onto the stoop after hearing some noise and seeing this guy on the ground. She didn't know what was going on. A couple of minutes later the police showed up and then the SWAT teams and she began to wonder just how quiet this place really was. For the most part, though, it was okay.

But, it turned out, not completely. When I was about five or six, I remember she was held up by some guy. He got her engagement ring and whatever money she had and then threatened to come to the house. She panicked and ran and the guy started shooting his gun. Our dog started barking when she ran up the steps, it was quite a scene. After, she went to the police station to look at mug shots.

Other than that it was pretty quiet.

I never felt like I grew up on the streets of Brooklyn. My best friend in high school was from Carroll Gardens, and I used to hang out with him and his friends. I went to Hunter High School in Manhattan, which took kids from all over the city, which is why we knew each other even though we were from different neighborhoods.

I remember marveling at how different Carroll Gardens was from Park Slope. In the Slope everyone stayed in their houses. In Carroll Gardens, because the houses are all recessed, the older people especially would sit outside on lawn chairs yelling at the kids running around while we'd hang on the corners drinking beer out of cans in small paper bags. We hung out in Carroll Gardens because no one hung out in Park

Slope. What was interesting to me was that I was a product of gentrification, living in Park Slope, while they were the guys being gentrified and they didn't like the new people who were moving in. Also, it felt so exciting being in a real neighborhood where guys did hang out on street corners, even though I wasn't really one of them. I really loved it, even though it got scary every once in a while. These kids were connected to each other, and tough.

One New Year's Eve I remember we got jumped by some other guys. My forehead was cut open and I had to get six stitches at the hospital. After, my parents really wanted to pursue these kids, to get the cops after them, but my friend told them they simply couldn't do that. We'd have to move out of Brooklyn if we did—it was as simple as that.

RABBI JACOBSON: Somehow Eastern Parkway held on because Rebbe Schneerson took a stand that no Jews should run. He said it was not responsible, that it meant leaving others behind, and that was wrong. He essentially drew a line in the sand. I remember that my block turned white to black within the period of a month, but my family didn't move because of Rebbe Schneerson.

We did make a small move, but within the community, from St. Marks to a place called Sullivan Place, a small street just south of Eastern Parkway. We lived there until 1969. I remember that year we went away to the Catskills for that summer and when we returned, the whole block had turned from Jewish to black. There were what were called at the time block busters, real-estate sharks who convinced people that they'd better sell their houses immediately or they would see the values plummet. "You can get thirty thousand for your house? Next month you'll only be able to get ten thousand." So people sold their houses overnight, and one day I woke up to find we were the only white family left on Sullivan Place.

In 1970 my parents bought a house on Montgomery Street, where to this day my mother still lives. We needed to move because I was the oldest of five children, and by the time the last one came along there was simply no more room for us to live. I lived there with my parents until 1983, when I got married and bought a house of my own on Eastern Parkway: Crown Heights.

It was a very depressing situation. Real estate prices dropped, stores went out of business. I remember in my childhood days that Utica Avenue had once been a bustling commercial area, Rogers Avenue, Nostrand, and one by one they fell. Windows were boarded up as if a hurricane was coming. But the stand that was taken in our community changed everything, all because of Rebbe Schneerson, our spiritual mentor.

Some of my classmates did leave, but not out of fear. They did it intentionally, as part of the rebbe's outreach program, to go out and build Jewish centers all over the world, from Australia to Israel. Nevertheless, the community lives on, as does the rebbe's message.

Those who remained created what they called "Chebro." This was a community fund where people bought shares in the fund that was then used to buy buildings, in an attempt to revive the community. As the stability returned, houses were renovated, and we were able to see major change. We bought buildings that had been taken over by the city because they were defaulted. A lot of poverty housing took its place, which was a breeding ground for drugs. That created a high level of street crime.

In 1972, slowly, it started changing, probably the first steps in what is today a tremendous renaissance going on throughout Brooklyn. By the late 1970s, visible signs of the revival could be seen in the upswing in local businesses; the price of houses started to rise. Houses that had once been abandoned were cleaned up, renovated, and sold by the city to the middle-class. Even the blacks in the community began to benefit. A lot of them happen not to be African American but from the Caribbean. The biggest parade every Labor Day is the Caribbean one.

THE SEVENTEENTH-CENTURY DUTCH settlers purchased woodlands from the Canarsee Indians and renamed the area Bedford. One of the earliest Dutch developers was Thomas Lambertse, who built Bedford's first inn in 1668. Lambertse sold land in Bedford to Lefferts Pieterse (Peter Lefferts) of Flatbush. Over the years the Lefferts family grew land-wealthy, and managed to endure through the Revolutionary War's famous Battle of Brooklyn, one of George Washington's early and most ignominious defeats on his way to eventual victory over the British. Members of the Lefferts family owned slaves, as did other white settlers in the area, and a significant proportion of the area's population was black. After New York State outlawed slavery in 1827, many free blacks settled in two towns about a mile apart, known as Carrville and Weeksville. Weeksville was a thriving community, thick with schools, churches, an orphanage, and one of the nation's first black newspapers, the *Freeman Torchlight*. The first female African American physician in New York State (and the third in the country) was a product of Weeksville. As time passed and development moved in, black residents were pushed out of the area; all that remains of Weeksville today are a few wooden houses on Hunterfly Road.

In the mid-1960s, historian James Hurley, who was conducting a Pratt Neighborhood College workshop on Brooklyn, began to investigate the history of Weeksville. From a plane, Hurley was able to identify four ramshackle houses as its last vestiges. Joan Maynard, who was one of the founders of the Society for the Preservation of Weeksville and Bedford-Stuyvesant History in 1968, became involved in the project, and eventually the society bought and restored the houses and created exhibitions about the area that were installed in two of the houses.

As wealthier white residents moved in, the area's wood-frame housing stock was replaced by brownstone row houses and even the occasional mansion. With the extension of the subway to the area in the early twentieth century, access became easier, and working-class residents, many of them Italian, Irish, or Jewish, moved in as the middle and upper classes moved out. Between the wars, many blacks from the South and immigrants from the Caribbean settled in the area, but the Depression and white flight sent the area into a decline.

Another neighborhood that experienced significant demographic change was Crown Heights, south of Bedford-Stuyvesant. In the late nineteenth century Crown Heights, like its neighbor Bedford-Stuyvesant, was a wealthy enclave. Its upper-class population left for the suburbs, and was replaced with poor Jews from Eastern Europe, African Americans, and Caribbean immigrants. After World War II, the area became home to an Orthodox Jewish community known as the Lubavitcher, who stayed in the neighborhood even as other whites left in the 1950s. The population shifts and encroaching poverty meant that, again like Bed-Stuy, Crown Heights entered a spiral of decay. On several occasions racial tensions erupted, but the most horrific spasm of violence occurred in August 1991.

The summer of 1991 was a particularly hot and humid one. Areas like Crown Heights were still reeling from a citywide economic collapse two years earlier that had put a halt to the promised economic redevelopment of the deteriorating ghetto. Many African American residents felt economically exploited and blamed the area's Orthodox Jews for the neighborhood's failure to improve, believing the Lubavitcher were so entrenched in their own traditions they they were unwilling to give way to modern, upscale city-subsidized housing development. The Hasidim, meanwhile, believed the growing crime rates on the streets were related to drug sales and blamed the area's African Americans. In apportioning blame for the neighborhood's general blight, both sides ignored the larger failures of city, state, and federal governments. But in the close proximity of urban street life in Crown Heights, cultural differences and economic tensions twisted around each other like the ends of a lit fuse.

The spark that led to the explosion happened on the evening of August 19, 1991, when a station wagon driven by Yosef Lifsh, part of the Lubavitch grand rebbe's motorcade, ran a red light, hit another vehicle, veered onto a sidewalk, and hit two young children. Seven-year-old Gavin Cato, the child of Guyanese immigrants, was trapped under the car, and his cousin Angela was severely injured. Lifsh, it was

said, immediately got out of his car to try to help the children and was
set upon and beaten by a small but infuriated crowd of African Americans. This began a series of race riots the likes of which had not been
seen in New York City since the draft riots of the Civil War.

RABBI JACOBSON: I remember the night that Crown Heights, as it came to
be known, happened. It was terrible. Cops were nowhere to be seen for
two whole days and because of it fear was in the air, windows were
being broken, looting was rampant, and the police did nothing about it.
I believe they were told to lay off, to let the blacks vent. It was a night of
complete lawlessness, not unlike what happens after a major disaster,
like a blackout or a flood. Hundreds of thousands of dollars of damage
was done.

The real point, though, was that the media badly distorted the truth
of what happened. The media made it seem as if the blacks and the Jews
were at war in Brooklyn.

RUDOLPH GIULIANI (three months before he defeated David Dinkins for
mayor): For three days people were beaten up, people were sent to the
hospital because they were Jewish. There's no question that not enough
was done about it by the city of New York.

AL SHARPTON: If the Jews want to get it on, tell them to pin their yarmulkes
back and come over to my house.

During the riots, an Australian student, Yankel Rosenbaum, was
stabbed and killed by attackers shouting anti-Semitic remarks. One
of the attackers, Lemrick Nelson, Jr., was acquitted of the murder. But
in 1998, nearly seven years later, he was found guilty by a Federal court
of violating Rosenbaum's civil rights and sentenced to 19 ½ years in
prison.

The case dragged on in one form or another for nearly fifteen years.
In 1997, five years after being acquitted of the murder of Rosenbaum,

Nelson was found guilty by a federal court of violating Rosenbaum's civil rights, but an appeals court overturned the verdict. A new trial ended in 2003 with his conviction, and Nelson was sentenced to ten years. As part of a plea bargain that included an admission of his guilt, Lemrick Nelson, Jr., was sentenced to ten years, but the time he had previously served meant that he could be released from prison to a halfway house in 2004, and from the halfway house in 2006.

It was a far different Brooklyn that Nelson found waiting for him on the outside. The Crown Heights district that had come to define the racial tensions of the 1990s was hardly recognizable, its population changed by a continuing flow of immigrants: West Indians, Jews, Asians, Africans.

JIMMY BRESLIN: The neighborhood's changed twice already.

DR. STEVEN RUDOLPH: I am actually not from Brooklyn, but from the Lower East Side, but had always heard about it from my aunt Rose, who lived on Ocean Parkway. I wound up going to Brooklyn College of the City of New York. Financial issues made the decision where I was going quite simple. We didn't have a lot of money in my family and, at the time, if you were accepted, Brooklyn College was free. You couldn't beat that deal.

I remember learning how to take the subway from Manhattan to the junction of Flatbush Avenue and Nostrand, the subway stop for Brooklyn College. The first time I did it I felt like I had emerged into a different world. That Brooklyn of 1969 was not the same as the Brooklyn of the first decade of the twenty-first century. The demographics were completely different. Brooklyn keeps on renewing itself with immigrant populations. In our stroke unit, 30 percent of the patients speak Russian as their native tongue. Traditionally, Maimonides serviced a specific tradition, in this instance Jews.

As you may or may not know, Jewish hospitals were built all over the United States because of the need of that particular group of immigrants to take care of itself, because other hospitals simply wouldn't. If you were poor and you were Jewish in New York City, for example, you could not go to Lenox Hill or New York Hospital. They would not admit you or put Jewish doctors on their staffs. Absolutely not. Today it's just the opposite, but even up until the seventies, there were still issues about admitting Jewish doctors to staffs, or even being on staff and hiding what they were. What changed it all was the civil rights movement of the sixties.

First of all, it made discrimination illegal, not just for the African American community, but for all minorities. It made it possible for a lot of different kinds of people to be in the workplace, if you wear a turban, or a yarmulke, or if you have head coverings, that's all covered by the civil rights laws that were enacted. If you go back to Brooklyn before then, you'll find that there were great Jewish hospitals, like Beth-El, which is now Brookdale, in East New York, or Brownsville. There was Brooklyn Jewish, now called Interfaith, near Crown Heights. That was a hospital that had world-famous doctors on its staff, in many different fields. Diseases were discovered there. Crohn's disease, for example. And don't forget that Jewish hospitals were not exclusively for Jewish patients. Maimonides, the hospital I'm affiliated with, was originally called Israel Zion Hospital. It was renamed Maimonides in the mid-1940s. It served anyone in the community, regardless of race, creed, or color. Maimonides became quite a big hospital, and had a tradition of teaching. There was always a lot of training going on, as well as treatment. It was, and remains, a community hospital, without pretensions to being Cornell or Columbia or Mt. Sinai. We've always had a dedicated staff.

Fifty years ago the Jews that lived here were either new immigrants or the children of new immigrants from the turn of the century. There were many Jews from that group born here and working here, working in civil service, the post office and other places. Maimonides took care of them.

Now we take care of the Chinese, who live two blocks away in Chinatown, on Eighth Avenue, and the Russians who live in Brighton Beach and Bensonhurst, and the Italians who still live in Bensonhurst, and the Orthodox Jews who live in Borough Park and Flatbush. Those are the communities that we predominantly serve.

The big difference between Brooklyn when I was a student and Brooklyn now is that people don't mix. If you lived in a Jewish and Italian neighborhood back then, everyone mixed together. Today that just doesn't happen. Chinese stay with Chinese. Russians stay with Russians. Jews stay with Jews. Italians stay with Italians.

The Russians are interesting. They want to go to a Jewish hospital when they need care, if they're Jewish, because of their lingering fears of anti-Semitism, left over from their experiences in the Soviet Union, whereas the Orthodox Jews born in the United States or of European origin don't care, they'll go to Lutheran Medical Center, or Methodist. In fact, they often think it's better somewhere else.

Nearly half the populace doesn't speak English at home. I think it's 47 percent now of the families that speak another language at home. That's the old-style redefining of Brooklyn. Then there's the gentrification of Park Slope and the area around Manhattan Bridge, and Cobble Hill, and all these areas that are "improving." "Improving," to me, means the rents have gone up. There was nothing wrong with a neighborhood that may not have been "improved," but you knew everybody, in a nice atmosphere. I grew up in an Italian neighborhood. We all knew each other. As my father used to say, "We were rich, we just didn't have money."

LOUIS SAVARESE: I'm from Brooklyn, born and raised in Bensonhurst. I went to an all-boys vocational high school, William E. Grady, where I learned all about electrical insulation. It wasn't much fun without the girls. I was part of a group of twenty-five guys that hung out on my block. All we did was play ball, hang out, cause trouble, whatever. All the houses on my block were private houses We were all slightly upper-middle-class, all Italian. Maybe one Irish, two at the most. That was fifty years ago. Today it's a lot of different nationalities, super-blended. Now I think the Italians are the minority. I think the Asians have taken over Bensonhurst. Asians and Russians.

As kids we couldn't wait to get up and go out and play ball in the street, the park, hang out. There was always enough players, enough kids to make a good game. On weekends and every day in the summer we were out from eight in the morning until twelve at night. We had to be dragged in. We never wanted to do anything like watch TV. That was for when you got sick. Today, kids don't go out at all. They stay home, play video games, use their computers, and miss out on all the good things. We had a blast. The older kids would get together on street corners and harmonize. I was too young to sing, but I'd love to listen to it. My generation's music was acid rock. We'd take some LSD, some mescaline, psilocybin, all the psychedelics, sometimes for months on end. I think I was once on a double dose of LSD, orange sunshine for a month straight. How was it? *Great!* It brought my head and my heart together. Drinkin', hangin' out, sleepin' on the beach, whichever beach was closest, Rockaway, Manhattan Beach, Riis Park. In 1969 I was on my way to Woodstock but I got so shit-faced I never made it.

I was a sanitation worker for the city of New York. No mob stuff, that was private and all gone now anyway. The city sanitation was clean. I worked for fifteen years and then retired after an injury. I was thirty-nine years old. Not bad. At three-quarters retirement I make more money now than I did then. I don't have to work no more. I'm good. I'm over sixty, and I just want to play racquetball with my boy, golf with the other guys, and I never need to go away. What for? You go on vacation when you work. When you don't work, there's no reason to go anywhere. I'm happy where I am, in Bensonhurst.

RALPH BEATRICE: I was born and raised in Brooklyn in an area near Kings County Hospital, an old-time Jewish and Italian area called "Pigtown." At one time there had been a number of pig farms there. It was very ethnic, and also a stone's throw from Ebbets Field. I had an uncle of mine that was a mechanic. Every day, religiously, he ate in a diner on Rogers

Avenue and Empire Boulevard called Toomey's, a famous place at the time. The Brooklyn Dodgers ate there all the time. A couple of the club owners too. I mean, it was a hangout. Every Sunday after I went to church, my uncle would take me to Toomey's for breakfast.

I went to a high school in Bed-Stuy, St. John's Prep, a private Catholic school, but I lived around the corner from Wingate, so people thought I was a student there. A friend of mine's mother was working in the cafeteria, so we hung out in the yard and the park around the corner. I spent 75 percent of my day back then there, playing ball on the courts. There were two great basketball players, one that played for Wingate and one that played for Boys High. They went pro—Roger Brown and Connie Hawkins, they were like the best players in the world. Connie used to come down once or twice a week, choose up, and play. Two very dominant players and four white kids who wished they could play one-tenth as good. We had a great time. You slept outside in the yard with a little net over you to keep cool at night.

ANTHONY PETROCINO: Bensonhurst, of course, was the locale for Jackie Gleason's *The Honeymooners* sitcom, and I think it was portrayed very well on that show. As Ralph Kramden, all of Gleason's phrases, his volatility, his scheming, his buddy Norton, and his maternal wife were very Brooklyn.* We saw in him what we saw in ourselves, and the reason it still resonates today is that we are a bunch of guys who are still kids inside married to women who are like our mothers.

TOMMY SPIONI: We used to play the Italian guys from north Manhattan, what they call the Bronx, in stickball. The Arthur Avenue boys. They used to wear gloves when they played. I couldn't believe it. Gloves with a rubber ball!

ANTHONY PETROCINO: None of us ever go to Manhattan. Oh, sometimes you might want to go, to splurge, but the average Brooklynite doesn't go.

---

* The Kramdens and the Nortons resided at 328 Chauncey Street, in Bensonhurst.

We got all the restaurants, all the finest food you want at a much more reasonable price right here.

BUDDY FANTO: Every fifth or sixth person in America can trace the development of their family tree either starting in or passing through Brooklyn. That kind of thing leads to a lot of myth making, out of fondness and sentimentality. Brooklyn is, in a sense, everyone's home, no matter where they're really from. They're really from Brooklyn, see?

There was a store on Thirteenth Avenue and Fifty-third Street, right in the middle of Borough Park. Big wide-open street. The place was owned by David Geffen's mother. She would yell at him, she would beat the shit out of him, because she was old world and he was a wild kid. Wild in the sense of ambition, when the old world mentality was mind your own business, stay close to home, stick with the family and continue the business. Buddy Hackett lived on the same street, I believe. Maybe Fifteenth Avenue. Snooky Lansen, the singer "with the voice from the heart," was from around there too. Jeff Chandler went to New Utrecht High School. Dane Clark, Johnny Saxon, Susan Hayward, they all came from that same neighborhood and all went to the same high school. You can see some of their pictures still hanging there in the hallway. Ray Romano and Andrew "Dice" Clay went there too.

DAVE TAWIL: I deal with the Haitian community in school. These are hardworking people. Yes, there's some gang stuff going on there but for the most part the Haitians remind me of the Jews and the Italians when they first came in. They're busting their ass. Go into their neighborhoods. They're beautiful down there on Flatbush Avenue. Unfortunately, you get white people up and down Flatbush, they're terrorized. That's bullshit. They're just immigrants, doing the same thing, selling fruits, vegetables, opening little shops, barber shops, beauty shops. The Russians on Brighton Beach—it's beautiful to see what they've done there. There's a whole other culture in Brighton Beach about possession and commercialism that is quite revealing, I think. It's brilliant, the revitalization that's going on throughout Brooklyn. I get a lot of Arab kids who are just coming here now. I deal with several of them in my sports classes and groups. A lot of the immigrant kids are working two and three jobs just to keep their heads above water and to help the family. There's very little of "I got it coming to me" among them.

AL BROWN: Everyone's connection to anywhere is their family. My parents were the children of immigrants from Ireland. They laid their roots in downtown Brooklyn and eventually came out to Flatbush. They used to "go out to Flatbush." I don't know why, but the older people always said it that way, as if they were going on a journey to get there. They settled near Holy Cross, and as the borough expanded so did we, moving further south, down by the junction. That's where I was born, in 1954.

For the first ten years of my life I remember adults walking around in suits, ties, dresses, and hats. That's my first image of Brooklyn, that men and women didn't go out of the house unless they were dressed really well. That's all changed now, of course, but back then it was a very purposeful thing. On Flatbush and Nostrand they had trolleys that ran on electricity with the cables above the surface. You can still see the tracks if you go over to certain places, along with the cobblestones that were there for the horses. Certain things remain. I'm a fireman and here at the firehouse there are check marks on the concrete floors, from the days when horses pulled the fire wagons, and they were kept in certain parts of the station so they didn't slip on wet concrete and have to be put to sleep.

The firehouse I work out of, in Canarsie, was built in 1907. At the time it was the only building on the street. I've been here since 1984. Before that I worked in downtown Brooklyn. There have been enormous changes in the neighborhood in those twenty-plus years. When I first arrived it was mostly Jewish and Italian, and very tight-knit. As time went on, a lot of them moved on and out. Long Island was flourishing in the seventies and the eighties, Staten Island was being expanded for living, New York suburbia was spreading and somebody had to buy those houses. That created a vacuum and where the Jews and Italians moved out, other groups moved in. What always irritates me is the way people point to Canarsie and Brooklyn and claim that it's a neighborhood and a borough of racial polarization. I remember, though, in the early eighties, Hauppauge was just being developed, and Smithtown, and all of Staten Island, which was, essentially, farmland full of cows. It was the vacuum that was created by those who were, in a way, considered traitors by those who stayed, and those who left were subsequently blamed by those who stayed, or had to stay, for creating the so-called polarization that evolved.

So when I grew up everyone was white and spoke the same language, English, even if they spoke another one at home. The neighborhood today is mostly black, Caribbean, Haitian, some Africans, it's hard to differentiate, say, the Caribbeans from the Haitians. But it's not hard to know they're here, because their culture is so different. They eat different food, for example. Nowhere in this neighborhood anymore can you go out and find an Italian salami store. They used to be on every street corner. That's all gone. We used to go out from the firehouse whenever we wanted and grab something to eat across the street. Now we have to send somebody, or take the truck, to a neighborhood that has delis, bakeries, groceries. Their customs, of course, are tied to their food and vice versa. It's a strange kind of segregated integration. To an outsider, it's all the same. To Brooklynites, it's highly individualized. The best we can do for each other is pick up as much as we can from each other.

Fire, of course, is a devastating thing. To have a neighborhood sustain an actual building fire every day can decimate a neighborhood in five years, much like it did the South Bronx in the seventies. Two or three small fires every day will do it. In times gone by, when I first got here, there would be one, maybe two fires a week and there would be days when you might have three in twenty-four hours. Post-9/11, in my opinion, New Yorkers have "gotten religion" and become more aware of things–they're practicing a little more conservative of a lifestyle.

Everybody was called in that day. I was there that day. The firehouse and the apparatus wasn't there. A crew remained at the house and the remainder of the men were shifted into Manhattan. We worked twenty-four on and twelve off for the first week or so. They cut back when they realized how hopeless any rescue operation was going to be. One thing that will always stick in my mind is how one of our muster points was on the Manhattan Bridge and when we arrived there, in city buses, the people, civilians, evacuating Manhattan were just starting to come over it and they were pretty beat up, torn up pretty good. They were very upset and very afraid. I can just remember [when they saw us] carrying the colors you can see a kind of reassurance in the faces. Their government was there. As upset as we all were, it was as reassuring for us to see them as it was for them to see us.

When I came back to Brooklyn that night we came across the Brooklyn Bridge, on pickup trucks, we were packed into them. There was an army tank on either side of the bridge, sandbags, a Hummer with .50 caliber machine guns at the plaza, things I thought I'd never see in my hometown. Stepping into Brooklyn felt like I was stepping into a safer zone. That little strip of water that separates Manhattan from Brooklyn felt like an ocean. I felt like I was safe and home.

✕ ✕ ✕

MORE FAMOUS BROOKLYNITES

SANDY KOUFAX (1935–): Legendary southpaw and three-time Cy Young Award winner. Played his entire professional baseball career with the Brooklyn and Los Angeles Dodgers. In 1965, pitched the first perfect game by a lefty since 1880, one of four no-hitters he achieved during his relatively brief career, which ended when he was thirty by arthritis.

MARTIN LANDAU (1931–): Began his career at the age of seventeen as a cartoonist for the New York *Daily News*. Attended the Actors Studio, appeared in several movies. Gained fame as a cast member of the highly successful sixties TV series *Mission: Impossible*. Won a Best Supporting Actor Academy Award for his performance in Tim Burton's 1993 film *Ed Wood*.

VINCE LOMBARDI (1913–1970): The son of Italian immigrant parents, attended Fordham University on a full football scholarship. Was head coach of the

Green Bay Packers from 1959 to 1967, during which time they won five national championships. Famously declared, "Winning isn't everything, it's the only thing."

FRANK MCCOURT (1930-): Born to Irish immigrant parents, taught in the New York City public school system for twenty-seven years before publishing *Angela's Ashes*, which won the Pulitzer Prize.

BERNARD MALAMUD (1914-1986): One of the most important American novelists of the postwar era. Child of Russian Jewish immigrants. He attended Erasmus High School, CCNY, and Columbia, earned an M.A. in English. His morally probing and sometimes allegorical work included *The Fixer* and *The Magic Barrel* (both won National Book Awards) and *The Assistant*. Baseball novel *The Natural* made into a popular film starring Robert Redford.

BARRY MANILOW (1943-): Singer-songwriter and arranger began his career working with Bette Midler. Has had several solo number one hits and albums and regularly plays Las Vegas as a major headliner.

BARRY MANN (1939-): Along with Cynthia Weil wrote some of the greatest rock/pop tunes of all time, including "On Broadway," "He's Sure the One I Love," "Uptown," and the single most-played song on radio of all time, "You've Lost That Lovin' Feeling," as sung by the Righteous Brothers.

DANIEL MANN (1912-1991): Popular film and television director.

HERBIE MANN (1930-2003): American jazz flautist and major recording artist.

BIZ MARKIE (1964-): A proponent of Brooklyn-style hip-hop. Best known for his humorous songs, such as "Just Like a Friend." Sometimes referred to as the "clown prince of hip-hop." Use of sampling from Gilbert O'Sullivan's "Alone Again Naturally" helped define the parameters for legal sampling. Later became associated with the Beastie Boys.

SAMANTHA MATHIS (1970-): Favored co-star of Gen X actors, including Christian Slater and the late River Phoenix, with whom she was involved romantically.

PAUL MAZURSKY (1930-): Film actor and director, best known for directing *Next Stop, Greenwich Village; Bob and Carol and Ted and Alice;* and *An Unmarried Woman*. In his youth, played one of the juvenile delinquents in *Blackboard Jungle*.

DEBRA LYNN MESSING (1968-): Actress and comedienne best known for her role as Grace in the long-running TV sitcom *Will and Grace*.

AL MICHAELS (1944-): TV sports commentator and play-by-play man.

ISAAC MIZRAHI (1961-): Fashion designer, TV personality. Attended High School of Performing Arts and Parsons School of Design.

MARY TYLER MOORE (1936-): TV and film actress, best known for her 1970s sitcom *The Mary Tyler Moore Show*.

ZERO MOSTEL (1915-1977): Film, stage, and TV actor, born Samuel Mostel, blacklisted in the 1950s. Most famous for playing Tevye in the original Broadway production of *Fiddler on the Roof* and co-starring role in the non-musical film version of *The Producers*.

CHRIS MULLIN (1963-): Pro basketball player, attended Xaverian High School of Bay Ridge. Was a star at small forward at St. John's University. He played sixteen years in the NBA.

EDDIE MURPHY (1961-): Actor, comedian. Was a regular on *Saturday Night Live*. Starred in *Beverly Hills Cop* and its sequels.

LORENZO MUSIC (1937-2001): Was a writer, voice-over actor, television producer, and musician. Best known as the voice of the cartoon character Garfield, he also was the voice of Carlton the doorman on the TV series *Rhoda*, wrote for *The Mary Tyler Moore Show*, created *The Bob Newhart Show*.

HARRY NILSSON (1941-1994): Songwriter, singer, painter, guitarist. Drinking buddy of John Lennon's during Lennon's split from Yoko Ono in the early 1970s. Wrote "Everybody's Talkin' at Me," used as the theme from the movie *Midnight Cowboy*.

THE NOTORIOUS B.I.G. (1972-1997): Born Christopher Wallace, aka Biggie Smalls. Shot to death after attending a music function in Los Angeles.

PAUL O'DWYER (1907-1998): Born in Ireland, grew up in Brooklyn. New York liberal, became a member of the City Council.

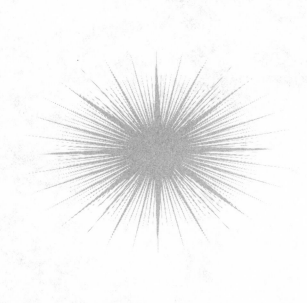

CHAPTER EIGHT

ON THE WATERFRONT

Mayor Opdyke had appealed for assistance to Brigadier General
Harvey Brown, commanding the garrison in the harbor forts.
General Brown brought three hundred troops into the city. The
Brooklyn Navy Yard sent a detachment of marines. Some soldiers
and marines were detailed to guard Federal buildings which offered
tempting prizes to the rioters, among them the Sub-Treasury and
Arsenal. The rest were assigned to work with the police. The Navy
Yard stationed two armed ships in the lower Hudson and East
Rivers, where their guns covered the financial district. . . . Riot
had taken on the look of revolution.

    —A DESCRIPTION BY LLOYD MORRIS OF THE ANTI-DRAFT RIOTS
    IN MANHATTAN AND BROOKLYN, JULY 4–16, 1862

T HE Brooklyn Navy Yard occupies the site of New York's first shipyard, built in 1781 by John Jackson and his brothers on land purchased from the descendants of the first Dutch settlers in the area. It is today a massive fenced-in enclosure bordered by Dumbo (Down Under the Manhattan Bridge Overpass), Fort Greene, Clinton Hill, and Williamsburg. The yard's history is long, glorious, and complex. Its greatest years were those leading up to and including World War II, when more than seventy thousand civilians were employed by the six dry docks that operated seven days a week, twenty-four hours a day. The Navy Yard is where the battleship USS *Maine* was built, presaging the United States' involvement in the Spanish-American War. Its ships also delineated in iron the beginning and ending of World War II: It built the USS *Arizona*, which was ignominiously sunk at Pearl Harbor, and the USS *Missouri*, upon whose deck the Japanese surrendered in 1945, ending the war in the Pacific. During its heyday it served as a sort of official Hollywood backdrop on a series of on-location New

York City–based movies, most famously the opening and closing sequences of Stanley Donen's and Gene Kelly's 1949 film version of the Broadway musical *On the Town*. During the 1970s financial downturn that affected the city, the state, and most of the country, what had once been a colorful and thriving waterfront had turned into a place where scrap metal scavengers routinely came to pick at the pieces of the past.

Today, after decades of neglect, corruption, racketeering, and political scandal, the waterfront—from the Brooklyn Army Terminal in Sunset Park to the site of the burned-out Greenpoint Terminal Market, an area that includes Red Hook—has been declared one of the eleven most endangered sites in the country by the National Trust for Historic Preservation. The problem, according to the Trust, is the massive destruction and reconstruction that has taken with it some of the most important buildings in the borough's history, such as the Old Dutch Mustard Company in Williamsburg, and threatens several others, including the Domino Sugar Refinery, a brick Romanesque Revival structure that once housed one of the largest refineries in the world, where more than half the sugar consumed in the United States was processed. The areas most at risk are all located at the Greenpoint-Williamsburg waterfront, which has been rezoned by the New York City Council, allowing for the razing of 180 blocks to make room for new and larger buildings. The nearby Atlantic Yards has been the focus of a major battle for the right to either preserve or destroy nearly eight million square feet of neighborhood to make room for high-rise co-ops and condos, office space, and a new basketball arena.* Bringing down the physical structures on the waterfront would dramatically reconfigure an area that from the nineteenth century through the end of World War II was for many people more than simply a place to go to work—it was the very best definition of the American dream.

* For the full Atlantic Yards story, see pages 271–72.

JULIUS ZOCAMPO: I was born in Brooklyn on Hamilton Avenue in Red Hook in 1927—the year the Babe hit his sixty, the year Esso came out with the first gasoline and Lindbergh crossed the Atlantic; a pretty good year. In those days Red Hook was all piers, mostly on Union Street. I remember my parents bought a house in the late twenties right after I was born for about $15,000, which was a lot of money in those days. Seven years later they sold it for $7,000 and took on a much bigger mortgage for the next one. Those were the facts of Depression life in Brooklyn. Not so different from today in one respect: you have to work an awful lot of hours to pay the mortgage. Numbers change, life doesn't change.

As soon as I was old enough, I worked for the Cosmopolitan Shipping Company. They had cruise liners, passenger ships, cargo ships, oil tankers. I was very happy in my job. I was getting paid well, working for a fellow called Boyce, who had come out of the Maritime Administration to head our company. Eventually they called him back to Washington to help run the Marshall Plan after World War II.

While I worked I went to school at night to study accounting, and climbed up the ladder until ten years later I was assistant treasurer of Cosmopolitan; four years after that I was secretary-treasurer. We had interests in Argentina. When they couldn't pay us in pesos down there, they gave us a company instead, one that made air conditioners. So we inherited this company called Field Argentina and we built a thousand houses in Brazil and Argentina. We also acquired an interest in a manganese mine in Brazil when we got paid with two small submarines and turned them into tenders. It was an interesting time.

On the passenger side, we were the forerunner of what the United States Line became. We operated a company called America-France, a passenger cruise operation, in the twenties until it was stolen away by other interests. We kind of got screwed over on that. We also had tankers in the days when you could have charter parties, meaning you could rent out the tankers to carry oil from one place to another, and the fee would be enough to cover the entire cost of the ship. In other words, we would buy a tanker for $2 million, have a $5 million charter party for two or three years, and all of a sudden we'd have $5 million in the bank and a tanker. Some of them we didn't need, so we would scrap them for the metal and the capital gain advantage.

That continued until 1969, when the United States government finally changed the tax laws and it no longer was possible to make a profit on anything but bulk cargo. But by then we had our fleet of tankers and were doing great business. It was a terrific time for shipping in New York City.

The Defense Department announced in 1964 that it would be closing the once-thriving Navy Yard within two years. This announcement came six years after the Dodgers had departed Brooklyn, a time when the glorious venues of downtown Brooklyn were disappearing one after another and long-standing neighborhoods were crumbling as white flight hit its peak.

In 1965 Robert F. Kennedy, then senator from New York, visited the Navy Yard and promised to do whatever he could to save the jobs of the remaining eleven thousand civilians who depended on it for their livelihood. A year later, the storied Brooklyn Navy Yard officially shut down for good, and its future became a prize that various political figures, including Meade Esposito, tried to use to enrich themselves.

Esposito was born in Brownsville in 1907 and, after dropping out of high school, rose through the borough ranks. In 1960 he was elected the Democratic district leader from Canarsie, winning on a platform to weed out corruption and implement across-the-board reform within the corrupt factions of his party. However, by the time he "retired" in 1983, he had become a multimillionaire through a series of overtly corrupt operations, the most notorious of all having to do with what happened to the Brooklyn Navy Yard after the Department of Defense decided to close it.

His mob connections didn't hurt his ambitions. He was always cozy with the Brooklyn-based Genovese family, particularly Federico "Fritzy" Giovanelli, whose mob specialties were loan sharking, bookmaking, gambling, and extortion, and who answered only to Vincent "the Chin" Gigante, godfather of the Genovese family. It was Fritzy who dubbed Esposito the Genoveses' "goombah," a term of affection within the hierarchy of the mob. It was the Chin's liking of and appreciation for the practically unlimited power of Esposito that saved the politico's life when he called Fritzy at home one Thanksgiving morning to wish his family a happy holiday. Unfortunately, when Fritzy's wife answered, Esposito called her "Gail," the name of Fritzy's *comare*, or mistress.

Otherwise, Esposito was a canny operator who had a piece of virtually every business and real-estate deal in Brooklyn between 1969 and 1987, a span of years that almost exactly coincides with Brooklyn's economic decline. Whatever Esposito made, Gigante got his percentage, in return for which he proudly dubbed Esposito "the undisputed boss of the whole fucking state." As described by Jack Newfield and Wayne Barrett in their powerful exposé of the corruption of late-twentieth-century politics in New York City, Esposito was "menacing, funny, smart, tough, obscene, Machiavellian, volatile, sentimental, and quotable. He was devious but acted like a noble primitive, without guile or guilt." It was this that made him so effective and gave him the means to acquire nearly unlimited power.

Esposito was able to influence Mayor Ed Koch's choice of who would run the city corporation that administered the Brooklyn Navy Yard, leasing parts of the property to private owners as a way to keep those who had worked at the Navy Yard employed. Esposito also made a hefty profit off every ship that docked at the facility, thanks to the fact that the company controlling two-thirds of the yard's rental space was a client of the insurance brokerage firm in which Esposito was a principal. Another revelation was that the hot dog vendor at the yard had somehow managed to cash hundreds of thousands of dollars in city checks made out to other, nonexistent vendors and employees, money that was then used as kickbacks to city administrators, Esposito chief among them. But when the corruption surrounding the Navy Yard's operations was finally cleaned up, much of the dry-dock business that was left at the Navy Yard dried up, and a great, gray stillness came over the yard, even as the city's economic fortunes improved in the 1990s.

Then, in April 1999, the Academy Award-winning actor Robert De Niro and the independent film moguls Harvey and Bob Weinstein—all native New Yorkers—were approached by Mayor Rudy Giuliani about the possibility of building a Hollywood-sized, fully operational movie studio on the site of the Brooklyn Navy Yard. While that deal was still in the works, out of nowhere a competing bid came in for the property from Douglas Steiner, of Steiner Equities, who also wanted to build a movie studio, and before anyone knew what was happening, Steiner's offer was accepted.

De Niro and the Weinsteins were furious, publicly accusing the mayor of having played them off Steiner to jack up the price of the deal. Giuliani was angry, too, because he'd been caught flat-footed—incredibly, no one in Giuliani's administration had bothered to clear the finalizing of the Steiner deal with the mayor until after it was signed, sealed, and delivered. How could such a thing have happened? insiders wondered. Part of the answer lay in an ongoing rivalry between two of Giuliani's most powerful underlings, Randy L. Levine, the deputy mayor who was responsible for corporate economic development in the city who had strongly supported the De Niro bid, and Rudy Washington, head of business services for the city, who favored the Steiner Equities plan.

If Giuliani, De Niro, the Weinsteins, and Levine were unhappy, Steiner and his partners in the project were ecstatic. As it was put by Lou Madigan, a computer consultant who, with Cary Hart, a movie set designer, were partners with Steiner in the joint venture: "This is the coolest thing to happen to Brooklyn since the Dodgers won the World Series at Ebbets Field."

Doug Steiner: I was born in Newark, New Jersey. I am now in charge of the largest studio project on the East Coast, 280,000 interconnected square feet, built on the Brooklyn Navy Yard, which is 261 acres. The yard itself is now an industrial park, with a view of the financial district of Manhattan. The original site, with its barracks and its officers' club on twenty-five acres of greenery, already looked very much like the perfect spot for a major movie studio back lot.

The studio actually was conceived before I got involved, by two men who were doing some work in the Navy Yard [Louis Madigan and Cary Hart] and thought the two unused administration buildings that existed would be perfect for making movies. One was in the set construction business, the other had an Internet business. They took it as far as they could, but they were not experienced developers and didn't have a whole lot of capital, so, eventually, we stepped into their shoes and took over. Before I got involved, the two were partnered by the city with Miramax, and Robert De Niro's company, Tribeca Productions. They quickly got mired down in negotiations that lasted for more than a year, some of it reportedly contentious, and at that point I saw an opening and I made a move. The old saying is true—the real estate business in New York City is a contact sport. In March 1999 I stepped into the breach that had developed. I'm a real tenacious son of a bitch and made an offer to the city that, in terms of what we wanted and what we could contribute, turned out to be the right one, and six weeks later I had completely taken over the project. The day I moved my office from New Jersey to Brooklyn was the day I knew I was in the movie business for real.

Five years later, despite an avalanche of doubters and naysayers, all of whom have since changed their minds, we opened our doors in November 2004. The first production made with our facilities was *The Producers*, which had an incredibly beautiful set. Everyone who came to see it from Hollywood said the same thing, that the quality of workmanship was incredible, the best in the world. And we've been full ever since, employing over a thousand people a day. We've just completed the first-ever Disney film made in New York City, called *Enchanted*. Disney's coming to Brooklyn is as significant, I think, as when it first came to Broadway with *Beauty and the Beast*, to Forty-second Street and the reestablishment of the Amsterdam Theater, and by extension, midtown Manhattan.

The unused yard was a diamond in the rough, waiting for someone to come along and unleash its potential, which we did. It had been down on its luck in pre-Giuliani New York. Today, if Giuliani's legacy is, apart from his heroism during 9/11, the rebirth of New York City, Bloomberg's will surely be the amazing rebirth and transformation of Brooklyn. Twenty years ago New York City, and Brooklyn especially, was an entirely different city.

The Navy Yard itself, located at the confluence of the Manhattan Brooklyn Bridge and Williamsburg Bridges on one side, and the Brooklyn-Queens Expressway on the other, is not something most New Yorkers born after World War II are all that familiar with, because for so long it was private and not at all open to the public. It was not even a factor for tourists who wanted to see what they believed were the crucial sites of New York City–the Statue of Liberty, the Empire State Building, Times Square, Rockefeller Center.

This is a purpose-built facility, really a boutique hotel for outside production, if you will, a fabulously deluxe service organization. We don't as yet produce our own shows or movies, but we hope to. We can service any production with everything from sets to writers, facilities, and state-of-the-art equipment.

The weather in New York City is not the weather in California, but the crews here are not used to having California facilities; they're used to working in decrepit armories where the roofs leak and there's no power, and they are able to adapt to almost any condition, no matter how difficult. What we provide are ideal conditions, the best in New York City, certainly, if not the entire East Coast. We have ambitious plans to continue to expand, to accommodate set construction, add writers' cottages, special effects laboratories, screening rooms, TV production facilities, all of which will make us even more autonomous.

We have a master plan in conjunction with the city and the Navy Yard to develop more stages and support space, over time evolving to what is the equivalent of the old Hollywood Universal, Paramount, and MGM lots. We are, right now, state of the art, the equal of or better than anything in L.A. We don't see our competition as the West Coast but all the other places that have come on as major motion picture production centers, like Toronto, like North Carolina, or even Eastern

Europe, who provide huge tax-incentive programs. We also want to take some business back from Canada and put it in Brooklyn. Film is one of America's greatest products, and all the money it generates belongs here, not overseas.

I see this studio complex as a vision of twenty-first-century Brooklyn. We've already brought tens of thousands of direct and indirect jobs back into the borough of Brooklyn. Traditionally, the film business in New York has never been more than a $5 billion industry at its peak. We think we can double that, to $10 billion, and that $20 billion annually is easily attainable in the next ten years.

Brooklyn is undergoing profound optimal conditions for development and, really, what amounts to a renaissance. We are now the safest major city in the United States. In Manhattan, there are virtually no bad neighborhoods left. In Brooklyn, there are still a few, but where we are, in Williamsburg, it's perfectly safe. As a rite of passage, kids getting out of college anywhere in the country no longer have the kind of reluctance to move to New York that was prevalent when I was younger. All the outflow of the second half of the twentieth century has reversed itself. Now, NYU's film school, Columbia's film school, and all the talent that wants to live here—stars, directors, and producers—are all great for the film business. Students, in particular, no longer seek to make the migratory trek out west, as it were, to join the industry. The industry has come east and joined them. We have an internship program with Brooklyn College, and in the future hope to expand that to other schools in the vicinity. One day we hope to bring one of the major film schools aboard to work with us.

Finally, what's truly great about Brooklyn, I feel, is that it's more of a community than Manhattan. The first thing I hear Brooklynites ask each other is, "What high school did you go to?"

In 2007, Steiner announced that he was doubling the size of his studio. His goal, he says, is to create "Burbank on the East Coast." Stranger and more unbelievable things have happened in Brooklyn.

✖ ✖ ✖

MORE FAMOUS BROOKLYNITES

JOHN PACELLA (1956-): Pitched in the major leagues between 1977 and 1986 for both the Mets and the Yankees, as well as for other teams.

BRUCE PALTROW (1943-2002): Television and film producer. Husband of Blythe Danner, father of Gwyneth Paltrow.

JOSEPH PAPP (1921-1991): The son of Russian Jewish immigrants. Founded the New York Shakespeare Festival in 1954 and, in 1967, the legendary Public Theater (now called the Joseph Papp Public Theater).

JOE PATERNO (1926-): Graduated from Brooklyn Prep and attended Brown University. At the age of eighty, completed his fiftieth year as head coach of Penn State's football team.

FLOYD PATERSON (1935-2006): Former heavyweight boxing champion of the world.

JOE PEPITONE (1940-): Colorful first baseman for the New York Yankees from 1962 to 1969. Introduced hair dryers into the locker room.

RHEA PERLMAN (1948-): Actress best known for her role on the TV sitcom *Cheers.* Married to actor/producer/director Danny DeVito.

RICO PETROCELLI (1943-): Americo Peter "Rico" Petrocelli was a major league shortstop. Played his entire career for the Boston Red Sox.

NORMAN PODHORETZ (1930-): Born to Jewish immigrants from Central Europe. Raised in the Brownsville section of Brooklyn. Editor of *Commentary* magazine from 1960 until his retirement in 1995, after which served as editor-at-large. Wrote the influential essay "My Negro Problem—and Ours" in 1963. Father of syndicated columnist John Podhoretz.

DOC POMUS (1925-1991): Born Jerome Solon Felder. Legendary blues singer and Brill Building songwriting alumnus. Co-wrote (with Mort Shuman) dozens of pop tunes for the biggest acts of the sixties, including the Drifters, Elvis Presley, Andy Williams, Bobby Rydell, the Coasters, the Beach Boys, the Byrds, the McCoys, and Dion.

PRISCILLA PRESLEY (1945-): Born Priscilla Beaulieu (aka Priscilla Ann Wagner). Married Elvis Presley.

LOU REED (1942-): Singer-songwriter, guitarist, member of the Velvet Underground.

THELMA RITTER (1905-1969): Movie, TV, and stage character actress. Received six Academy Award nominations. Appeared with James Stewart and Grace Kelly in *Rear Window*.

MAX ROACH (1924-2007): Pioneering jazz drummer. Played with such be-bop greats as Charlie Parker, Miles Davis, and Clifford Brown.

CHRIS ROCK (1965-): Born in South Carolina, Rock grew up in Bed-Stuy. Stand-up comic, movie star, creator of the autobiographical TV sitcom *Everybody Hates Chris*. Hosted the Academy Awards. Was a member of the *Saturday Night Live* ensemble for three seasons.

MICKEY ROONEY (1920-): Born Joseph Yule Jr. into a vaudeville family. Changed his name to Mickey Rooney and became the biggest Hollywood box-office star of the 1930s. Appeared in hundreds of movies and TV shows. Has been married eight times.

HERBERT ROSS (1927-2001): Film director, producer, choreographer. Won the Los Angeles Film Critics Association award for Best Director and a Golden Globe for Best Director for *The Turning Point* (1977).

CARL SAGAN (1934-1996): Astronomer, astrobiologist.

ALBERT SALMI (1928-1990): Theater, screen and TV character actor. Proponent of Lee Strasberg's Method acting.

ADAM SANDLER (1966-): Brooklyn-born actor, producer, comedian. Former cast member of *Saturday Night Live*.

LAWRENCE SCHILLER (1936-): Journalist, collaborator (with Norman Mailer, Albert Goldman, and others). Winner of an Emmy Award for the miniseries *Peter the Great* (1986).

CHARLES SCHUMER (1950-): U.S. senator from New York.

ERICH SEGAL (1937-): Son of a rabbi. Attended Midwood High School. Most famous for writing the popular romantic novel *Love Story*, the basis for the highest-grossing movie of 1971. Taught at Harvard, Yale, Princeton, and Oxford.

MAURICE SENDAK (1928-): Son of Polish Jewish immigrant parents. Writer and illustrator of children's books, including 1963's *Where the Wild Things Are*. Was heavily influenced by the animated stylings of the Walt Disney studio.

JERRY SEINFELD (1954–): Stand-up comic, best known for his TV series *Seinfeld*.

IRENE MAYER SELZNICK (1907–1990): Theatrical producer. Daughter of MGM mogul Louis B. Mayer, wife of David O. Selznick.

CHAPTER NINE

WHADDYA GOT TO EAT?

Every day after school we'd go to one of the Jewish delis
that were on every corner. We would bust our butts to get
a frank, with sauerkraut, mustard, a knish, an egg cream,
all of it for under 50 cents.

—BILLY DAWN SMITH

MMIGRANTS BRING WITH THEM new types of food and new techniques to prepare it, and Brooklyn has benefited from this great bounty. It has been the home of some of the nation's best ethnic restaurants, which cater to an immigrant clientele while serving the entire city. Jamaican restaurants flourish in Flatbush alongside Trinidadian, Guyanese, Barbadian (fantastic coo-coo), and Haitian places. On Fulton Street the offerings include dishes from Senegal, Guinea, Ghana, and Nigeria. In Coney Island, there are Russian ravioli walkins, Pakistani curry houses, places that serve Turkish, Georgian, Uzbek, Tajik, Afghan, and Israeli specialties. On Atlantic Avenue and in Bay Ridge there are Yemeni, Egyptian, Moroccan, Syrian, and Lebanese offerings. Sudanese snacks are plentiful in Bed-Stuy. On the Coney Island boardwalk, Shatzkin's knishes are eaten off the wax paper they come in, drowned with spicy brown mustard or perhaps a little of Tillie's hand-ground horseradish.* And, of course, the single most identifiable "Brooklyn" food of all, the hot dog, especially the ones served up fresh and tasty from Nathan's on Coney Island.

Alas, some of the most legendary places no longer exist, such as the late and greatly lamented Ebinger's bakery, renowned the world over for its classic crumb buns and insanely perfect blackout cake. A Brooklyn fixture for half a century, Ebinger's, a modest chain that linked Brooklyn's neighborhoods via sweet tooth, finally went under in the 1970s. Like the Dodgers, Ebinger's remains irreplaceable.

Junior's is an altogether different story. In downtown Brooklyn, where it has been since the borough's glory years after World War II, Junior's Deli is still renowned for its hot pastrami and corned beef and worshipped for its legendary cheesecake. Situated near the first Brooklyn stop on the D train headed out of Manhattan, Junior's takes up the entire corner of DeKalb Avenue and the Flatbush Avenue extension.

Entering Junior's wide front doors, the first thing a visitor notices is the aroma of freshly baked pastries coming from the right side: still-warm pans of coffee rings, Danish, crumb-topped pies made with every fruit imaginable, and of course that famous cheesecake. To the left is the deli take-out counter, where the aroma of pickles and garlic hangs in the air. Beyond the entrance, a ballroom-sized main dining room awaits, where waitresses and waiters outfitted in orange and white stripes serve up heaping portions of the food that defines how the good life should taste.

Junior's, like so many of Brooklyn's best restaurants, is still family-owned. Its original owner, Harry Rosen, the child of European Jewish immigrants arrived in the New World at the close of the nineteenth century and settled on Manhattan's Lower East Side. By the age of six-

---

* During the Depression, the original Brooklyn-based Tillie did all the grinding by hand, while her husband sold it from a pushcart. Today, Tillie's is based on Long Island and is the largest manufacturer of horseradish in the world.

teen, Harry and his brother Mike were running their own luncheonette, the Enduro Sandwich Shop, in Manhattan, with an eye toward
expansion. They soon had four Manhattan locations, and began thinking of adding a fifth restaurant in Brooklyn.

Their timing couldn't have been better. By the late 1920s, all of
Brooklyn was thriving. The waterfront was employing tens of thousands of longshoremen and truckers, private industry was building factory after factory to manufacture everything from glass works to
stoves. Domino Sugar had built its main plant in the borough. The
fabled cellophane-wrapped Drake's cakes, a breakfast staple for native
New Yorkers, were made in Brooklyn. Yuban roasted its coffee beans
in the borough, Boar's Head manufactured its cold cuts there, and the
legendary Fox's U-Bet syrup was being made and bottled in Brownsville
(where it still is to this day). The pharmaceutical company Pfizer built
a plant in Williamsburg, and John Mack, the founder of Mack Trucks,
shifted his gears in Brooklyn.

The borough's nightlife was jumping as well, with vaudeville the main
after-work attraction. The Albee Theater, at Fulton and DeKalb, head-
lined such legendary live acts as Bill "Bojangles" Robinson. Robinson's
1925 opening night at the Albee was an event of such importance and
prestige that it was attended by many of the biggest names in show
business, including Eddie Cantor, Ed Wynn, and Al Jolson. Three years
later the Brooklyn Paramount opened its doors, offering live shows
plus a feature-length movie. Not long after, the competing Fox chain
opened the Brooklyn Fox a block south, at Nevins and Fulton, boast-
ing the largest pipe organ in the world (until Radio City installed an
even bigger one).

With so much going on, a lot of people needed to be fed. In February 1929, Harry Rosen decided the time was perfect to expand. His
new Brooklyn eatery, in a storefront rented from the Dime Savings
Bank, offered a rich menu of Jewish delicacies—corned beef, roast
beef, tongue, brisket, egg salad, whitefish salad, all served on freshly
baked breads. The restaurant caught on and was making a lot of money
until the stock market crash in October 1929. Soon, however, business

dried up and the Rosens were forced to sell off the Manhattan location so they might salvage just this one.

It wasn't until 1932 and the repeal of Prohibition, when beer and wine could be put back onto the menu, that the restaurant business began to show signs of renewed life in downtown Brooklyn. Not long after, Rheingold, Schaefer, and Piels all opened breweries in Brooklyn, which overnight became the largest beer-producing center in the United States.

MARVIN AND WALTER ROSEN: The repeal of Prohibition spurred my father to imagine a more full-scale restaurant, not just a sandwich shop but one with casual dining and a bar. Once the shop next door was vacated, my father expanded the space and the menu. As part of the new Enduro, he created a unique bar, one that surrounded an elevated bandstand. The Enduro Sandwich Shop became the Enduro Restaurant and Café, complete with cocktails and live entertainment.

Soon, at the corner of Flatbush and DeKalb, in the heart of downtown Brooklyn, Enduro was *the* place for a cocktail and dinner before attending a show at the Paramount or Albee, and afterward it was the obligatory stop for coffee and cheesecake, a malt, or an ice cream soda.

MARVIN AND WALTER ROSEN: Into the 1940s, Brooklyn was the world. At least that's what we thought. Nearly 2.5 million people from all over the world–Italians, Irish, African Americans, Jews, Poles, Russians, Arabs, Greeks, Chinese, Japanese, Scandinavians, Swedes, Germans, Puerto Ricans, West Indians, and Cubans lived here, all mixed together in some twenty-five different sections of Brooklyn. . . . The thrilling thing was that all of Brooklyn belonged to everybody–from Nathan's Famous hot dog stand in Coney Island to the posh Roof Top Restaurant of the Hotel Bossert in Brooklyn Heights; from Abe Stark's Men's Clothiers on Pitkin Avenue in Brownsville to Frederick Loeser's department store on Fulton Street; from a corner grocery in Flatbush to the huge Wallabout Market by the Navy Yard; from Lundy's seafood in Sheepshead Bay to the

tender steaks and chops at the Enduro across from the Brooklyn Paramount. It was all yours, mine, anybody's for a nickel, the cost of a trolley ride.

In 1942, the Enduro expanded further, all the way to the corner, as
it continued to do huge business among the workers and servicemen
who came over from the bustling Navy Yard.

MARVIN AND WALTER ROSEN: When the Paramount premiered *It Happened
in Brooklyn* [1947], the blocks stretching either side of Flatbush Avenue
Extension and DeKalb swarmed with thousand of fans. Frank Sinatra,
Jimmy Durante, and Peter Lawford, who starred in the picture, had
trolleyed over the Brooklyn Bridge for opening day. I don't think we saw
crowds like that again until later in the 1950s when the rock 'n' roll idols
played the Paramount. The Enduro was always packed. During those
years it seemed as if we never closed.

Although it seemed the high life would last forever, a noticeable
downturn began within weeks after the end of World War II. Peacetime brought an end to the borough-wide economic boom that had
emanated from the Navy Yard. As if to mark the end of the good times,
the famous nickel subway and trolley ride, the city's long-standing symbol for nearly a half century of working-class freedom, suddenly rose
to a dime. The trolley then disappeared altogether, replaced by the
automobile, the favored vehicle of the peacetime middle class.

Anticipating the coming middle-class exodus, the automobile
allowed shoppers to head for the new suburban malls, thus cutting
down on the pedestrian traffic in downtown Brooklyn. By 1949, just
three years after Enduro's best one, the Rosens were forced to close
the place down.

But Harry Rosen was a fighter, and he refused to believe the shut-
tering of the Enduro meant the end of his long run on Flatbush and
DeKalb. In a last-ditch effort he went to the Dime Savings Bank and

managed to negotiate a reduced rent, surrendered some of the space he had taken over during the good times, and reopened as a new, family-style restaurant he christened Junior's in honor of his two sons.

At first it was tough going. Many of the larger surrounding retail operations eventually went under. The Brooklyn Paramount didn't make it through the sixties, nor did the Fox or the Albee. Downtown Brooklyn was particularly hard hit. In the seventies the neighborhood took on a bombed-out look as hundred-year-old buildings either decayed or burned down, more often than not set afire by their owners for the insurance.

Things finally started turning around for the city in 1973, when a onetime accountant named Abe Beame, Brooklyn-born and Tammany-bred, won the mayoralty from John Lindsay and set about restoring some economic stability. That same year, Manhattan-centric *New York* magazine's highly influential "Underground Gourmet" traveled over the bridge for the first time to see what was up with Brooklyn's famed eateries and chose Junior's as an example of the finest the borough had to offer. Not long after, the *Village Voice* voted Junior's as having the best cheesecake in the city, and tour guides began to travel over the Brooklyn Bridge to include Junior's on their routes.

RON ROSENBAUM: Junior's cheesecake is the simultaneous experience of creamy and dense impenetrable richness, it is a single enthralling bell-toned flavor, and a bewilderingly complex play of many exciting and subtle flavor overtones. It makes—as Carl Reiner and Mel Brooks once said—your mouth want to throw a party for your tongue. Most people who taste it the first time are unable to suppress an involuntary moan and shudder.

Peter Luger's Steakhouse, in the Williamsburg section of Brooklyn, has been in existence since 1887 (there is one more Peter Luger's, farther out on Long Island) and is considered by New Yorkers of all boroughs to be the best steakhouse in the city. If it's hip to go to the

Palm or Gallagher's, both of which are in Manhattan, it's even hipper to be willing to venture all the way into Brooklyn for a steak, *if* that steak comes from the kitchen of Peter Luger.

ALAN KING: Peter Luger is one of the great steakhouses of the world. I lived in Williamsburg when I was a kid. I can remember at lunchtime, all the Wall Street moguls would get in their limousines and would come over the Williamsburg Bridge to Peter Luger for lunch. From twelve to two the entire street was filled with limousines. I used to take my lunch, in a brown bag, an egg salad sandwich on a kaiser roll, and stand on a little box and stare into the window. I'd see those porterhouse steaks and those hash brown potatoes and the fried onions as big as your fist. Someday, I'd tell myself, I'm going to be able to afford to eat at Peter Luger. Of course, now I can buy Peter Luger, but the irony is I can't eat there because of my dietary restrictions—no red meat!

Peter Luger's for steak and Junior's for cheesecake, and for that last after-coffee piece of candy, a chocolate-covered marshmallow twist (preferably frozen), a chocolate-covered cherry ring, or a half-moon of halva—Milton Berle used to say that whenever he was asked what halva was, he'd reply, "An Oh Henry! candy bar dipped in cement!"—these are just a few of the many delicacies turned out by the Brooklyn-based family-owned Joyva Company, whose headquarters have been located in the same factory building since 1929.

RICHARD RADUTZKY: We've heard halva described as tasting like everything from sawdust to mortar to caulking. Some think it's like a Butterfinger bar, only smoother.

MILTON RADUTZKY: How the Jews latched on to it, I don't know. Maybe Daddy was instrumental in making it happen. We were fortunate to ride with the flow of European-to-Brooklyn heritage. My dad, Nathan, came over from Kiev, Ukraine, in 1904 to escape political upheaval, with this recipe for making halva. He was in the grain business there, so that's how he knew about sesame and sesame seeds. It was more of a food in the old country than a candy. You'd come home from school, you'd schmear some halva on a roll, and it was nourishing.

He landed in Ellis Island, like all the immigrants did. I don't believe he had any relatives here; I think he was the first to come over. He located with his wife on the Lower East Side, and two years later, in 1906, opened a little retail and wholesale store on Orchard Street, where he sold to the public and also to the pushcarts that were prevalent in the day, to sell the halva and other candies he made. Two years after that they decided to leave the East Side and move to Brooklyn.

Actually, halva had been around for quite a while. Its origins are Middle Eastern. *Halva* is Turkish for "sweetmeat." I don't know if he stole the recipe, or whatever, but he made it his own in the United States. The original company was called Independent Halva and Candies, Inc. That name was changed much later to "Joyva" when my brother's daughter gave birth to a girl named Rosalind Joy. He was friendly with someone in an ad agency in Baltimore who came up with the name of the Joyva Corporation. Joy was his daughter's name, hence Joyva. The famous corporate symbol, the Turkish man with the turban, was also from the ad agency. These days I'm not so sure it's the best advertising for us. At one point we even thought of changing it.

RICHARD RADUTZKY: After September 11, interestingly enough, we received a fair share of hate mail and phone calls for our sultan symbol. Amazingly, they associated him with terrorists! But we kept him because he was pretty recognizable as a brand, and besides, we trusted him and knew he wasn't capable of anything worse than a potential case of heartburn.

MILTON RADUTZKY: Once in Williamsburg, my father opened up another store, a little bigger than the last, and stayed there for about four years, until 1918, when he started having children. In 1916 we moved into the location where we still are, on Varick Avenue in Williamsburg. Nathan had four boys, of which I am the baby. He came to Brooklyn after he'd brought his two brothers and three sisters from the Old World and simply needed more room. Williamsburg offered more space than the Lower East Side, and an opportunity came along to get the plant, which was already built. I don't know what it was used for, but there was a horse barn next to it, so who knows. Maybe they made hot dogs there.

Our products were real candy-store-counter items, which is one of the reasons they were so popular in Brooklyn and parts of the rest of the city, where there were always a lot of corner candy stores. In those days, back in our first years, there were no supermarkets, just mom-and-pop stores. At first, we sold our goods off a wagon or a little truck, traveling from store to store. We'd walk in and ask the proprietor to sell our candies. We had a decent product, and usually they'd say yes. We were always very friendly, and kept up relationships on a one-to-one level, which was extremely important as a way of doing business in the neighborhoods. The candies, ours and our competitors', tasted more or less the same. It was service and attitude that made the difference, and of course, quality control of the product. There were tons of candy stores, especially in Brooklyn, hundreds along Pitkin Avenue alone, sometimes two or three on every block. I don't know what you can relate it to today. Maybe neighborhood bars.

RICHARD RADUTZKY: Yeah, it was the place where everybody hung out. There were pinball machines, jukeboxes, egg creams, and tons of our candy on the counter.

MILTON RADUTZKY: We had the one plant, and eventually added two or three buildings to it, as the product line extended, from halva to jellies, marsh-mallows, to sesame candies and tahini. Somewhere along the way tahini became a viable product all its own, especially in health food stores because of its protein, antioxidant qualities, and polyunsaturation.* We got new equipment to make the new candies, and we continued to make all our products right in these buildings, from the processing of the

---

* Tahini is sesame seed paste.

sesame seeds to the packaging and delivering. We began with the moon shapes, and then the square logs.

RICHARD RADUTZKY: I have to say, though, that as much as a survivor as we are, it's been getting exponentially harder to keep doing business in Brooklyn and New York. It's expensive, the labor—we employ up to seventy people—the overhead, the energy, all these costs have gone through the roof. Taxes too. Yet it's a trade-off because it's a great place to do business, at least for us. With our sesame products alone we do twenty-five thousand pounds a day, maybe more on the halva side. We are the largest halva producer in the country, all of it mixed by hand. When we introduced it here in Brooklyn, both halva and Joyva became associated with the borough as its original birthplace, which of course it is not.

Our biggest customer base is within a hundred-mile radius for us, although we do do business in the major markets throughout the country. In Los Angeles, for instance, there's a huge Russian area, and they are big customers. In Miami we also do a lot of business, because there are so many transplanted Brooklynites down there. It's not as accessible in some other markets, say South Carolina, but it's available and it's there, and we get a lot of calls from people who say, "Oh my God, I grew up in Brooklyn, where can I find your candy? I miss my childhood!" It's nostalgia, to be sure, but it's also a very real, nostalgic link to the memories of childhood for a lot of kids who grew up on the streets and in the neighborhoods of Brooklyn for most of the twentieth century. When young men went to war in the '40s, we used to get requests for care packages of our candy, and we always sent them out to thank the boys for all they were doing and to give them a little taste of home.

We had, at one time, three or four competitors, but we survived because we were better operators, and had what I'd like to think was a better product. My granddad had a great business sense, and he had cheap labor, meaning his sons.

MILTON RADUTZKY: Many big candy companies have tried to buy us out through the years, but we wouldn't go for it. We never wanted to work for anybody else. We were and are a family business. We all got along and that was the key. That's always been our strength. We are a Brooklyn family business, handed down from generation to generation, and we are not looking to become second cousins to a Snickers bar. We understand and appreciate the fact that Brooklynites are really nuts about their halva.

We bring out a new product every five hundred years. My oldest brother, Alex, did come up with the idea of "Miss Joyva," a contest that we ran in the fifties that was enormously popular. It was essentially a beauty contest, with all the girls dressed like harem girls. We held the event at Krum's chocolate shop. We were selling them some stuff and figured because they had so much room it would be the perfect place to hold the Miss Joyva contest. We were coming out with a new line of candy and wanted something that would catch the public's eye. We hired the chorus line from the Copacabana night club. We also gave a special award to Henny Youngman that night for mentioning halva so much in his act–a fifty-pound box of halva. The winner of the contest, by the way, was Joyce Stewart, one of the Copa's "pony girls." She became the official 1951 Joyva Queen.

RICHARD RADUTZKY: East Williamsburg, where our factory is, has been regenerated two, maybe three times. Same as the Lower East Side in Manhattan. It almost follows the same pattern. Upgrading one's life, looking for the greener pastures, the shortage of real estate, the rediscovery of certain neighborhoods once considered low-rent, the whole cycle. All of that. Today there are second, third, and fourth generations presently working for the company.

We have a big kosher-for-Passover business. It's like our Valentine's Day or Halloween. We actually prepare for Passover maybe six months in advance. A rabbi comes in and makes sure that all the ingredients are right.

MILTON RADUTZKY: At my bar mitzvah, they made me sit for a bust made out of halva. It was a family tradition.

RICHARD RADUTZKY: Times have changed, we're still here and still going strong. Why? Who knows. Maybe because sesame seeds are considered by some cultures to be aphrodisiacs.

Finally, what would a trip through Brooklyn food be without a little bravado between belches?

JOHN "CHA CHA" CIARCIA: I was born and raised in Little Italy, Mulberry Street, Manhattan, New York, my whole life, but always went to Brooklyn. To us, Brooklyn was an extension of the Lower East Side, just on the other side of the Manhattan Bridge, closer than midtown Manhattan. I hung out there half my life. A lot of my friends, my family and several businesses are in Brooklyn. There's a reason it's the fourth largest city in the country. Everybody loves it there. It's got a great zoo, for one thing. Brighton Beach, Sheepshead Bay, the Brooklyn Cyclones—where else you gonna find a borough, or a city even, like Brooklyn? Remember Jahn's, the ice cream parlor? We used to go into Brooklyn just to have some of their ice cream specialties.

I got back into Brooklyn on a more regular, business basis when I opened a bar in Coney Island. Then, in 2003, I went to Coney Island with the idea of starting an ice cream franchise. I realized after three weeks that it was a failure. Coney Island wouldn't accept gourmet Italian ice cream and ices. Go figure—they were willing to pay $3.50 for a hot dog, but they wouldn't pay $3 for a gelato, I guess because they were used to buying Italian ice and regular ice cream for a dollar. Being that I already had my café and a liquor license, I decided to turn the place into a nightclub. We called it "Cha-Cha's of Coney Island—the Home of Wild Women and Wise Guys."

We did things like wet T-shirt contests. After seeing a couple of them, I said, "Wait a minute. My name is on this place. I have to stop doing them because I don't want the vice squad coming down and locking me up one of these days." So we became a rock-and-roll funky Coney Island kind of place. We've been doin' great ever since.

The site of the club has a lot of history. At one time it was a place with singing waiters, like Eddie Cantor. Al Capone was a bouncer there. Durante, Bob Hope, a lot of them started there when it was called the Club Atlantis. It always had a roof deck, for entertainment and also for sunning in the summer, right there on the beach. For a while it was known as the Cowboy Bar, in the fifties. There was a big horseshoe bar in the middle of the club and there was this cowboy singer, a Gene Autry kind of guy, sitting in a chair playing country and western tunes. That was very successful. Then it was closed for a couple of years before reopening as the Atlantis Latino night club. After, they broke off a piece of it and leased it to Nathan's and it became a hot dog jernt. Until I came back and resurrected the Atlantis nightclub. And that's the history in a nutshell, so to speak.

Oh, one more thing. I'm opening a hot dog stand right opposite Nathan's, on Stillwell and Surf. I'm calling it "Big Al–the Hot-Dog King of Chicago." I'm gonna put a big picture of Al Capone in the dining room and feature Chicago-style hot-dogs and White Castle hamburgers.

I don't know how I can go wrong.

The financier and landlord of Cha Cha's hot-dog shop? Doug Steiner and Thor Equities.

✖ ✖ ✖

MORE FAMOUS BROOKLYNITES

HUBERT SELBY JR. (1928-2004): Nicknamed "Cubby." Selby lived on the same Bay Ridge block as his childhood friend writer Gilbert Sorrentino. Incapacitated by tuberculosis after a stint in the merchant marine. He turned to writing and produced a notorious novel of waterfront life, *Last Exit to Brooklyn,* which became an international outrage and sensation. Other novels included *The Room* and *Requiem for a Dream,* made into a well-regarded film.

BEN SHAHN (1898-1969): Lithuanian-born muralist, social activist, photographer, and teacher. Best known for his 1957 philosophical work *The Shape of Content.*

RAY SHARKEY (1952–1993): Film and TV actor. Winner of a Golden Globe for his performance in *The Idolmaker* (1980).

IRWIN SHAW (1913–1984): Playwright, novelist, screenwriter. Born Irwin Shamforoff. Graduated from Brooklyn College. Best known for his novel *The Young Lions*.

MORT SHUMAN (1936–1991): Singer-songwriter. Member of the Brill Building generation. He often collaborated with Doc Pomus. Wrote several of the most well-known rock/pop tunes of the sixties.

BENJAMIN "BUGSY" SIEGEL (1906–1947): Organized-crime figure. Built Las Vegas into a gambling mecca, killed before he could fully realize his dream. While living in Hollywood, Siegel was known as "King of the Sunset Strip." Partnered with Meyer Lansky to form the Jewish wing of Murder, Inc., a mob enforcement gang.

BEVERLY SILLS (1929–2007): Born Belle Miriam Silverman. Opera singer known for her coloratura soprano. After retiring from singing, Sills became, in succession, general manager of the New York City Opera, chair of Lincoln Center, and chair of the Metropolitan Opera.

HENRY SILVA (1928–): Puerto Rican character actor often cast as Asian. Minor, second-tier member of Sinatra Rat Pack.

PHIL SILVERS (1911–1985): Actor, comedian. Silvers was best known for his starring role as Sergeant Bilko in *The Phil Silvers Show*, aka *You'll Never Get Rich*. He appeared in several movies and Broadway shows.

GILBERT SORRENTINO (1929–2006): Prolific poet, critic, and writer of "metafictional" novels. Known for his seriocomic masterpiece *Mulligan Stew*. Much of his work rooted in native Bay Ridge, particularly *Steelwork*. Raised on the same block as childhood friend Hubert Selby Jr. Attended Fort Hamilton High School and Brooklyn College. Worked as an editor for Grove Press (where he edited *The Autobiography of Malcolm X*). Taught for many years at Stanford University before moving back to Bay Ridge in his last years.

PAUL SORVINO (1939–): Character actor, singer. Father of actress Mira Sorvino.

MICKEY SPILLANE (1918–2006): Novelist best known for his Mike Hammer novels.

BARBARA STANWYCK (1907–1990): Born Ruby Stevens. Became an internationally known Hollywood actress. Was nominated for four Academy Awards, including one for her best-remembered performance in Billy Wilder's 1944 suspense classic *Double Indemnity.*

CONSTANCE TALMADGE (1897–1973): Silent-film star.

VINNY TESTAVERDE (1963–): Football quarterback. Played for the New York Jets, among other teams.

IRVING THALBERG (1899–1936): Film producer at MGM. Known as "the Boy Wonder" until his early, untimely death.

GENE TIERNEY (1920–1991): Fashion model, actress.

MARISA TOMEI (1964–): Actress. Won the Academy Award for Best Supporting Actress for her performance in *My Cousin Vinny* (1992).

JOE TORRE (1940–): Baseball player, manager of multiple championship New York Yankees teams. Manager of the Los Angeles Dodgers. As a child rooted for the New York Giants.

RICHARD TUCKER (1913–1975): Born Ruvn Ticker. American tenor, cantor.

MIKE TYSON (1966–): Former world heavyweight boxing champion. Often called "Iron Mike." Once bit off a piece of his opponent's ear during a championship bout.

JERRY WALD (1911–1962): Hollywood producer, screenwriter.

ELI WALLACH (1915–): Actor. Star of dozens of movies. Exemplar of the Actors Studio method.

BISHOP F. D. WASHINGTON (1903–1988): Renowned Pentecostal minister of Brooklyn's Washington Temple Church of God in Christ. Ordained the Reverend Al Sharpton when Sharpton was nine years old.

WENDY WASSERSTEIN (1950–2006): Born to Polish immigrants (her father left Poland after being accused of spying on the government). Internationally renowned playwright, recipient of the 1989 Tony Award for Best Play and the Pulitzer Prize for *The Heidi Chronicles.*

MAE WEST (1893–1980): Actress, sex symbol, playwright, screenwriter.

HENNY YOUNGMAN (1906–1998): English-born. Grew up in Brooklyn. Violin-playing king of one-liners: "Take my wife—*please!*"

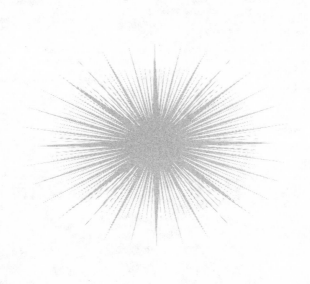

Leaving Brooklyn
Fuhgeddaboudit
Marty Markowitz
Borough President
Michael R. Bloomberg
Mayor

CHAPTER TEN

POLITICS AND POKER

BROOKLYN BOROUGH HALL—originally City Hall—was conceived in 1802, nearly a hundred years before the City of Brooklyn would be incorporated into the greater City of New York and reduced to one of the outer boroughs, though construction didn't even begin for another three decades and the building was not completed until 1848. It is now the headquarters of operations for Brooklyn's borough president, a position some consider more powerful than that of the mayor of New York.

From 1977 to 2001 that position was held by Howard Golden, under whose leadership Brooklyn underwent one of the most dramatic transformations in the history of urban enclaves.

HARVEY SCHULTZ: I was the executive assistant to Howard Golden, the Brooklyn borough president, from 1977 through 1986. Howard was a city councilman, a Borough Park–based Democrat, before he was the borough president, and was elected to that post first by the Council delegation and then again by the people.

There is a strong Democratic tradition in Brooklyn. A lot of people think it's mostly because of the large amounts of immigrants, who felt more represented by the Democratic Party than the Republicans, that the Democrats stood for the best interests of the working class, and the Republicans did not.

The Democratic organization in Brooklyn is the largest in the city and has a rich history. Through the years, Brooklyn-based Democrat leadership has always been made up of colorful characters, such as Meade Esposito, whom Howard Golden succeeded as councilman. The reason for that comes out of the tradition of the nineteenth-century Tammany Hall, or clubhouse politics, which many people then thought of as *good* for working-class people, and still do to this day. For many years, it was the *only* government Brooklyn knew, since Brooklyn Democrats, whether Stanley Steingut, Stanley Fink, Mel Miller, or Esposito, had the state government completely under their control. Most people don't realize or remember that in terms of politics, Brooklyn was far more powerful than Manhattan, because [Brooklyn] controlled the City Council. The majority leader of the City Council was always Democratic, always from Brooklyn, and the council, by virtue of representation, controlled the State Assembly. In addition, there used to be a Board of Estimate, also solidly Democratic and traditionally led by party bosses. Today, of course, state legislators are more independent, but tradition is a hard thing to let go of, mainly because it got politicians elected, *because it worked.*

Howard Golden was borough president during the height of this Brooklyn-favored state-dominating council power. He became borough president in 1977 and remained in that position until he was eventually forced out by term limits, which made room for Marty Markowitz, the present borough president, to succeed him. Howard came to office at a time when New York City in general and Brooklyn in particular were still recovering from the major population changes that were taking place throughout the city.

During the early days of his presidency, the older, Eastern European contingency of the city was leaving it en masse, some scurrying to the safety of the suburbs of Westchester, Long Island, Staten Island, others moving further south, mostly to Florida or the Southwest. They were all were replaced by a new generation of immigrants, coming up from the south, or from Puerto Rico, or the Caribbean, Asia, and Africa. New minorities were replacing old ones, and as a result the city experienced a major transition that some would define as an upheaval.

At the same time, much of the physical housing shortage wasn't being properly invested in by the private sector. Not only that, there was a lot of *dis*investment. I'd have to say, even if it sounds harsh, at least part of the reason was those population shifts. The people who owned the residences they'd once bought no longer wanted to live in the neighborhoods where their homes were. They wanted to sell off their houses as quickly as possible, mostly out of fear for their personal safety as well as the market values that seemed to be falling out of the bottom, and because of it, most of them wound up in the hands of speculators. As a result, there were less owner-occupied units.

The new residents had less experience living in urban centers, since most had come from rural places. They were not aware of what it took to live in the density that was Brooklyn. That provided more wear and tear, on the borough and on the residences. Housing stock rapidly devalued as it deteriorated. At the same time there had been a great influx of public housing in various neighborhoods in the fifties and sixties, especially in places like East New York and Brownsville that encouraged a whole new wave of immigration into those neighborhoods, which in turn elevated the fear level among those who had lived there for decades.

I grew up in a Jewish/Italian/Slavic neighborhood in East New York, and once the word spread that "the neighborhood is changing," people began to leave. They simply got into their cars and found new places to live. This massive turnover lasted into the seventies. Brooklyn, along with the rest of New York, was not helped by the great blackout [of 1965], the rapid downturns in the economy, and the city's growing fiscal crisis. Everyone remembers "Ford to City: Drop Dead," the famous October 30, 1975, headline the *Daily News* ran to underscore both the inner problems the city was having and the lack of any apparent interest or compassion by the federal government, which didn't want anything to do with New York City.

In Brooklyn, the results were particularly devastating. All the big hotels closed, all the major department stores except A&S [Abraham and Straus] closed, and the storied Fulton Mall in downtown Brooklyn changed overnight from a place that serviced the middle class to a lower-class hangout.

That was more or less the arena that Howard Golden stepped into when he became borough president. Fortunately, community boards were just coming into power, so there was something of a resurgence in community-level involvement going on. Howard was a fierce and passionate person, and said he was going to fight for the survival of Brooklyn to make sure that no matter what, its people got their fair share from the city, and the city, in turn, from the federal government. How, he demanded to know, and quite loudly, could Brooklyn, the equivalent of the fourth largest city in the country, have no more decent hotels? Without them, he asked, how could anyone want to or be able to conduct serious business in the borough?

He knew he couldn't turn Brooklyn completely upside down in a year, but he believed he could do it. As soon as he was elected he began to forge new relationships with the big banks and utilities of the day—Manny Hanny [Manufacturers Hanover Trust], Bankers Trust, Brooklyn Union Gas. "We're here," he told them, "we're not going away, and we deserve better!"

Howard was a savvy politician who knew what he wanted and how to get it. If there was going to be any further development in the city, he wanted some of it for Brooklyn. He particularly wanted to save the storied downtown area, which he considered to be Brooklyn's central business district.

Because he took on these battles so fiercely, he wasn't liked all that much, particularly by the mayor of New York City, Ed Koch. Howard looked at what the mayor was trying to do with Forty-second Street, for instance, and complained that Brooklyn was being short-shrifted and needed to get its fair share. As far as Howard was concerned, Koch represented a Manhattan juggernaut whose interest in their own cultural institutions and financial investments far outweighed what Brooklyn needed and was fairly entitled to. Howard took Koch and his people on. He used the City Council leadership, the state leadership, his influence at the Board of Estimate, and, most effectively, his own bully pulpit.

Whenever he felt he wasn't getting his fair share he simply put the brakes on and didn't cooperate, and, because of the strategic power he held via the City Council, he could bring Manhattan and at times the state to an impasse, if not an outright grinding halt. Back then, particularly in Brooklyn, there was a tremendous concentration of power, and Howard Golden was at the helm of it all. He had the courage and the ability to argue with Koch, and could make him blink; he had that much political clout.

Yes, Howard was irascible; yes, he had a big personality; yes, he said what he thought; and yes, he could be outrageous at times. But he got things done. Once people in power realized he wasn't going away, he was able to get a hell of a lot accomplished.

Under his auspices, the one overwhelming thing that changed was, ironically, the one thing that wasn't under his control. The trends that had created the difficulties in the city were finally beginning to reverse themselves. For all the credit that Howard and others deserve for turning Brooklyn around, the events statewide, nationally, and internationally all contributed. Money became more available, jobs opened up, and the immigrant lower middle class settled into being what the group was that it had replaced–the middle middle class. The desperations that had initially plagued the immigrant Eastern Europeans, the Latins, the Asians all began to fade as the leadership at the local level gradually included them. They began to take an interest in bettering their communities, and while Howard didn't initiate it, he certainly took advantage of it.

Because of it he was extremely popular among the people, much more so than the other politicians. He got along with all the neighbor-hood leaders and they got along with him. He believed everyone had a right to representation from the community level on up. Later on into his tenure and continuing after he left office, it was due to his policies that newer waves of immigration from all over the world wanted to come and live in Brooklyn, USA, where they thought they would be treated fairly and without bias. You go out to Sunset Park now, or Eighth Avenue, you see predominantly Asians. Go out to Brighton Beach, you'll see the Russians. Different neighborhoods have extraordinary combinations of Pakistani and Indians. It's amazing. It's called democracy.

Today, Brooklyn's economy is surging. There continues to be a major revival of upper-scale commerce right in line with the needs and the desires of the populace who shop locally. Lots of Eastern European mer-chants have set up businesses and a new generation of mom-and-pop stores has grown and expanded. It took many, many years for this to happen, for the neighborhoods and the business districts to reestablish themselves, for crime to go down. I'm not talking about organized crime, which I don't think was a priority in the years that Howard was in office. I'm talking about the crime where people were afraid to walk in the streets out of fear of being mugged.

Of course, organized crime did have a deleterious effect on every-one, since most street crime could be traced sooner or later, in most cases sooner, to drugs, and drugs were operated by the five Brooklyn crime families. Mostly, though, organized crime was perpetrated against one another, and that was not a governmental concern at the time.

Everyone in New York City, in or out of Brooklyn, benefited from the Golden era; it was a real renaissance and everybody in the country knows it, whether they know the name of Howard Golden or not. Peo-ple are no longer struggling to get out of Brooklyn. These days they're struggling to get in. Will there ever be a statue of Howard Golden for all he did? I don't think so. Politicians are rarely, if ever, considered heroes. There is a statue of Jackie Gleason as Ralph Kramden at the Port Author-ity bus terminal, and here in Brooklyn there is one of Pee Wee Reese and one of Jackie Robinson, out where the Cyclones play on Coney Island. These are more typically Brooklyn heroes.

CHARLES HYNES: I came out of law school and bounced around from job to job and finally ended up with the Legal Aid Society. After a couple of years I went into private practice. In 1969 a new DA was elected in Brooklyn, a former defense attorney—or, as I like to call them, a recovering defense lawyer, like me. He tried to recruit me and I decided it might be a good idea to go into the DA's office, learn all their dark secrets, and then go out and beat them over the head with it. I stayed on for six years because I kept on getting promoted, and then in the early seventies I became chief of the Brooklyn Rackets Bureau.

I was about to return to private practice in 1974 when the nursing home scandal blew up across the state. I was appointed by Governor Carey and Attorney General Louis Lefkowitz to investigate it. I stayed another six years doing that, until I was recruited by Ed Koch to become his fire commissioner. I did that for two years, then went back to private practice, where I was making a good living until called upon by the new governor, Mario Cuomo, to become the corruption prosecutor. I accepted the position and was the chief prosecutor in the famous Howard Beach case that happened in Queens, where the African American kid was chased onto the Belt Parkway by a crazed white mob, where he was hit by a car and died. I convicted three of the four charged for homicide, and they got substantial jail sentences.

I was about to return to private practice when the Brooklyn district attorney, Elizabeth Holtzman, was leaving to run for comptroller and I was encouraged to run as her replacement. I had no money, I think I raised all of $200,000, but I had a lot of notoriety and name recognition because of the Howard Beach case and managed to get elected to be the next Brooklyn district attorney. I had the support of the African American community and the broad spectrum of the Jewish community and that was enough. I had all of the African American community because the victim in the Howard Beach case was black. As for the Jews, I grew up in an eighty-four-family apartment house in Brooklyn, where the only two *goyish* families were the super and mine. I probably speak more Yiddish than most Jews. I was always accepted in their community and I'm proud of it. At one point, that connection–between me, an Irish Catholic, and Jews–was what Brooklyn was all about. A lot expressions that eventually became part of the English lexicon originally came out of the Brooklyn Yiddish idiom, like *chutzpah*, for example.

At the time I was elected, we had extensive organized crime activity in the borough. The so-called five families were operating in various locales throughout the county. The most exciting thing we did was something called the "Gold Bug," nicknamed after the district attorney at the time, Eugene Gold. It had to do with a listening device we planted in a trailer in the East New York section of Brooklyn that was run by a guy named Paulie Vario.

In the course of fifteen months, we had surveillances both inside the trailer from the listening device as well as observations made by detectives who were placed around the area. We were able to connect at different times members of each of the five organized crime families visiting Vario and involved in various deals with him. When we took the case down it was on the front page of every newspaper, not just in Brooklyn and in the country, but all over the world.

We had a long grand jury investigation and served hundreds of grand jury subpoenas. At the end of two years we had amassed about 150 convictions, everything from insurance fraud to extortion to illegal sports betting to attempted murder. It was a very successful operation.

Unfortunately, the long-term effect wasn't very much. The incredible amount of money that is generated by organized crime in Brooklyn doesn't lend itself to elimination. Even today, with the federal government's RICO program, the government can obtain jail sentences of up to a hundred years for conspiracy and have put some pretty important people away using it, but there's always someone new coming up to take their place.

Why did the five families huddle in Brooklyn in the first place? They were entrenched from the time they first came over as immigrants, and that's about the best answer. It was their long-term base of operations, in Bensonhurst, East New York, Canarsie; it was not only the place they lived but the place they were active in their operations. Long before I was involved, there were well-founded suspicions of links between organized crime and politicians and the judiciary. In other words, they had the law in their pocket and were able to operate pretty much with impunity until Gold came in and a new generation of law enforcement took over.

Organized crime continues to thrive in Brooklyn because it's such an enormous cash cow, which begins with illegal sports betting and finances every other illegal activity they do, including drugs and prostitution. That alone probably accounts for something between $35 and $40 billion across the country annually. In New York City it generates about $15 to $20 billion a year. In 1990, my first year as DA, we had a Super Bowl sweep on Super Bowl Sunday, and every year thereafter. It got to be nearly comical. One time I went into a restaurant in the Bay Ridge section of Brooklyn to have dinner with my wife. As we were leaving, I noticed some wise guys at the bar. "Hey, Mr. DA," one of them said, "you doing the roundup this year?"

Back then, in 1990, Brooklyn was the fifth most violent place in America, per capita. We had about 170,000 indexed crimes of the seven major felonies. We had a body count of about 750 a year. In 2006, we went under 40,000 indexed crimes and 200 murders. A lot of it had to do with two factors. One, tremendous support in the community for law enforcement. Two, hard-nosed prosecution that does not plea-bargain violent crime while also recognizing prevention strategies like long-term mandatory drug treatment as an alternative to prison. We're only one of two prosecutor's offices in the country that has its own reentry program. We take people coming out of prison and match them with providers of job training and placement.

Community activism has turned this community around dramatically, especially in places like East New York, which used to have a hundred murders a year and now has maybe fifteen or twenty. Housing, on the other hand, now runs about $350,000 to $500,000 a house. In other words, the reduction of crime has increased the real estate values throughout Brooklyn. In 2003 *Money* magazine said that Brooklyn had become one of the ten best places in America to live. Yuppie kids are discovering Brooklyn; young people who can't afford to live in Manhattan have decided to come across the river.

Ironically, Brooklyn itself is becoming unaffordable in so many different places, and we're not doing enough to provide for those who were here during the cleanup who can no longer afford to stay and are being shoved out by escalating real-estate values and an extraordinary amount of upscale redevelopment. We should be putting investment into low-income housing so we don't lose our diversity. I think that's a real ongoing problem. Unfortunately, most developers are not the least bit interested in putting that into the equation. Ultimately, though, the overall progress is very good for the borough.

We now have three Chinatowns in Brooklyn. One is on Eighth Avenue, which was all Latino at one point. One is down by what used to be called Gravesend Bay, and one is on the opposite end of Avenue U going towards Flatbush. That's the newest one. The Asian population is exploding and they tend to stay together, just like all the other ethnic cultures that emigrated to the United States via Brooklyn. They're pretty well behaved, although we did have some trouble with Fujian gangs, whose members originally came from Fujian province in China, in the early nineties, but the feds took care of that fairly quickly. The Dominican drug dealers and the Jamaican drug dealers have also virtually disappeared due to strong law enforcement and their own economic and educational development. More often than not, the culture will overwhelm the criminal element and get rid of it themselves and become strong legitimate political voices.

The Russian population began in Brighton Beach and has expanded into Bensonhurst and Bay Ridge. In fact, one-seventh of all the people in the United States can trace their roots in America back to Brooklyn, this unique place where people live apart in their own communities and together at the same time.

In 2002, after twenty-five years of Howard Golden in Borough Hall, Marty Markowitz became Brooklyn's new borough president, the crowning achievement to twenty-three years of civil service as a state senator, representing at various times Flatbush, Crown Heights, Sheepshead Bay, and Midwood. He is consistently jovial and incessantly upbeat, if at times a bit oblivious to the realities of political life. For instance, during the 1991 Crown Heights riots, Markowitz decided to make a public appearance in that very neighborhood, dressed in an all-white tuxedo, hosting a B. B. King concert, eating Shabazz pie, while Bed-Stuy burned.

Markowitz had unsuccessfully challenged Golden for borough president in 1985. Coming up against Golden's political machine, Markowitz not only lost but was eventually charged with failing to disclose a campaign contribution from a local businessman. He pleaded guilty to a misdemeanor and was fined $8,000 and ordered to perform seventy-five hours of community service.

Markowitz's conviction put a serious dent in the cult of personality politicians in New York City. Mayor Beame, Koch's predecessor, had been a product of the Brooklyn Democratic machine, as were Governor Carey, Tom Cuite, the majority leader of the City Council, and the notorious Stanleys, Steingut and Fink. In 1991, scandals in Queens eventually led to that borough's president, Donald Manes, committing suicide, and helped bring down Ed Koch (and, indirectly, Howard Golden), resulting in the Board of Estimate being dissolved and shorter term limits for elected officials. It was no longer possible for any single figure to amass the type of political power and influence that Howard Golden once had. Because of it, power in the city became more centralized under Mayors Giuliani and Bloomberg, with Brooklyn's influence lessened and Manhattan's significantly expanded.

Once elected, Markowitz shrewdly retuned the duties of his office as more public relations than backdoor politics, in the hopes of attracting new and major investment money. "Only in Brooklyn," he loves to proclaim, "can you go from China to Russia in fifteen minutes!" Virtually no public speech he makes ever fails to mention Junior's cheesecake. For a borough-wide weight-loss campaign, the slightly round Markowitz stripped down to his shorts at Borough Hall (he had lost eleven pounds during the campaign, after which he promptly regained it). And one of Markowitz's first moves as borough president was to have signs put up at points of entry to and exit from the borough: "How Sweet It Is!" on the Brooklyn Bridge, "Leaving Brooklyn—Fuhgeddaboudit!" on the Gowanus Expressway, en route to the Verrazano-Narrows Bridge. ("Leaving Brooklyn—Oy Vey!" was rejected by the Department of Transportation for being "distracting and uninformative.")

ANTHONY PETROCINO: I was in a restaurant one time with Borough President Markowitz and actually an Italian guy came up to him and said he was a little insulted by those signs. "Whaddaya mean, 'fuhgeddaboudit'? How would you like it if I said something Jewish?" Markowitz smiled and said, "I wouldn't mind. I would have used one myself if I could have come up with a good one."

Brooklyn's ongoing renaissance includes one minor-league ballpark, Keyspan Park, home of the Brooklyn Cyclones, a Class A affiliate of the New York Mets. Markowitz has also set his sights on bringing a major sports franchise back to Brooklyn. He built his 2001 campaign on the promise he would do everything in his power to bring the New Jersey Nets to Brooklyn (as well as on a wacky plan to have Brooklyn secede from New York and once again become a full-blown city—a plan that disappeared shortly after his election). Once in office, Markowitz approached Nets owner Bruce Ratner about the possibility of his bringing his basketball team to Brooklyn.

Thus was born one of the most ambitious and controversial renewal projects in the history of New York City. Ratner pledged to raise $2.5

billion through his development company, Forest City Ratner, to build a new stadium for his Nets in Brooklyn and along with it a brand-new neighborhood complete with an enormous housing and commercial development, to be called Atlantic Yards, that would be built on the edge of Pacific Street in Prospect Heights, in the heart of downtown Brooklyn. The key to getting all the approvals needed, not to mention the necessary tax abatements, was his promise to build much-needed moderate-income housing.

To no one's surprise, it didn't exactly work the way he planned.

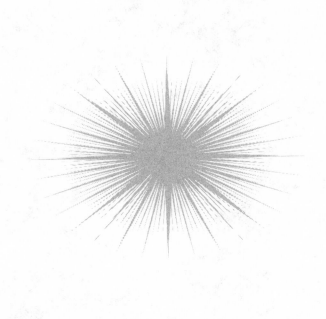

CHAPTER ELEVEN

BACK TO THE FUTURE

We lived in Williamsburg when I was a little boy. My older brother and I used to go to the pickle store down the street. I hadn't been there for thirty years. One day I got in my car and drove back to the old neighborhood and couldn't believe that the pickle store was still there, owned by the same people. I went in and told the fellow I used to come in as a little boy and that I hadn't been back in thirty years, and he said, without missing a beat, "What took you so long?"

—MARTY ASHER

B ROOKLYN'S FUTURE IS a roller-coaster ride back to its glory days, making it the place to be rather than the place to flee. The high costs that have plagued Manhattan and threaten to turn it into a cultural and artistic wasteland have helped create not just a generation of young and vital expatriate and never-were Manhattan-ites who have chosen instead to live in Brooklyn.

The revitalization of Brooklyn is quite vividly reflected in its classic architecture. The landmarked Brooklyn Academy of Music (BAM), at 30 Lafayette Street, once upon a time served as *the* gathering place for Brooklyn's most talented artists. The renovation and reconstruc-tion of its exterior is nothing less than "an emblem for the revitaliza-tion of the borough as well as BAM," according to Karen Brooks Hopkins, the Academy's president. In what's being called the BAM Cul-tural District, the Theatre for a New Audience's $22 million theater, created by Frank Gehry and Hugh Hardy, now stands proudly along-side the Brooklyn Museum's $63 million new entry pavilion, designed by James Stewart Polshek; the $39 million expansion of the Brooklyn Children's Museum, designed by Rafael Vinoly; and the Brooklyn Public Library's new Visual and Performing Arts Library, designed by Enrique Norten.

KAREN BROOKS: When you add all those projects to the glorious Art Deco of the Williamsburg Bank Building, you have to say that the future architectural epicenter of New York City will be right here in Brooklyn.

Though the final cost of the renovation of BAM's exterior alone came to more than $10 million, the project was enthusiastically approved by Brooklyn's City Council and given a hearty thumbs-up by Borough President Marty Markowitz. This restoration, like the others mentioned above, was conceived in the mid- to late 1990s, when the stock market was running high and fast and tenants throughout the city were running even faster to keep up with the skyrocketing cost of apartment rentals, co-ops, and condos. This real-estate upswing swept through Brooklyn as it did the rest of the city and swept out a lot of economic debris in the wake. It had a devastating effect on the existence of Brooklyn's most cherished working- and middle-class laborers and artists. But the corporate thinking went, "So what?" Mayor Michael Bloomberg, the most corporate (and wealthiest) mayor in the history of New York City, shrugged it off as the price one has to pay to live in the "greatest city in the world." Or, to put it another way, someone has to pay for all those "improvements."

BAM currently sits in what was designated in 1978 as an entire historic district. In 1861 the Brooklyn Academy of Music opened at 176-194 Montague Street in Brooklyn Heights. That building was destroyed by fire in 1903; ironically, the value of the site was so great that BAM's stock price actually went *up* the day of the fire. The Academy made plans to rebuild in Fort Greene, a fashionable neighborhood at the edge of the business district.

The design of the new facility became the subject of a spirited contest between the most celebrated architects of the day, and was won by the firm of Herts and Tallent.* Their Italian Renaissance Revival façade would eventually be copied by the Williamsburg Savings Bank in 1929, whose tower still dominates (but not for long) as the tallest in the Brooklyn skyline.

The neglect that befell the Academy in the second half of the twentieth century began when the Board of Education, looking for solutions to the overcrowding the new wave of post–World War II immigrants had created, took it over and divided its once grand halls into classrooms. As if to signal the shift in priorities, the building began to be neglected, its terra-cotta ornaments and brickwork crumbling, its cornice torn off.

The latest restoration of BAM, begun in 2002, signals what city planners have called a renaissance of artistic expression. But what constitutes that renaissance? A multiplex movie theater run by the Rose Corporation, a second-floor performance space, a high-end restaurant, an independent bookstore that is part of a small chain of independents in the city, and a theater (for which there is no longer any room in the main building, and which is being housed in a nearby Fulton Street facility).

As a sign that the renaissance was succeeding, and proof that it was the cause of the resurrection of the surrounding neighborhood, city planners loudly waved pages of statistics to the press that "proved" attendance was up in 2004 by half a million. However, according to the *New York Times*, 55 percent of that half million, or about 275,000 visitors, were coming to BAM from Manhattan, with little or no money being spent for food or lodging in Brooklyn itself. Nevertheless, according to Hugh Hardy, founding partner of Hardy, Holzman, Pfeiffer Associates, the firm in charge of the restoration, "the building, and

---

* Henry Herts and Hugh Tallent were among the most successful and influential turn-of-the-century architects. Among their many achievements were Manhattan's Longacre and New Amsterdam theatres.

everything that BAM is, now has a real constituency in the community." In 2005, Joseph V. Melillo, executive producer of the Brooklyn Academy of Music, was awarded the Order of the British Empire for his great work in "showcasing British art in America." So much for the preservation and promotion of local artists.

But Brooklyn still is the place young, upcoming artists want to be. Yesterday's Greenwich Village is today's Bushwick. Somewhere in the vicinity of Bed-Stuy, art-school graduates, a large contingent from NYU, have set up shop in studios whose exposed brick walls, vast spaces, and seedy vestibules are a convenient step or two from Richie's Candy Store, the Showdown Barbershop, the Greene Avenue public basketball courts, and the little storefront selling cuchifritos, all of which recall nothing so much as the glory boho days of the prewar Village. The only real difference between then and now is the necessity of enforced communal living. No one who is starting out with ambitions to be an artist, sculptor, painter, writer, poet, designer, or conceptual artist and who was born without a trust fund is likely to be able to afford the past luxury of living alone in Brooklyn.

It is indeed ironic that the left-wing romanticism of Depression-era Greenwich Village was kept alive by artists and writers, who managed somehow to wangle vast lofts, rooftop gardens, skylit apartments, and walk-throughs that matched the length of some of the smaller subway stops in the vicinity. The new crop of upwardly mobile young creatives are void of any apparent political unity, their goals narrowed to simply making enough to afford to live in one-bedrooms with a starting rent of around $2,500 a month. They routinely live in threes and fours, as many of their forefathers did in downtown Moscow in the old Soviet Union. The romanticism of individual expressionism includes shared kitchens and bathrooms and windowless bedrooms.

Word of a citywide new-housing boom that had effectively blanketed "all corners of the city" made the front page of the New York Times in 2004 This was seen by many as a good thing, attributable to the stock market boom of the 1990s and mid-2000s, low interest rates,

a significant drop in street crime, and government programs, the latter the engine that, according to city officials, "has affected every borough and most neighborhoods, reshaping their physical form, ethnic
makeup and collective memories."

Throughout Brooklyn, the result of this boom was twofold. The first
was the destruction of thousands of one- and two-family homes, many
of which had been occupied for generations by the same families, and
their replacement by nondescript six-story cookie-cutter-style square
brick buildings, low in style but high in price and almost 100 percent
co-op or condo, sold to the new, moneyed immigrants from the once-
impoverished countries of the Old World and Asia. Less affluent residents, many either the children or grandchildren of immigrants, were
farmed out to places such as Florida and Arizona for retirement. After
all, the city had more pressing (and more profitable) matters to deal
with than providing low-cost housing for them, such as what to do with
the approximately $2.2 billion it took in from real estate transfer taxes
that year alone.

Still, as the mayor was quick to point out, some low-to-middle-
income housing was being built. L&M Equity Partnerships set about to
solve the situation for the city's poor by building co-ops in Harlem and
Bedford-Stuyvesant, two of the city's predominantly African American neighborhoods, with prices starting at $140,000 and going up to
$300,000, still a bargain in Bloomberg's expensive city. Unfortunately,
those prices doubled in less than two years as first-time buyers became
first-time sellers, and most of the new occupants were upwardly mobile
whites willing to pay upward of half a million dollars for housing on
blocks that had once been the site of apartments that went for a
few hundred dollars a month to the aged and the lower class of New
York City.

BOB GANS: Brooklyn is coming back, but in a different capacity. People
who are coming to Brooklyn now are those who have been displaced
out of Manhattan or couldn't afford it in the first place, who are "redis-

covering" Brooklyn but were not born and raised there. They may have grown up in Long Island or the Midwest or other countries, and they come first to Manhattan, prices are what they are, so they come to Brooklyn, to Park Slope, to Greenpoint, or other areas, and think to themselves, "Wow, this is a great neighborhood." And as they find out just how great Brooklyn is, as they discover all the great sights, the restaurants, the foods, they decide they want to stay there while they pursue their careers, and that begins the cycle of gentrification.

ANDREW MILLER: I discovered that a couple of people who lived on my block in Park Slope were in publishing, long before I knew what publishing really was. Once I got into the business, it seemed like everyone I knew was either living in or moving to Park Slope. My first response to all the bars and restaurants that were opening up and catering to this crowd was, "Hey, this neighborhood is going down the tubes!" However, it wasn't very long before I realized the scene was quite different from anything happening in Manhattan. For one thing, it was a real neighborhood. It had all these things you could never get in Manhattan. House parties, for instance. No one had house parties in Manhattan. Park Slope became more of a destination, not just for those people trying to get away from the high rents in Manhattan, but for those who wanted a real taste of city life. After living for a while in Manhattan, I moved back to Park Slope. I love this community of people around. As soon as I got back it felt like, "This is exactly where I should be." I began to realize that Manhattan is a place where people come and go, but the outer boroughs are where people actually live.

BOB GANS: Sooner or later, as has happened so many times before in so many other places, they want to rebuild those places, neighborhoods, and houses that were left to rot, to die on the vine. Through that rejuvenation, the awareness of Brooklyn grows, and the prices start to go up. One of the most telling signs is what happened to Coney Island's blighted Sea Park, an affordable housing project on Surf Avenue built in 1964 as a Mitchell-Lama affordable-housing building that was eventually converted to condos and underwent a $77 million redevelopment.* Its neighbor Sea Gate is now a gated community where medium-sized two- and three-family houses are approaching the million-dollar level.

As far as [developer Bruce] Ratner, and the Ratners of the world who have invested heavily into Brooklyn, are concerned, they are creating a different Brooklyn that natives like me knew. We didn't grow up surrounded and shut off from the sky by all these high-rise luxury apartments. At the end of the day, what will be there may be terrific, but it won't have anything to do with Brooklyn. Ratner is a wonderful developer, but he's building something new; he's not restoring anything. And maybe fifty years from now his housing will be looked back upon as some great nostalgic experience. However, the Brooklyn-born-and-raised pride will simply not be there. Even for those few who may actually have been born and raised there.

Brooklyn will never be what it once was, and becomes more and more like Manhattan with every passing day.

SUKETU MEHTA: About 38 percent of Brooklynites are foreign-born. If you include their children, their numbers jump to more than 55 percent. This isn't the Jewish Brooklyn of Woody Allen or the Italian Brooklyn of *Moonstruck.* There are people living in Brooklyn who have no idea what stickball is, what stoop sitting is, who the Dodgers were or why they left Brooklyn. These people play cricket in Marine Park, barbecue suckling pigs in their backyards, listen to Russian matinee idols in Brighton Beach nightclubs, and worship not Kobe Bryant and Derek Jeter but Diego Maradona, an Argentine soccer player, and Sachin Tendulkar, an Indian cricket star. They are inventing their own Brooklyn, a Brooklyn their kids will be nostalgic about twenty years from now.

---

* State-subsidized public housing, with preference according to need, as determined by income. The program was launched in 1955, named for its co-sponsors, state senator MacNeill Mitchell and assemblyman Alfred Lama.

STEVE ETTLINGER: If the public will really own it, why did Barclay's Bank agree to pay Mr. Ratner $400 million so [the arena] could be called the Barclay's Arena?

MARTY MARKOWITZ: I can't tell you how many residents have told me . . . they are looking forward to Brooklyn's most exciting project, the major-league sports arena and the affordable housing that Atlantic Yards will bring to Brooklyn.

Bruce Ratner, a commissioner of New York City's Department of Consumer Affairs during the Koch Administration, has the blessing of the Empire State Development Corporation, which approved his proposed $4.2 billion, twenty-two-acre, Frank Gehry–designed redevelopment project along the old Long Island Rail Road yards situated between the intersection of Flatbush and Atlantic Avenues, surrounded by Fort Greene, Park Slope, Prospect Heights, Boerum Hill, and downtown Brooklyn.* Both the city and the state governments support the new upscale development despite the uproar of thousands of middle- and lower-class citizens about to be uprooted from their neighborhood because of it. The reasons are obvious: the city alone stands to earn an additional $1.5 million in taxes from the Atlantic Yards project in its first year in existence, not counting what it will make from taxes, parking, and other ancillaries associated with a major league sports revenue. The state will make even more.

DANIEL GOLDMAN: To justify eminent domain, Bruce Ratner wants to argue that the neighborhood is blighted. It is not. This is his attempt to create "developers' blight."

* As of the publication of this book, the budget for this part of the development has escalated to 9.2 billion, with a completion date now set for 2012. According to Joe Chan, the president of the Downtown Brooklyn Partnership, "We're talking about a number of prominent, tall buildings designed by great architects like Frank Gehry emerging from what is now parking lots and underused buildings."

STEVE ETTLINGER: The bottom line is that Mr. Ratner had eyed this site years ago and has engineered an abuse of eminent domain to acquire the land he needs.

ROSIE PEREZ: I've lived here all my life and I'm glad we don't have skyscrapers. The size of the project doesn't respect the character of the neighborhood, and I think the thing that really hurts is the people being displaced.

Maybe the $358,000 in lobbying costs Ratner's company has thus far shelled out will change Rosie Perez's mind.

Sometimes, however, even if you can't stop the train altogether, you can succeed in slowing it down a bit. In September 2006, in the wake of a furiously growing campaign of protests impossible for the city (or politicians seeking reelection) to ignore, Ratner announced that the size of the Atlantic Yards Project budget would be reduced by 6 to 8 percent.

Ratner's apparent concession, no matter how token it may have appeared, nevertheless stood as a symbol of victory for the anti-project coalition. Overlooked was the fact that the revised total for new low- and moderate-income apartments to be built now stood at 2,250, against more than 5,000 luxury apartments, in what had been an historic working-class neighborhood.

CHRIS SMITH: Brooklyn is vast, so it would be arrogant and silly to say how Atlantic Yards will change the borough. Maybe they won't feel a thing in Sheepshead Bay and Greenpoint and East New York and Crown Heights . . . I'm no spaldeen-and-egg-cream nostalgic, but Brooklyn has always been different and better because it's been closer to the ground. That's a significant thing to lose.

And so it goes. Brooklyn continues to grow at the fastest pace in its history and will soon overcome the great population drain caused by the mass exodus of the sixties, seventies, and eighties and exceed the record 2.75 million residents the borough had during the first years of the postwar baby boom.* Is Ratner really the villain of all of this, or is he just one more opportunist in what has become the uncontrollable destiny of all cities with too many people and not enough places to put them?

In 2007, the overall average price of a condo in Brooklyn rose 24 percent from a year earlier, to just under half a million dollars; Williamsburg saw a 19 percent increase. And if daily gossip columns are to be trusted at all, most of the primary tenants in these tonier places seem to be celebrities. Academy Award–winning actress Jennifer Connelly gave up what she described as a "cramped" apartment in Manhattan for a spacious loft in Park Slope; character actor John Turturro, writer Paul Auster, character actor (and part-time fireman) Steve Buscemi, actor Rory Kennedy, and actress Annabella Sciorra all have become Brooklynites. In Sciorra's case, the price of admission to the neighborhood via a three-bedroom, two-and-a-half-bath corner apartment was a cool $1.2 million.

The non-famous, too, are trying to work their way into the upscale act. Dilapidated fixer-uppers on Coney Island's Ocean Avenue are routinely going for a swift half million *as is*. To date, the top price paid so far for a townhouse in Brooklyn is $20 million.

Perhaps one of the reasons Williamsburg has attracted so many artists, writers, and actors is because of the burgeoning (way) off-Broadway theater movement happening there. The Galapagos Art Space, the Streb Lab for Action Mechanics (SLAM), the Glass House Gallery, the Charlie Pineapple Theater, the Brick, and hundreds of others are popping up everywhere, in abandoned storefronts and unheated lofts. The scene is young, vibrant, and exciting, its partici-

---

* The population of Brooklyn in 1950 was 2,738,175. The population in 2007 was 2,508,820. The projected population by the year 2020 is 2,628,211. Source: The Mayor's Office, the City of New York.

pants pumping with hope and enthusiasm. Many of them have never attended a theatrical performance in Manhattan and express no interest in doing so. However, among all the optimism, there is this perhaps chilling voice of caution, from one of the co-founders of the Brick theater.

MICHAEL GARDNER: When I saw the bodega across the street turn into a realty office last week, I started to get nervous.

But not everyone is nervous or afraid of change.

MARK LOTTO: In Brooklyn, the older yuppies bitch and bellyache and theorize about the younger yuppies moving in, as if this latest batch of arrivistes into Brooklyn were the flood of Muslim immigrants into France. Best to take it with a grain of salt. The public defenders bitched about the corporate lawyers, the artists about the professionals, the immigrants about the artists, the New Netherlanders about the New Englanders, the Delaware Indians about the Dutch . . . Established celebs of the Slope–Turturro, Auster, etc.–aren't thought of as neighbors per se but as landmarks, as well-worn and familiar as the Prospect Park band shell.

BRUCE RATNER: Each generation is judged, rightly or wrongly, by its ability to prepare for future generations. We are fortunate that we have the resources and the vision to leave behind a city that is greater than the one we inherited, with better housing and mobility and improved health care and education. Brooklyn, in many ways, is a model for the change our city is experiencing. Twenty years ago, when Forest City Ratner opened in the downtown area, we were called foolish. Many thought the area, long in disarray, could not be developed and would not attract jobs. Today Brooklyn is celebrated as a world-class destination, the home to diversity in all of its glory, with great food, parks, and cultural attractions. We are proud to be part of both our borough's past and its future.

And that may be the prevailing sentiment. As a new generation comes of age in Brooklyn, too young to remember the storied way it was, old memories are inevitably replaced by new ones, as surely as old structures give way to new. The Brooklyn that they will know is the only Brooklyn they will have ever known.

A Representative List of Films Made in or About Brooklyn

Brooklyn Bridge (1896). A five-minute one-reel short made on location by Edison Manufacturing Company, showing pedestrians descending from the Brooklyn Bridge (Edison did not give director credit for its films).

Fun on the Steeplechase (Edison Manufacturing Company, 1897).

Shooting the Chutes at Luna Park (Edison Manufacturing Company, 1903).

Execution of Topsy (Edison Manufacturing Company, 1903). This is one of the most controversial, little-seen movies ever made. It shows the real-time electrocution of a Luna Park elephant. It was filmed during the initial construction of the park at the personal directive of Thomas Edison, who filmed various animals being electrocuted as a way to promote his preferred DC (direct current) method of delivering electricity. At the time Edison was competing against his competitor's use of AC current. Despite his movies, Edison eventually lost that campaign.

Monday Morning in a Coney Island Police Court (Biograph Studios, 1908). Directed by D. W. Griffith.

At Coney Island (Keystone Film Company, 1912). Directed by Mack Sennett. With Sennett and Mabel Normand.

A Coney Island Princess (Famous Players Studio, 1916). Directed by Dell Henderson. A wealthy pursuer falls in love with a hootchy-cootchy dancer and disgraces himself by taking a job as a piano player to woo Tessie, "The Princess of Coney Island." Fifteen years later, Josef von Sternberg would borrow this property, which had, in the interim, been acquired by Paramount in its merger with Famous Players, and use it as one of the bases for his movie *The Blue Angel* (1930); the other was Heinrich Mann's novel *Professor Unrat*.

Fatty at Coney Island (Comique Film Company, distributed by Paramount Pictures, 1917). Directed by Roscoe "Fatty" Arbuckle. Madness ensues when Buster Keaton dresses as a girl and passes as Fatty's date for a ride on the Shoot-the-Chutes.

The Crowd (MGM, 1928). Directed by King Vidor. The life of a man and a woman in New York City. The exteriors filmed at Luna Park, interiors of the fun house filmed on the Venice Pier in California. With James Murray, Eleanor Broadman, and Bert Roach.

Symphony of Six Million (RKO, 1932). Directed by Gregory La Cava. A young man temporarily abandons his Jewish roots in an attempt to enter high society. The Cyclone may be seen operating in several shots. With Irene Dunne and Ricardo Cortez.

Manhattan Melodrama (MGM, 1934). Directed by W. S. Van Dyke. A childhood friendship between two orphans continues into adulthood as they live lifestyles on the opposite side of the law. With Clark Gable, William Powell, and Myrna Loy. Some scenes shot on location at Coney Island.

Every Day's a Holiday (Paramount, 1937). Directed by A. Edward Sutherland. A notorious confidence woman keeps on selling the Brooklyn Bridge to gullible buyers. With Mae West.

Cowboy from Brooklyn (Warner Bros., 1938). Directed by Lloyd Bacon. An actor fakes being a real cowboy to get a job in radio. With Ronald Reagan, Dick Powell, Pat O'Brien, and Priscilla Lane.

The Nurse from Brooklyn (MGM, 1938). Directed by S. Sylvan Simon.

A tough Brooklyn nurse's brother is killed and she helps find who did it. With Sally Eilers and Paul Kelly.

The Shopworn Angel (MGM, 1938). Several scenes shot on location at Coney Island during the couple's courtship in this romantic comedy. With James Stewart and Margaret Sullavan.

The Devil and Miss Jones (RKO, 1941). A love story about a shop owner who goes undercover to spy on his employees. Several scenes were shot on location at Coney Island. With Robert Cummings and Jean Arthur.

'Neath the Brooklyn Bridge (Monogram, 1942). Directed by Wallace Fox. Starring Leo Gorcey and the East Side Kids. Trouble 'neath you know where.

Coney Island (20th Century-Fox, 1943). Directed by Walter Lang. Starring Betty Gable and George Montgomery. A turn-of-the-century musical set in the amusement parks filmed entirely in Hollywood.

Lifeboat (20th Century-Fox, 1944). Hitchcock's World War II adventure filmed entirely in a lifeboat. One of the floaters, William Bendix, talks out loud about his beloved Dodgers as he lay dying. With Bendix, Tallulah Bankhead, Walter Slezak, and Hume Cronyn.

When Strangers Marry (Monogram, 1944). Directed by William Castle. Psychological thriller with some scenes shot on location in Coney Island, including at the "Human Pool Table." With Robert Mitchum, Kim Hunter, Dean Jagger.

A Tree Grows in Brooklyn (20th Century-Fox, 1945). Directed by Elia Kazan. Poor but happy family with alcoholic father, growing up in Brooklyn circa 1900, based on the beloved novel by Betty Smith. With Joan Blondell, Dorothy McGuire, Lloyd Nolan, James Gleason, James Dunn (Best Supporting Actor).

The Blonde from Brooklyn (Columbia, 1945). Directed by Del Lord. Brooklyn blonde poses as Southern-bred beauty to win a man. With Lynn Merrick and Bob Stanton.

The Kid from Brooklyn (Samuel Goldwyn Productions, 1945). Directed by Norman Z. McLeod. Shy milkman somehow becomes contender for heavyweight champion of the world. With Danny Kaye, Virginia Mayo, Vera-Ellen, Steve Cochran, and Eve Arden.

It Happened in Brooklyn (MGM, 1947). Directed by Richard Whorf. A young man joins the navy and gets homesick for his old Brooklyn neighborhood. With Frank Sinatra, Kathryn Grayson, Jimmy Durante, and Peter Lawford.

On the Town (MGM, 1949). Directed by Stanley Donen and Gene Kelly. Three sailors on twenty-four-hour leave in New York City. Based on the Bernstein/Comden/Green Broadway musical. With Gene Kelly, Frank Sinatra, Betty Garrett, Ann Miller, Jules Munshin, Vera-Ellen.

Bela Lugosi Meets a Brooklyn Gorilla (Jack Broder Productions, 1952). Directed by William Beaudine. Brooklyn vs. mad scientist with a gorilla thrown in for good measure. With, surprise surprise, Bela Lugosi.

The Little Fugitive (Joseph Burstyn Productions, 1953). Directed by Morris Engel, Ray Ashley, and Ruth Orkin. A young boy runs away to Coney Island after believing he has killed his brother. Shot on location. With Ricky Brewster and Richie Andrusco.

Imitation of Life (Universal-International, 1953). Directed by Douglas Sirk. An unwed mother tries for a career in movies, with the help of her African-American housekeeper. Many location shots of Coney Island. With Lana Turner and John Gavin.

The Landlord (United Artists, 1970). Directed by Hal Ashby. Race relations in pre-gentrified Park Slope. With Beau Bridges, Lee Grant, Diana Sands, Pearl Bailey, Louis Gossett, Jr., Susan Anspach, and Robert Klein.

Carnival of Blood (Kirt Films International, 1971). Directed by Leonard Kirtman. Psychopathic killer let loose in Coney Island. Exteriors shot on location. With Earle Edgerton and Judith Resnick

Lords of Flatbush (Columbia, 1974). Directed by Martin Davidson and Steven Verona. A group of teenagers from Brooklyn forms a gang. With Sylvester Stallone, Henry Winkler, Susan Blakely, Perry King.

Dog Day Afternoon (Warner Bros., 1975). Directed by Sidney Lumet. True story of inept Brooklyn bank robbers, shot on location. With Al Pacino, Charles Durning, John Cazale.

Saturday Night Fever (Paramount, 1977). Directed by John Badham. A talented working-class boy tries to extend the boundaries of his young and limited life through creative dancing. Based on an article by Nik Cohn. Shot on location in Brooklyn. With John Travolta and Karen Gorney.

Annie Hall (United Artists, 1977). Directed (and written) by Woody Allen. Several Brooklyn location shots, including one of the Cyclone, during the courtship phase of this Academy Award–winning comedy-romance. With Woody Allen and Diane Keaton.

The Wiz (Universal, 1978). Directed by Sidney Lumet. African-American updated remake of *The Wizard of Oz*. Several scenes of singing and dancing at the Cyclone. With Diana Ross and Michael Jackson.

American Hot Wax (Paramount, 1978). Directed by Floyd Mutrux. The story of Alan Freed's 1950s Brooklyn Paramount rock and roll shows that changed the course of popular culture. With Tim McIntire, Fran Drescher, Jay Leno, and Laraine Newman.

Boardwalk (Atlantic Releasing, 1979). Directed by Stephen Verona. An elderly Jewish couple struggles to survive in a Coney Island that has seen better days. Some opening-credit exteriors shot on location. With Ruth Gordon and Lee Strasberg.

The Warriors (Paramount, 1979). Directed by Walter Hill Starring. The Bronx's and Brooklyn's rival street gangs go to war. Some exteriors shot at Coney Island. With Michael Beck and James Remer.

The Goodbye People (Castle Hill Productions, 1983). Directed by Herb Gardner. A man tries to build a new career on the beach at Coney Island. Some exteriors shot on location. With Judd Hirsch and Pamela Reed.

Over the Brooklyn Bridge (Cannon Films, 1984). Directed by Menahem Golan. A Brooklyn Jewish restaurant owner is about to borrow money from his uncle to open a place in Manhattan until his family finds out his girlfriend and business partner is Catholic. A few scenes shot on location using the Cyclone. With Elliott Gould, Margaux Hemingway, and Sid Caesar.

Crossover Dreams (Miramax, 1985). Directed by Leon Ichaso. Salsa performer from Brooklyn tries to make it in show business. Many exteriors shot on location at Coney Island. With Ruben Blades and Shawn Elliot.

Heaven Help Us (HBO Films, 1985). Directed by Michael Dinner. Life at St. Basil's Catholic Boys School in Brooklyn during the sixties. Several location shots of the Boardwalk, The Wonder Wheel, The Parachute Jump, the beach, and the Boardwalk. With Donald Sutherland, Mary Stuart Masterson, and Andrew McCarthy.

She's Gotta Have It (40 Acres and a Mule Filmworks, 1986). Directed by Spike Lee. African American woman and her three lovers. With Tracy Camilla Johns, Tommy Redmond Hicks, John Canada Terrell, Spike Lee.

Remo Williams: The Adventure Begins (Orion, 1986). Directed by Guy Hamilton. Police action-adventure shot on location in New York City. Several exteriors shot at Coney Island, highlighted by a fight scene on The Wonder Wheel and backgrounds of The Cyclone. With Fred Ward, Joel Grey.

Streets of Gold (20th Century-Fox, 1986). Boxing melodrama. Some exteriors shot at Coney Island. With Klaus Maria Brandauer, Wesley Snipes.

Angel Heart (Carolco, 1987). Supernatural thriller. Several scenes shot on location at Coney Island. Starring Mickey Rourke, Lisa Bonet, Robert De Niro.

Shakedown (Universal, 1988). Cops and robbers, drugs and deception. Several scenes filmed at Coney Island. Extended fight sequence filmed on The Cyclone. With Peter Weller, Sam Elliott.

Do the Right Thing (40 Acres and a Mule Filmworks, 1989). Directed by Spike Lee. Hatred and bigotry explode out of a pizza parlor in Bed-Stuy on the hottest day of the summer. With Danny Aiello, Ossie Davis, John Turturro, Rosie Perez, Samuel L. Jackson.

Enemies: A Love Story (Morgan Creek, 1989). Married Holocaust survivor lives in Coney Island, has an affair. Based on a novel by Isaac Bashevis Singer. Several scenes shot on location at Astroland. With Angelica Huston, Ron Silver.

Goodfellas (Warner Bros., 1990). Directed by Martin Scorsese. Based on the nonfiction classic *Wiseguys* by Nicholas Pileggi. The life of Henry Hill, small-time Brooklyn street gangster. With Ray Liotta, Robert De Niro, Joe Pesci, Lorraine Bracco.

Last Exit to Brooklyn (Allied Filmmakers, Bavarian Films, 1990). Directed by Uli Edel. Union corruption, prostitution, lower-depths marriage, and violence. Shot mostly in Germany. Based on the groundbreaking novel by

Brooklyn-born Hubert Selby Jr. With Steven Lang, Jennifer Jason Leigh, Burt Young, Jerry Orbach, Stephen Baldwin.

Little Odessa (New Line Cinema, 1994). Directed by James Gray. Murder mystery involving assassin and younger brother. Many scenes shot on location at Coney Island. With Tim Roth and Edward Furlong.

Straight out of Brooklyn (American Playhouse, 1995). Directed by Matty Rich. African-American urban street violence. Pioneering film in the African-American independent filmmaking movement. With Larry Gilliard, Jr., George T. Odom, Ann D. Sanders, Matty Rich.

Smoke (Miramax, 1995). Directed by Wayne Wang. Improvisational situation in a Brooklyn candy store, scripted by Park Slope literary celebrity Paul Auster. Harvey Keitel, Jared Harris, William Hurt, Stockard Channing.

Blue in the Face (Miramax, 1995). Directed by Paul Auster, Wayne Wang. Improvisational situations in a Brooklyn candy store (sequel to *Smoke*). With Lou Reed, Michael J. Fox, Roseanne, Jim Jarmusch, Lily Tomlin, Jared Harris.

Vampire in Brooklyn (Paramount, 1995). Directed by Wes Craven. Urban fangs. With Eddie Murphy, Angela Bassett.

A Brooklyn State of Mind (Miramax, 1995). Directed by Frank Rainone. Low-grade *Sopranos*. With Danny Aiello, Vincent Spano, Maria Graza Cucinatta, Abe Vigoda, Tony Danza.

He Got Game (Touchstone, 1998). Directed by Spike Lee. Realistic street-drama set in housing projects and basketball courts. With Denzel Washington, Milla Jovovich, Ray Allen, Rosario Dawson.

Went to Coney Island on a Mission from God . . . Be Back by Five (Phaedra Cinema, 1998). Directed by Richard Schenkman. Two friends search for a third. With Jon Cryer and Ione Skye.

Disappearing Acts (HBO Films, 2000). Directed by Gina Prince-Bythewood. A Brooklyn couple struggles to stay together, based on the bestselling novel by Terry Macmillan. With Sanaa Lathan, Wesley Snipes, Regina Hall, Lisa Arrindel Anderson.

Brooklyn Babylon (Artisan Entertainment, 2001). Directed by Marc Levin. Brooklyn rapper falls in love with Jewish girl. With Tariq Trotter, Karen Goberman, Bonz Malone, David Vadim.

Requiem for a Dream (Artisan, 2001). Directed by Darren Aronofsky. Drug addicts prey on themselves, family in decrepit Coney Island. Several scenes shot on location. Based on the Hubert Selby Jr. novel. With Ellen Burstyn, Jared Leto, Jennifer Connelly.

Uptown Girls (MGM, 2003). Directed by Boaz Yakin. A nanny and her charge go to Coney Island, where the little girl runs away and hides among the rides. Several scenes shot on location at The Wonder Wheel and The Teacups ride. With Brittany Murphy and Dakota Fanning.

Brooklyn Lobster (Galloping Films, 2005). Directed by Kevin Jordan. Traditional Brooklyn family lobster-farming saga. With Danny Aiello, Jane Curtin.

The Squid and the Whale (Samuel Goldwyn Films, 2005). Directed by Noah Baumbach. Two young boys deal with their parents' divorce in 1980s Brooklyn. With Owen Kline, Jeff Daniels, Laura Linney, Jesse Eisenberg, William Baldwin, Anna Paquin.

Half Nelson (Hunting Lane Films, 2006). Directed by Ryan Fleck. Inner-city Brooklyn teacher with drug problems relates to students in a special way. With Ryan Gosling, Jeff Lima, Shareeka Epps, Nathan Corbett, Tyra Kwao-Vovo.

NOTES

CHAPTER ONE: CONEY ISLAND

11 "I actually rode it . . ." Gerald Howard, Author Interview. Unless otherwise noted, all interviews are A.I.

12 In 1871, Charles Feltman staked his claim: Some background information on Feltman's is from Jeffrey Stanton, "Coney Island, Nickel Empire," 1997, available at http://www.westland.net/ coneyisland/articles/nickelempire.htm.

14 "My grandfather . . ." Brian Gari. A.I.

14 "The story goes . . ." Bill Handwerker, quoted in the 2006 documentary *History of the Hot Dog,* produced by Atlas Media Corporation for the History Channel. All quotes from Bill Handwerker are from this source.

15 "In 1934 . . ." Mickey Freeman. A.I.

17 "After a few jobless weeks . . ." Cary Grant's quote is from his autobiography, which was ghostwritten by Joe Hyams and appeared in serial form in the *Ladies' Home Journal* in 1963 under the title "Archie Leach."

18 "You know what . . ." Don K. Reed. A.I.

19 "Coney Island . . ." Powers, A.I.

20 "I used to go . . ." John "Cha Cha" Ciarcia. A.I.

21 Sitt began buying up the rights: Some additional information and quotes regarding the

restoration of Coney Island come from Joseph Berger, "In Coney Island's Future, Looking to Past Glory," *New York Times*, April 18, 2005.

21 "I was born . . ." Joe Sitt. A.I.

25 "This is going to be . . ." Diana Carlin. Quoted in the *New York Post*, June 14, 2007.

CHAPTER TWO: SHEEPSHEAD BAY

35 "My friend Alan Colmes . . ." Brian Gari. A.I.

36 "All the New York City . . ." Mickey Freeman. A.I.

37 "I went into comedy . . ." Joan Rivers. A.I.

38 "I felt like . . ." Joey Gay. A.I.

CHAPTER THREE: MUSIC

45 At Erasmus Hall . . . "Looking for an Echo," composed by Richard Reicheg.

46 "I been in music . . ." Billy Dawn Smith. A.I.

47 "Once you got into . . ." Lee, p. 30.

48 "If you weren't . . ." Kenny Vance. A.I.

50 "Maybe it was . . ." Neil Sedaka, in Monti, p. 183.

50 "I was born and raised . . ." Neil Sedaka. A.I.

53 "I was born . . ." Don K. Reed. Interview with author.

54 "I remember Brooklyn . . ." Ben Vereen. Interview with the author. All quotes A.I. unless otherwise noted.

56 "By the time . . ." "Cousin" Brucie. Interview with the author. All quotes A.I. except where otherwise noted.

57 "Brooklyn had a sound . . ." Johnny Maestro. Interview with author. All quotes are from A.I. unless otherwise noted.

59 "Summer nights in Brooklyn . . ." John Karlen. A.I.

59 "I lived in Canarsie . . ." Marty Asher. A.I.

61 "We always used . . ." "Little Anthony" Gourdine. A.I.

63 "I was the lead . . ." Cleveland "Cleve" Duncan. Interview with author. All quotes A.I. unless otherwise noted.

68 "There was something odd . . ." Gerry Howard. Interview with author. All quotes from Howard A.I. unless otherwise noted.

69 "To me Brooklyn hip-hop" Brian Bergner. A.I.

70 "I'm twenty-three . . ." Jeanelia. Interview with author. Lyrics used with permission.

74 "If hip-hop . . ." Pete Hamill. A.I.

CHAPTER FOUR: DEM BUMS
AND OTHER ASSORTED SPORTS

79 "I was on a ship . . ." Pee Wee Reese, quoted in Allen, p. 3.

80 "Everything in Brooklyn . . ." Bob Gans. A.I.

80 "We'd hang out . . ." Mel Brooks. A.I.

80 "Basically, our neighborhood . . ." Pete Hamill. A.I.

81 "There was a lot . . ." Frank LoGrippo. A.I.

82 "At Ebbets Field . . ." Herb Cohen. A.I.

83 Background on early baseball comes from several sources, primarily Burrows and Wallace.

85 "There was great . . ." Hamill, pp. 7-8.

87 "I often get mail . . ." Erskine, p. 1.

88 "Mr. Rickey was . . ." Erskine, pp. 26-27.

89 "After an early season . . ." Allen, p. 148.

90 "The fans were . . ." Shapiro, pp. 55-56.

90 "Historically, it seemed . . ." Lee, pp. 35-36.

92 "When we lost baseball . . ." Rosen, p. 117.

93 "But the Yankees . . ." Lee, p. 36.

93 "I never knew . . ." Podres, Allen, p. 203.

94 "Dad was so proud . . ." Ben Vereen. A.I.

94 "The 1955 World Series . . ." Erskine, p. 88.

95 "I was a delivery . . ." Allen, quoted by Lee, p. 173.

95 "When Don Mueller . . ." Thompson, quoted by Ray Robinson, *New York Times*, September 30, 2006.

95 "I grew up . . ." Gerald Howard. A.I.

96 "I've never lived . . ." Selwyn Raab. A.I. (via e-mail).

96 "The Dodgers emphasized . . ." Bruce Wulwick. A.I.

97 "I remember in 1951 . . ." Herb Cohen. A.I.

97 "After visiting Japan . . ." Erskine, p. 169.

99 "Baseball was traditionally . . ." Erskine, pp. 4-5.

99 "I'll never forget . . ." Reed. A.I.

103 "I heard . . ." Markowitz, quoted in Mead.

103 "'We were betrayed . . .'": Richard Radutzky. A.I.

105 "I was the first . . ." Cha-Cha Garcia. A.I.

105 "Even in Coney Island . . ." Darcy Frey, p. 4.

106 "I followed . . ." Lee, p. 23.

106 "We have some things . . ." Lee, p. 171.

107 "I was born . . ." Lenny Wilkens. A.I.

108 "For me . . ." Stephon Marbury. A.I.

111 "My nickname is . . ." Tawil. All quotes from Tawil are A.I. unless otherwise noted.

CHAPTER FIVE: THE WAY WE WERE . . . AND WEREN'T

118 "My mother's maiden name . . ." Mel Brooks. A.I.

119 "I tend to have . . ." Herb Cohen. A.I.

120 "When I grew up . . ." Joan Rivers. A.I.

124 "My baptized name . . ." Frank LoGrippo. A.I.

125 "In [public] school the first year . . ." Hamill, p. 9.

125 "When we were kids . . ." "Little" Anthony Gourdine. A.I.

129 "I was born . . ." "Cousin Brucie" Morrow. A.I.

134 "We used to hang out . . ." Don K. Reed. A.I.

140 "I was born on Fortieth . . ." John Karlen. A.I.

142 "There were immense . . ." "Hamill, pp. 96–97.

145 "I grew up . . ." Ben Vereen. A.I.

146 "I was born and raised . . ." Ivan Kronenfeld. A.I.

151 "As far as Jews go . . ." Rabbi Jacobson. A.I.

151 "My biggest regret . . ." Woody Allen, in Eric Lax, *Woody Allen: A Biography* (New York: Knopf, 1991), pp. 18–19.

152 "I was born . . ." Bruce Wulwick. A.I.

155 "I was born . . ." Bob Gans. A.I.

CHAPTER SIX: LITERARY BROOKLYN

166 "styling himself the representative . . ." "New Publications; The New Poets," *New York Times*, May 19, 1860.

166 "It is important . . ." Michael Frank, "Whitman's Multitudes, for Better and Worse," *New York Times*, November 18, 2005.

167 "Whitman taught . . ." Pete Hamill, from Vin Scelsa's "Idiot's Delight," WFUV, rebroadcast, December 24, 2005.

169 "so bohemian . . ." Louis MacNeice, quoted in Sherill Tippins, *February House* (New York: Houghton Mifflin, 2005), p. 91.

170 "Barney [my husband] . . ." Fanny Schneider Miller, in Manso, p. 18.

170 "Few who grew up . . ." Mills, p. 24.

171 "I doubt . . ." Mailer, quoted by Mills, p. 87.

171 Mailer's thoughts on Henry Miller are taken from several passages in the introduction of Mailer (Miller).

172 "I must have begun . . ." These Henry Miller quotes are from an interview with Miller by George Wickes, in London, September 1961, and are reprinted in Henry Miller and Frank L. Kersnowski, *Conversations with Henry Miller* (University Press of Mississippi, 1994), pp. 50, 51, 60, 58, 60.

173 "Writing in more or less . . ." Arthur Miller, *Timebends: A Life* (New York: Penguin, 1995), pp. 22, 119.

174 "Whitman, Miller, Mailer . . ." Kronenfeld. A.I.

174 "It's the time . . ." Hamill. A.I.

177 "I think it's just . . ." David Haglund. A.I.

178 "I was born . . ." Brian Bergner. A.I.

179 "I really don't think . . ." Amy Sohn. A.I.

180 "The 'new Brooklyn . . ." Jonathan Lethem. A.I. (via e-mail).

181 "I was born . . ." Debbie Boswell. A.I.

182 "I emigrated from . . ." J. K. Savoy. A.I.

183 "I am from . . ." Erica Townsend. A.I.

CHAPTER SEVEN: THE NABES

190 "Being a baby-boomer . . ." Kenney Jones. Interview with author.

191 "My paternal grandfather . . ." Rabbi Simon Jacobson. A.I.

194 "That's true." Marty Asher. A.I.

195 "My parents . . ." Andrew Miller. A.I.

201 "For three days . . ." Giuliani, New York *Daily News*, July 1, 1993.

201 "If the Jews . . ." Sharpton, *Newsday*, August 18, 1991.

202 "The neighborhood's changed twice already." Jimmy Breslin, quoted by Michael Kamber, "Faded Rage," *The Village Voice*, January 16–22, 2002.

202 "I am actually . . ." Dr. Steven Rudolph, director of the Stroke Center at Maimonides Medical Center. Interview with author. All quotes A.I. except where otherwise noted.

204 "I'm from Brooklyn . . ." Louis Savarese. A.I.

205 "I was born . . ." Ralph Beatrice. A.I.

206 "Bensonhurst, of course . . ." Anthony Petrocino. A.I.

206 "We used to play . . ." Tom Spiono. A.I.

207 "Every fifth or sixth person . . ." Buddy Fanto. A.I.

207 "I deal with the . . ." Dave Tawil. A.I.

208 "Everyone's connection . . ." Al Brown.

CHAPTER EIGHT: ON THE WATERFRONT

215 "Mayor Opdyke..." Morris, pp. 42-43.

217 Some background and information regarding the Waterfront development is from Pogrebin, Robin, "Brooklyn Waterfront Called Endangered Site," *New York Times*, June 14, 2007.

218 "I was born..." Julius Zocampo. A.I.

220 "menacing, funny, smart, tough, obscene..." Jack Newfield and Wayne Barrett, *City for Sale: Ed Koch and the Betrayal of New York* (New York: Harper and Row, 1988), p. 15.

221 Some background information re De Niro/Weinstein/Steiner/ Giuliani is from Dan Barry's article, "Hollywood, City Hall and a Production Deal That Wasn't," *New York Times*, October 10, 1999; Glenn Collins, "On Brooklyn Back Lot, Finally, Some Action; After Years of Talk, a Movie Studio Is Being Built at the Navy Yard," July 21, 2003.

221 "This is the coolest..." Madigan, quoted by Collins, *New York Times*, September 3, 2006.

221 "I was born..." Doug Steiner. A.I.

CHAPTER NINE: WHADDYA GOT TO EAT?

229 "Every day after school..." Billy Dawn. All quotes from Dawn are A.I. unless otherwise noted.

232 "a lot of..." Ron Rosenbaum, *The Village Voice*, July 1973.

233 "The repeal of prohibition..." Rosen and Rosen, pp. 19-20.

233 "Into the 1940s..." Rosen and Rosen, pp. 47-50.

236 "Peter Luger is one..." Alan King, in the documentary *A Walking Tour of Brooklyn*.

236 "We've heard halva..." Richard Radutzky. All quotes with Radutzky A.I. unless otherwise noted

236 "How the Jews..." Milton Radutzky. All quotes with M. Rudutsky A.I. unless otherwise noted.

241 "I was born and raised..." Cha Cha Ciarcia. All quotes with Ciarcia A.I. unless otherwise noted.

CHAPTER TEN: POLITICS AND POKER

248 Brooklyn Borough Hall: Background information in this chapter comes from Rebecca Mead, "Mr. Brooklyn," *The New Yorker*, April 25, 2005.

248 "I was the executive..." Harvey Shultz. All quotes from Shultz are A.I. except where otherwise noted.

254 "I came out of..." Charles Hynes. All quotes from Hynes are A.I. except where otherwise noted.

259 "I was in a restaurant..." Anthony Petrocino, A.I.

CHAPTER ELEVEN: BACK TO THE FUTURE

263 "We lived in Williamsburg . . ." Marty Asher. A.I.

264 Some background information on the landmarking of the Brooklyn Academy of Music is from Diamonstein, p. 454.

264 "an emblem . . ." Karen Brooks, quoted in Glenn Collins, "A Brooklyn Landmark Gets Its Crown Back," *New York Times*, May 17, 2004.

265 "When you add . . ." ibid.

266 BAM attendance figures for 2004 are from *New York Times*, May 17, 2004.

266 "the building . . ." Hardy, quoted in *New York Times*, May 17, 2004.

267 Background on the housing boom—Jennifer Steinhauer, "Housing Boom Echoes in All Corners of the City," *New York Times*, August 4, 2005.

268 "has affected every borough. . ." ibid.

268 Background and information on median prices for homes in East New York is from Dennis Hevesi's "The Boom Spreads to East New York, *New York Times*, August 7, 2005.

268 Brooklyn is coming back . . ." Bob Gans. A.I.

269 "I discovered . . ." Andrew Miller. A.I.

270 "About 38 percent . . ." Mehta, *New York Times*.

271 "If the public . . ." Ettlinger, *New York Sun*, November 16, 2007.

271 "I can't tell you . . ." Markowitz, quoted by Patrick Gallahue, *New York Post*, January 16, 2006.

271 "To justify . . ." Daniel Goldman, quoted by Nicholas Confessore in "Another Step for Downtown Brooklyn Project," *New York Times*, December 16, 2005

272 "The bottom line . . ." Ettlinger, *New York Sun*, November 16, 2007.

272 "I've lived here all my life . . ." Rosie Perez, quoted in *New York Post*, 200_

272 "Brooklyn is vast . . ." Chris Smith, "Mr. Ratner's Neighborhood," *New York Magazine*, August 14th, 2006.

274 "When I saw . . ." Michael Gardner, quoted by Ada Calhoun in the *New York Times*, February 6, 2005.

274 "In Brooklyn, the older . . ." Mark Lotto, *The Observer*, December 5, 2005.

274 "Each generation . . ." Bruce Ratner, quoted by Stephen Witt, "Changing the tide downtown," which appeared in "Brooklyn Tomorrow," a special supplement published in the *New York Post*, Spring 2007.

BIBLIOGRAPHY

Allen, Maury, *Jackie Robinson: A Life Remembered*, New York: Franklin Watts, 1987.

Burrows, Edwin C., and Wallace, Mike, *Gotham: A History of New York City to 1898*, New York: Oxford University Press, 1899.

Capote, Truman, *Selected Writings by Truman Capote*, New York: Curtis Publishing, 1959.

Diamonstein, Barbaralee, *The Landmarks of New York II*, New York: Abrams, 1988.

Erskine, Carl, *Tales from the Dodger Dugout*, Champaign, Il: Sports Publishing Inc., 2001.

Frey, Darcy, *The Last Shot*, New York: Houghton Mifflin, 1994.

Hamill, Pete, *A Drinking Life*, New York: Little, Brown, 1994.

Hamill, Pete, *Downtown: My Manhattan*, New York: Little, Brown, 2004.

Hershkowitz, Leo, *Tweed's New York*, New York: Anchor Press, 1978.

Hood, Clifton, *722 Miles*, New York: Simon and Schuster, 1993.

Jacobson, Simon, *Toward a Meaningful Life*, New York: Morrow, 1995.

Lax, Eric, *Woody Allen*, New York: Knopf, 1991.

Lee, Spike, *Best Seat in the House*, New York: Crown, 1994.

Lopate, Phillip, *Waterfront*, New York: Crown, 2004.

Mailer, Norman, *Genius and Lust: A Journey Through the Major Writings of Henry Miller*, New York: Grove Press, 1976.

Manso, Peter, *Mailer*, New York: Simon and Schuster, 1985.

Miller, Arthur, *Timebends: A Life*, New York: Grove Press, 1987.

Mills, Hillary, *Mailer: A Biography*, New York: Empire Books, 1982.

Monti, Ralph, *I Remember Brooklyn*, New York: Birch Lane Press, 1991.

Morris, Lloyd, *Incredible New York, 1850-1950*, New York: Bonanza Books, 1951.

Newfield, Jack, and Barrett, Wayne, *City for Sale*, New York: Harper and Row, 1988.

Rosen, Marvin and Walter, with Allen, Beth, *Welcome to Junior's!*, New York: William Morrow, 1999.

Shapiro, Michael, *The Last Good Season*, New York: Doubleday, 2003.

Shorto, Russell, *The Island at the Center of the World*, New York: Doubleday, 2004.

Taylor, B. Kim, *The Great New York Trivia and Fact Book*, Nashville, TN: Cumberland House, 1998.

Tippins, Sherill, *February House*, New York: Houghton Mifflin, 2005.

Ziga, Charles J., *New York Landmarks*, New York: Dovetail, 1999.

ADDITIONAL SOURCES

A Walk Around Brooklyn, produced by David McCarthy for WNET/ PBS, 2000.

Brooklyn Bridge, A Documentary Film by Ken Burns, Florentine Films, 1981.

ACKNOWLEDGMENTS

This book was originally conceived by Howard Kaminsky, a great writer, editor, and publisher, and now I'm proud to say, also a friend. I was asked to write about Brooklyn because of another book I'd done on the glorious history of New York that had been published in 2001: *Down 42nd Street*. Like its predecessor, *Brooklyn* took many years to write and its completion is due in no small part to my gallant, extremely patient, highly talented, incredibly involved, and totally committed Brooklyn-born editor, Gerald Howard. His hands-on approach—including recording his own recollections of growing up "Brooklyn" on tape, along with those of some of his friends and colleagues—helped make the book what (ever) it is. I appreciate his inexhaustible encouragement and enthusiasm. Thanks also to his assistant, Katie Halleron.

There are several people who deserve special mentions for their contributions. I don't know where to begin, really, but perhaps no greater nod of gratitude belongs to the wonderfully funny, generous, and insightful Mel Brooks (Howard Kaminsky's cousin), who not only made himself available during an extremely busy time in his schedule but, after a long, detailed, and lovely interview about his childhood memories of Brooklyn, he asked what I was thinking of calling the book. "Brooklyn," I said. "No, no," he said, without missing a beat, "'Song of Brooklyn.'" So it is that this work was titled. Thank you again, Mel Brooks.

For the past seven years, I have been fortunate to hold a regular place (once a week or so, sometimes more, sometimes less) in the rotation of has-beens, never-wases, wannabes, and actually done-somethings who occupy the so-called "roundtable" of dysfunctional family, friends, fellow entertainers, and devotees of the New York night, otherwise known as the Joey Reynolds Show, a nationally syndicated radio program. Through my association with the show I met many of the people who helped make this book possible. Thank you, Joey Reynolds, for your friendship and generosity.

One such fellow I met from the show (although we did not appear on it together, the show's "booker," Myra Chanin, put us together) is Kenny Vance. Kenny not only made himself completely available, but spent one entire summer driving me around the south of Brooklyn and introducing me to dozens of people, many of whom are in *Song of Brooklyn*. Kenny has become a close and dear friend. Thank you for your precious love, devotion, and invaluable help.

Don K. Reed was enormously gracious and helpful, and his memories are as golden as the songs he often played on his legendary CBS "Doo-Wop Shop." Thank you, Don K. Reed.

"Cousin Brucie," Bruce Morrow, is a prince. There is no other way to put it. He was a great addition to this book. Thank you, cousin.

My dear friend Zack Norman was instrumental on the West Coast.

Stephon Marbury, Lenny Wilkins, Pete Hamill, and Neil Sedaka were wonderfully cooperative, expansive, and illuminating. Pete Hamill was one of those writers who inspired me early in my life to think that maybe I could one day pick up a pen and express myself in words. Thank you, Stephon, Lenny, Neil, and especially Pete. All of you are great.

Dave Herwitz was a terrific assistant and organizer for me. His relentless tracking down of people was impressive and essential. Thank you, Dave.

My thanks to my fellow Friars at the Friars Club, so many of whom found their way into the pages of *Song of Brooklyn*.

My thanks as well to the following people for the contributions to this book: Marty Asher, Mike Berger, Brian Bergner, Debbie Boswell, Al Brown, Mahogany L. Brown, Brian Burns, John "Cha Cha" Ciarcia, Herb Cohen, Cleveland "Cleve" Duncan, Buddy Fanto, Mickey Freeman, Darcy Frey, Bob Gans, Brian Gari, Chris Gilman of the Palm West, "Little" Anthony Gourdine, David Haglund, District Attorney Charles Hynes, Jeanelia "J," Rabbi Simon Jacobson, Kenney Jones, John Karlen, Ivan Kronenfeld, Mark Lotto, Frank LoGrippo, Johnny Maestro, Andrew Miller, Deborah Nader, Anthony Petrocino, Milton Radutzky, Nathan Radutzky, Richard Radutzky, Joan Rivers, Marv and Walter Rosen, Dr. Steven Rudolph, Louis Savarese, Neil Sedaka, Harvey Schultz, Joe Sitt, Billy Dawn Smith, Amy Sohn, Tom Spioni, Doug Steinger, David Tawil, Erica Townsend, Ben Vereen, Ernest Wright, Bruce Wulwick, Julius Zocampo.

My thanks to Mel Berger, of the William Morris Agency, who brought this project to me and made it happen.

Finally, I thank you, my faithful readers, for the many years of your wonderful support. *I leave you now, but we'll surely meet again, a little further up the road . . .*